The Complete Reference to
to
Angels in the Bible

Also by Kermie Wohlenhaus, Ph.D.

How to Talk and Actually Listen to Your Guardian Angel
A Quick Reference Guide to Angels in The Bible

The Complete Reference to
Angels in the Bible

Kermie Wohlenhaus, Ph.D.

Kermie & the Angels Press   Tucson, Arizona

Copyright © 2014 by Kermie Wohlenhaus, Ph.D.

All rights reserved. No part of this book may be reproduced or transmitted in any form or by any means, electronic or mechanical, including photocopying, recording, or by any information storage and retrieval system, without permission in writing from the author.

Scriptures are taken from the King James Version of the Bible. All other versions of the Bible, except the New King James Version, tend to alter the references to angels and use other names for these heavenly hosts. This has caused reference guides to miss important verses regarding the angels.

To contact the author or order
additional copies of this book
Kermie & The Angels Press
P. O. Box 64282
Tucson, AZ 85728
www.KermieandtheAngels.com
KermieandtheAngels@gmail.com

This edition was prepared for publication by
Ghost River Images
5350 East Fourth Street
Tucson, Arizona 85711
www.ghostriverimages.com

Cover design by Kermie Wohlenhaus

ISBN: 978-0-9832300-4-5
Library of Congress Control Number: 2014908232

Printed in the United States of America
First Printing: May, 2014
10 9 8 7 6 5 4 3 2 1

Dedicated to the Divine and the Glorious Angels

Table of Contents

Introduction   19

Angels of the Angelic Hierarchy

Seraphim
  Isaiah 6:1-13 - Description of Seraphim and Holy Song   21

  Revelation 4:1-11 - Four Living Creatures (Seraphim) Give Glory to God and Holy Song   22

Cherubim
  Genesis 3:1-24 - Cherubims Guarding with a Flaming Sword the Tree of Life and the Garden of Eden   23

  Exodus 25:16-22 - Two Cherubim of Gold in the Two Ends of the Mercy Seat and Upon the Ark of the Testimony   25

  Exodus 26:1-37 - Make the Tabernacle with Cherubim of Cunning Work and with Cherubim Shall it be Made   26

  Exodus 36:1-38 - Tabernacle Made with Cherubims of Cunning Work   29

  Exodus 37:1-29 - He Made Two Cherubims of Gold, Beaten Out of One Piece at Two Ends of the Mercy Seat   32

  Numbers 7:89 - One Speaking to Moses from off the Mercy Seat from between Two Cherubims   34

  1 Samuel 4:1-22 - Ark of the Covenant which Dwells between Cherubims   34

  2 Samuel 6:1-23 - Ark of God that Dwells between the Cherubims   37

  1 Kings 6:11-38 - Two Cherubims Carved Out of Olive Wood   39

  1 Kings 7:13-36 - On the Borders that were between Ledges were Cherubims and on Plates of the Border's Ledges He Graved Cherubims   41

  1 Kings 8:1-24 - The Most Holy Place, Even Under the Wings of Cherubims and Spread Forth their Two Wings   43

2 Kings 19:1-37 - Lord God of Israel which Dwells between Cherubims ... 45

1 Chronicles 13:1-14 - Ark of God that Dwells between Cherubims ... 49

1 Chronicles 28:1-21 - Chariot of the Cherubims that Covered the Ark of the Covenant of the Lord ... 50

2 Chronicles 3:1-17 - Graved Cherubims on the Walls and Most Holy House, Two Cherubims Description ... 52

2 Chronicles 5:1-14 - Cherubims Spread their Wings over the Ark ... 54

Psalms 80 - Shepherd of Israel, Thou that Dwells between Cherubims ... 55

Psalms 99 - Lord Reigns and Sits between the Cherubims ... 57

Isaiah 37:1-38 - Lord of Hosts, God of Israel that Dwells between Cherubims ... 57

Ezekiel 10:1-22 - Position, Appearance and Duties of the Cherubims ... 61

Ezekiel 11:14-25 - The Cherubims Lift up their Wings ... 63

Ezekiel 41:1-26 - Cherubims and Palm Trees with Every Cherub had Two Faces ... 64

Hebrews 9:1-28 - Cherubims of Glory Shadowing the Mercy Seat ... 66

Thrones
Ezekiel 1:1-28 - Description of Thrones in a Vision of Enoch ... 69

Daniel 7:1-28 - Daniel Beheld till the Thrones were Cast Down ... 71

Colossians 1:9-18 - All Things Created, Thrones, Dominions or Principalities ... 74

Dominions
Daniel 7:1-28 - The Kingdom and Dominion ... 75

Colossians 1:9-18 - All Things Created, Thrones, Dominions or Principalities ... 78

Powers
- Matthew 24:1-37 - Immediately after the Tribulation . . . the Powers of Heavens shall be Shaken — 79
- Mark 13:1-37 - The Stars of Heaven shall Fall and the Powers that are in Heaven shall be Shaken — 81
- Romans 8:35-39 - For I am Persuaded, that neither Death . . . nor Powers — 84
- Romans 13:1-8 - Let Every Soul be Subject unto the Higher Powers — 84
- Ephesians 3:1-12 - To the Intent that now unto the Principalities and Powers in Heavenly Places might be known . . . — 85
- Ephesians 6:10-13 - For we Wrestle not against Flesh and Blood but against Powers — 86
- Colossians 1:9-17 - For by Him were All Things Created, that are in Heaven . . . whether they be . . . or Powers — 87
- Colossians 2:8-17 - And Having Spoiled Principalities and Powers — 87
- Titus 3:1-7 - To be Subject to Principalities and Powers — 88
- Hebrews 6:1-6 - Have Tasted the Good Word of God and the Powers of the World — 89
- 1 Peter 3:18-22 - Powers being Made Subject unto Him — 89

Principalities
- Jeremiah 13:16-18 - Your Principalities shall Come Down, even the Crown of Your Glory — 90
- Romans 8:35-39 - For I am Persuaded that neither Death nor Principalities — 90
- Ephesians 3:1-12 - Now unto the Principalities and Powers in Heavenly Places be Known by the Church, the Manifold Wisdom — 91
- Ephesians 6:10-13 - For we Wrestle not against Flesh and Blood but against Principalities — 92
- Colossians 1:9-17 - All Things Created whether they be Principalities — 92

Colossians 2:8-17 - Having Spoiled Principalities	93
Titus 3:1-7 - To be Subject to Principalities and Powers	94

Archangels

1 Thessalonians 4:13-18 - The Lord shall Descend from Heaven with the Voice of the Archangel	94
Revelation 8:1-2 - I Saw Seven Angels which Stood before God (Commonly thought to be the Seven Archangels in Christian Theology)	95

Michael

Daniel 10:1-21 - Michael shall Stand Up and none that Hold with Me these Things but Michael your Prince	95
Daniel 12:1-3 - Michael Stand Up, the Great Prince	97
Jude 1:1- 9 - Michael the Archangel Disputed about the Body of Moses	98
Revelation 12:1-10 - Michael and his Angels Fought against the Dragon	99

Gabriel

Daniel 8:1-27 - Gabriel, Make this Man Understand the Vision	100
Daniel 9:20-27 - Gabriel being Caused to Fly Swiftly and Touched Me	102
Luke 1:1-38 - Gabriel Speaking to Zachariah about Birth of Son John and Gabriel Proclaiming the Birth of Jesus to Mary	103

Angels in the Old Testament

Genesis 16:1-16 - Angel of the Lord Aiding Hagar and Ishmael	107
Genesis 19:1-28 - Two Angels to Sodom and Gomorrah	108
Genesis 21:1-21 - Angel of God Rescues Hagar and Ishmael	111
Genesis 22:1-18 - Angel of the Lord Stops Abraham from Slaying Isaac	112
Genesis 24:1-67 - Angel Finds Isaac's Wife	114
Genesis 28:1-22 - Angels of God Descending and Ascending on Jacob's Ladder	119
Genesis 31:1-13 - Jacob Explaining Dream from the Angel of God	121

Genesis 32:1-3 - Jacob Met Angels of God	122
Genesis 48:1-22 - Israel (Jacob) Asking Angel Blessing for Joseph	122
Exodus 3:1-22 - Moses and Angel of the Lord in Burning Bush	124
Exodus 14:1-31 - Angel of God Went before the Camp of Israel	127
Exodus 23:19-33 - God Sending an Angel before Moses and Israel	129
Exodus 32:1-35 - God Sending an Angel before Moses and Israel	131
Exodus 33:1-3 - God Sending an Angel to Drive Out the Inhabitants of the Promised Land	134
Numbers 20:1-17 - Moses' Messengers Retelling Story of God Sending an Angel Leading Israel out of Egypt	134
Numbers 22:1-41 - Balaam and the Angel of the Lord	136
Judges 2:1-7 - Angel of the Lord Prophesying about Israel's Disobedience to Joshua and Israelites	139
Judges 5:1-31 - Deborah's Song Including a Verse about the Angel of the Lord	140
Judges 6:1-40 - Gideon and the Angel of the Lord	143
Judges 13:1-25 - Angel of the Lord Prophesying Samson's Birth	146
1 Samuel 29:1-11 - Achish Calling David as an Angel of God	148
2 Samuel 14:1-23 - Joab Sending Wise Woman to King David – Wise as the Wisdom of an Angel of God	150
2 Samuel 19:24-27 - Mephibosheth Saying the King is Like the Angel of God	152
2 Samuel 24:1-25 - Angel of the Lord Destroying Jerusalem	153
1 Kings 13:1-34 - Bethel Lying about what Angel told Him	155
1 Kings 19:1-21 - Angel of the Lord helps Elijah to Escape	158
2 Kings 1:1-18 - Angel of the Lord gives Elijah a Message	160
2 Kings 19:1-37 - Angel of the Lord Kills 185,000 Assyrians	162
1 Chronicles 21:1-30 - King David and the Census of Israel - as Punishment, Angel of the Lord Destroys Jerusalem	166

2 Chronicles 32:1-33 - Isaiah Prays for Help and the Lord Sent an Angel	168
Job 4:1-21 - Eliphaz tells Job, God Charges Angels with Folly	171
Ecclesiastes 5:1-7 - What Not to Say before the Angel	173
Isaiah 37:1-38 - Angel of the Lord Kills 185,000 Assyrians	173
Isaiah 63:1-19 - Angel of His Presence Saved the Afflicted	177
Daniel 3:1-30 - Nebuchadnezzar Praises God and Angel for Delivering Shadrach, Meshach and Abed-Nego from Fiery Furnace	179
Daniel 6:1-28 - Angel Shut the Lions' Mouths for Daniel	182
Hosea 12:1-14 - Hosea Saying that Jacob Struggled with the Angel	185
Zechariah 1:1-21 - Zechariah's Visions of Angels	186
Zechariah 2:1-13 - Zechariah's Visions of Angels	188
Zechariah 3:1-10 - Zechariah's Visions of Angels	189
Zechariah 4:1-14 - Zechariah's Visions of Angels	190
Zechariah 5:1-11 - Zechariah's Visions of Angels	191
Zechariah 6:1-15 - Zechariah's Visions of Angels	192
Zechariah 12:1-14 - Zechariah's Visions of Angels	193

Angels in the Psalms

Psalm 8 - Humans a Little Lower than Angels	195
Psalm 34 - Angel of the Lord Encamps and Delivers Those Who Revere God	195
Psalm 35 – Let the Angel of the Lord Chase and Persecute Those Who Fight Against Me	197
Psalm 68 - Thousands of Angels	199
Psalm 78 - Manna, the Bread of Angels	201
Psalm 91 - God Gives Angels Charge Over You to Keep You in All Your Ways	206
Psalm 103 - Bless the Lord, Ye Angels	207
Psalm 104 - Who Makes God's Angels Spirits; Ministers of Flaming Fire	209
Psalm 148 - Praise God, All God's Angels	211

Angels in the New Testament

Angels in the Life of Jesus in Chronological Order

Luke 1:1-45 - Angel of the Lord Proclaims Birth of Son to Zacharias and Gabriel Foretells to Mary the Gender, Name, Destiny and that the Conception of her Child, Jesus, was from the Holy Ghost ... 213

Matthew 1:17-25 - Angel of the Lord in a Dream told Joseph about Taking Mary as His Wife and that the Baby was Conceived by the Holy Ghost and told Him the Child's Gender, Name and Destiny ... 216

Luke 2:1-20 - Angel of the Lord Announces the Birth of Jesus to the Shepherds, followed by a Multitude of Angels Praising God ... 217

Matthew 2:1-23 - Joseph Instructed in a Dream by the Angel of the Lord to Flee to Egypt and when to Return Safely to Israel ... 219

Mark 1:9-13 - Angels Ministered to Jesus after the 40-day Temptation ... 221

Matthew 4:1-11- Angels Ministered to Jesus after the 40-day Temptation ... 221

John 5:1-9 - Angel Troubled the Water at the Healing Pool in Bethesda ... 222

Luke 22:39-47 - Jesus Comforted by an Angel in His Agony at Mount of Olives ... 223

Matthew 28:1-8 - Angel of the Lord Rolled Back the Stone from Jesus' Tomb and Announced Jesus' Resurrection to the Women at the Tomb ... 224

John 20:1-18 - Angels Question Mary Magdalene's Grief at the Tomb ... 224

Matthew 13:1-58 - Parable of the Seeds and Angels to Harvest Righteous and Unrighteous for Jesus at the End of the Age ... 226

Matthew 24:25-31 - Jesus will send his Angels with a Great Sound of a Trumpet to Gather His Elect ... 230

Mark 13:21-27 - He Shall Send His Angels to Gather Together His Elect	231
Mark 8:34-38 - Jesus Comes with the Holy Angels	231
Matthew 16:24-28 - The Son of Man Shall Come in the Glory of His Father with His Angels	232
Matthew 25:31-46 - Son of Man Shall Come in His Glory and all the Holy Angels; He Shall Separate Them One from Another, the Devil and his angels	232
Luke 9:18-26 - He Shall Come in His Own Glory and of the Holy Angels	234
Revelation 5:1-14 - Many Angels Praise the Lamb	234
Revelation 12:1-17 - Michael and His Angels Cast Out Dragon	236

Jesus' Teachings Regarding the Angels

Matthew 18:1-10 - In Heaven, Children's Angels Do Always Behold the Face of God	237
Matthew 22:23-30 - Angels of God Do Not Marry	238
Matthew 24:34-37 - Angels of Heaven Do Not Know all that God Knows - Time of Jesus' Coming	239
Matthew 26:46-56 - Jesus Could Pray to God and God Would Send 12 Legions of Angels (72,000) to Save Him	239
Mark 12:18-25 - Angels Do Not Marry	240
Mark 13:31-33 - Angels Do Not Know but God Knows the Time of Jesus' Coming	241
Luke 9: 23-27 - Whosoever Shall be Ashamed of Me . . . of Him Shall the Son of Man be Ashamed When He Shall Come in His Own Glory and of the Holy Angels	241
Luke 12:8-12 - Whosoever Confesses Me before Men, Him Shall the Son of Man Also Confess Before the Angels of God	242
Luke 15:1-10 - There is Joy in the Presence of the Angels of God Over One Sinner that Repents	242
Luke 16:14-31 - The Humble Beggar Lazarus Carried by the Angels into Abraham's Bosom	243
Luke 20:27-36 - Angels Do Not Marry	244
John 1:44-51 - Ye Shall See Heaven Open and the Angels of God Ascending and Descending upon the Son of Man	245

Acts of the Apostles, Paul's letters, the General Letters
  Acts 5:12-29 - Angel of the Lord Frees the Apostles from Prison ... 246
  Acts 6:1-15 - Saw Stephen's Face as it Had Been the Face of an Angel ... 248
  Acts 7:22-40 - Stephen's Defense Against Charges Recounting the Angel of the Lord in the Burning Bush Appearing to Moses and Spoke to Him on the Mount of Sinai ... 249
  Acts 7:46-53 - Stephen Refers to Law Given by the Dispostion of Angels ... 251
  Acts 8:25-39 - Angel of the Lord Instructs Philip to Meet Ethiopian Eunuch ... 251
  Acts 10:1-35 - Angel of God Came to Cornelius the Centurion to Send for Peter ... 253
  Acts 11:1-18 - Peter Repeats to the Apostles and Brethren his Story about Cornelius and Gentiles Granted Repentance unto Life ... 255
  Acts 12:1-25 - Peter being Rescued from Prison by the Angel of the Lord ... 257
  Acts 23:1-11 - Paul being Questioned by Pharisees and Sadducees; Sadducees say that there are No Angels and Pharisees Defend Paul and say there are Angels ... 259
  Acts 27:1-44 - Paul Being Told by Angel of God that Ship would be Lost but No Loss of Life ... 260

  Romans 8:35-39 - Paul Asking who shall Separate them from the Love of Christ? Not Angels ... 263

  1 Corinthians 4:4-10 - Paul Saying how Apostles are made Spectacles unto the World and to the Angels ... 264
  1 Corinthians 6:1-8 - Paul Warns to not Judge and Telling Apostles that They shall not Judge Angels ... 265
  1 Corinthians 11:1-16 - Paul Instructs Women Covering their Heads while Praying and Prophesying because of the Angels ... 265
  1 Corinthians 13:1-3 - Speaking with the Tongues of Angels ... 266

  2 Corinthians 11:1-15 - Satan being Transformed into an Angel of Light ... 267

  Galatians 1:1-8 - Paul Instructing the Church that we or an Angel Preach any Other Gospel, let Him be Accursed ... 268

Galatians 3:18-20 - Paul Speaking of the Law Being Ordained by Angels in the Hand of a Mediator	269
Galatians 4:6-14 - Paul is Received as an Angel of God	269
Colossians 2:16-19 - Paul Warning to Let no Man Begile You of Your Reward in the Worshipping of Angels	270
2 Thessalonians 1:3-10 - When Jesus Shall be Revealed from Heaven with His Mighty Angels	270
1 Timothy 5:17-25 - Paul Charging Timothy to Carry out his Instructions by Jesus Christ and the Elect Angels	271
Hebrews 1:1-14 - Jesus Made Better than Angels, Let All the Angels of God Worship Him and Sit on Right Hand of God and Ministering Spirits of the Heirs of Salvation	272
Hebrews 2:1-18 - Word Spoken by Angels and Made Him a Little Lower than the Angels	273
Hebrews 12:18-24 - Innumerable Company of Angels in Heaven	274
Hebrews 13:1-2 - Entertain Strangers, Unwittingly Entertain Angels	275
1 Peter 1:1-12 - Angels Desire to Look into those Things Preached	275
1 Peter 3:18-22 - Angels Subject to Jesus Christ	276
2 Peter 2:1-10 - God not Sparing Punishment on the Angels who Sinned	277
Jude 1:1-6 - Angels who did not Keep their Proper Domain	278

The Book of Revelation and the Angels

Revelation 1:1-20 - Jesus Christ Sent and Signified Angel with this Revelation - Seven Stars are Seven Angels of the Seven Churches and Seven Candlesticks are the Seven Churches	279
Revelation 2:1-29 - The Angel of the Chruch of Ephesus, Smyrna, Pergamo and Thyatira Writes	281
Revelation 3:1-22 - The Angel of the Church of Sardis, Philadelphia and Laodicean Writes	283
Revelation 5:1-14 - Strong Angel Proclaiming Who is Worthy to Open the Book - Many Angels Around the Throne Praising God and the Lamb	285

Revelation 7:1-17 - Four Angels Standing on the Four Corners of the Earth, Another Angel Ascending from the East, Crying not to Hurt the 144,000 - All Angels Around the Throne Worshipping God ... 287
Revelation 8:1-13 - Seven Angels Which Stood Before God and Sound Four of Seven Trumpets ... 288
Revelation 9:1-21 - Three More Angels Which Stood Before God and Sound Trumpets ... 289
Revelation 10:1-11 - A Mighty Angel Came Down From Heaven ... 291
Revelation 11:1-19 - Seventh Angel Sounded ... 292
Revelation 12:1-17 - Heavenly War between Michael and His Angels Fought Against the Dragon ... 294
Revelation 14:1-20 - Angels in the Midst of Heaven ... 296
Revelation 15:1-8 - Seven Angels and the Seven Plagues ... 298
Revelation 16:1-21 - Seven Angels and the Seven Plagues ... 298
Revelation 17:1-18 - Seven Angels and the Seven Vials ... 300
Revelation 18:1-24 - Angel Come Down From Heaven ... 302
Revelation 19:1-21 - Angel Calling Standing in the Sun ... 304
Revelation 20:1-15 - Angel Casting Down Satan for 1,000 Years ... 306
Revelation 21:1-27 - Seven Angels and the Seven Vials ... 307
Revelation 22:1-21 - John Worshipping at the Feet of the Angel ... 310

Acknowledgements ... 313

About the Author ... 315

Introduction

There are over 180 scriptures regarding angels in the Bible. Many biblical scholars and theologians have glossed over the importance of these celestial beings in biblical dissertation and study. But now the study of angels – Angelology – is bringing these winged emissaries of the Divine back into focus and illuminating their great work in our sacred texts.

The word angel – from the Greek word "angelos" – is derived from the Hebrew "malakh" meaning "messenger." Angels are not limited to being *only* "messengers" of Divine Will, but are also known to be helpers, rescuers and guides – clearing the way. Angels were created by the Divine to fulfill Divine Will between God and creation. They talk to us in dreams and manifest physically. They come to give great proclamations and are known to punish, liberate and often save us.

We read in the New Testament that angels were very involved in the life of Jesus. They not only came to his unwed mother and proclaimed his conception, but were present at Jesus's birth, ministered to him throughout his life and were on hand to explain Christ's resurrection at the tomb.

The Complete Reference to Angels in The Bible contains the complete angelic verses as written in the King James version. The companion booklet, *A Quick Reference Guide to Angels in The Bible* by Kermie Wohlenhaus, Ph.D., is a fast, easy guide to all biblical angelic verses without the text included. Both are the perfect complement to any biblical study of angels.

This book begins with "Angels of the Angelic Hierarchy" created by Pseudo-Dionysius from Syria in the 6th Century. The Roman Catholic Church, which was the authorizing Christian Church for many decades, has used this Angel Hierarchy of angel orders and choirs since that time. Other Christian angelologists continue to utilize this as an important, but not the only, theory to this day. Because of its popularity, I have opened this reference with "Angels of the Angelic Hierarchy." They are: Seraphim, Cherubim, Thrones, Dominions, Powers, Principalities, Archangels (including Michael and Gabriel) and, of course, the Angels.

The next section is "Angels in the Old Testament" including "Angels in the Psalms." This is followed by "Angels in the New Testament," highlighting "Angels in the Life of Jesus In Chronological Order", "Jesus's Teachings Regarding the Angels" and "Acts of the Apostles, Paul's Letters and the General Letters." This quick reference guide finishes with "Angels in the Book of Revelation."

We read that angels not only protect but liberate, minister, prophesize, praise God and walk with us unawares. They also punish, kill and stop us and the donkey we are riding on in our tracks if they have a Divine reason for doing so. They are mighty and filled with Divine power and love.

I hope this book will encourage study and illuminate the Divine work that these great beings of light perform in our lives. May the angels continue to shower you with Divine blessings.

Kermie Wohlenhaus, Ph.D.
www.KermieandtheAngels.com

Angels of the Angelic Hierarchy

Seraphim

Isaiah 6:1-13 - Description of Seraphim and Holy Song

[1] In the year that king Uzziah died I saw also the Lord sitting upon a throne, high and lifted up, and his train filled the temple.

[2] Above it stood the <u>seraphims</u>: each one had six wings; with twain he covered his face, and with twain he covered his feet, and with twain he did fly.

[3] And one cried unto another, and said, Holy, holy, holy, *is* the LORD of hosts: the whole earth *is* full of his glory.

[4] And the posts of the door moved at the voice of him that cried, and the house was filled with smoke.

[5] Then said I, Woe *is* me! for I am undone; because I *am* a man of unclean lips, and I dwell in the midst of a people of unclean lips: for mine eyes have seen the King, the LORD of hosts.

[6] Then flew one of the <u>seraphims</u> unto me, having a live coal in his hand, *which* he had taken with the tongs from off the altar:

[7] And he laid *it* upon my mouth, and said, Lo, this hath touched thy lips; and thine iniquity is taken away, and thy sin purged.

[8] Also I heard the voice of the Lord, saying, Whom shall I send, and who will go for us? Then said I, Here *am* I; send me.

[9] And he said, Go, and tell this people, Hear ye indeed, but understand not; and see ye indeed, but perceive not.

¹⁰ Make the heart of this people fat, and make their ears heavy, and shut their eyes; lest they see with their eyes, and hear with their ears, and understand with their heart, and convert, and be healed.

¹¹ Then said I, Lord, how long? And he answered, Until the cities be wasted without inhabitant, and the houses without man, and the land be utterly desolate,

¹² And the LORD have removed men far away, and *there be* a great forsaking in the midst of the land.

¹³ But yet in it *shall be* a tenth, and *it* shall return, and shall be eaten: as a teil tree, and as an oak, whose substance *is* in them, when they cast *their leaves: so* the holy seed *shall be* the substance thereof.

Revelation 4:1-11 - Four Living Creatures (Seraphim) Give Glory to God and Holy Song

¹ After this I looked, and, behold, a door *was* opened in heaven: and the first voice which I heard *was* as it were of a trumpet talking with me; which said, Come up hither, and I will shew thee things which must be hereafter.

² And immediately I was in the spirit: and, behold, a throne was set in heaven, and *one* sat on the throne.

³ And he that sat was to look upon like a jasper and a sardine stone: and *there was* a rainbow round about the throne, in sight like unto an emerald.

⁴ And round about the throne *were* four and twenty seats: and upon the seats I saw four and twenty elders sitting, clothed in white raiment; and they had on their heads crowns of gold.

⁵ And out of the throne proceeded lightnings and thunderings and voices: and *there were* seven lamps of fire burning before the throne, which are the seven Spirits of God.

⁶ And before the throne *there was* a sea of glass like unto crystal: and in the midst of the throne, and round about the throne, *were* four beasts full of eyes before and behind.

⁷ And the first beast *was* like a lion, and the second beast like a calf, and the third beast had a face as a man, and the fourth beast *was* like a flying eagle.

⁸ And the four beasts had each of them six wings about *him*; and *they were* full of eyes within: and they rest not day and night, saying, Holy, holy, holy, Lord God Almighty, which was, and is, and is to come.

⁹ And when those beasts give glory and honour and thanks to him that sat on the throne, who liveth for ever and ever,

¹⁰ The four and twenty elders fall down before him that sat on the throne, and worship him that liveth for ever and ever, and cast their crowns before the throne, saying,

¹¹ Thou art worthy, O Lord, to receive glory and honour and power: for thou hast created all things, and for thy pleasure they are and were created.

Cherubim

Genesis 3:1-24 - Cherubims Guarding with a Flaming Sword the Tree of Life and the Garden of Eden

¹ Now the serpent was more subtil than any beast of the field which the LORD God had made. And he said unto the woman, Yea, hath God said, Ye shall not eat of every tree of the garden?

² And the woman said unto the serpent, We may eat of the fruit of the trees of the garden:

³ But of the fruit of the tree which *is* in the midst of the garden, God hath said, Ye shall not eat of it, neither shall ye touch it, lest ye die.

⁴ And the serpent said unto the woman, Ye shall not surely die:

⁵ For God doth know that in the day ye eat thereof, then your eyes shall be opened, and ye shall be as gods, knowing good and evil.

⁶ And when the woman saw that the tree *was* good for food, and that it *was* pleasant to the eyes, and a tree to be desired to make *one* wise, she took of the fruit thereof, and did eat, and gave also unto her husband with her; and he did eat.

⁷ And the eyes of them both were opened, and they knew that they *were* naked; and they sewed fig leaves together, and made themselves aprons.

⁸ And they heard the voice of the LORD God walking in the garden in the cool of the day: and Adam and his wife hid themselves from the presence of the LORD God amongst the trees of the garden.

⁹ And the LORD God called unto Adam, and said unto him, Where *art* thou?

¹⁰ And he said, I heard thy voice in the garden, and I was afraid, because I *was* naked; and I hid myself.

¹¹ And he said, Who told thee that thou *wast* naked? Hast thou eaten of the tree, whereof I commanded thee that thou shouldest not eat?

¹² And the man said, The woman whom thou gavest *to be* with me, she gave me of the tree, and I did eat.

¹³ And the LORD God said unto the woman, What *is* this *that* thou hast done? And the woman said, The serpent beguiled me, and I did eat.

¹⁴ And the LORD God said unto the serpent, Because thou hast done this, thou *art* cursed above all cattle, and above every beast of the field; upon thy belly shalt thou go, and dust shalt thou eat all the days of thy life:

¹⁵ And I will put enmity between thee and the woman, and between thy seed and her seed; it shall bruise thy head, and thou shalt bruise his heel.

¹⁶ Unto the woman he said, I will greatly multiply thy sorrow and thy conception; in sorrow thou shalt bring forth children; and thy desire *shall be* to thy husband, and he shall rule over thee.

[17] And unto Adam he said, Because thou hast hearkened unto the voice of thy wife, and hast eaten of the tree, of which I commanded thee, saying, Thou shalt not eat of it: cursed *is* the ground for thy sake; in sorrow shalt thou eat *of* it all the days of thy life;

[18] Thorns also and thistles shall it bring forth to thee; and thou shalt eat the herb of the field;

[19] In the sweat of thy face shalt thou eat bread, till thou return unto the ground; for out of it wast thou taken: for dust thou *art*, and unto dust shalt thou return.

[20] And Adam called his wife's name Eve; because she was the mother of all living.

[21] Unto Adam also and to his wife did the LORD God make coats of skins, and clothed them.

[22] And the LORD God said, Behold, the man is become as one of us, to know good and evil: and now, lest he put forth his hand, and take also of the tree of life, and eat, and live for ever:

[23] Therefore the LORD God sent him forth from the garden of Eden, to till the ground from whence he was taken.

[24] So he drove out the man; and he placed at the east of the garden of Eden <u>Cherubims</u>, and a flaming sword which turned every way, to keep the way of the tree of life.

Exodus 25:16-22 - Two Cherubim of Gold in the Two Ends of the Mercy Seat and Upon the Ark of the Testimony

[16] And thou shalt put into the ark the testimony which I shall give thee.

[17] And thou shalt make a mercy seat *of* pure gold: two cubits and a half *shall be* the length thereof, and a cubit and a half the breadth thereof.

[18] And thou shalt make two <u>cherubims</u> *of* gold, *of* beaten work shalt thou make them, in the two ends of the mercy seat.

¹⁹ And make one <u>cherub</u> on the one end, and the other <u>cherub</u> on the other end: *even* of the mercy seat shall ye make the <u>cherubims</u> on the two ends thereof.

²⁰ And the <u>cherubims</u> shall stretch forth *their* wings on high, covering the mercy seat with their wings, and their faces *shall look* one to another; toward the mercy seat shall the faces of the <u>cherubims</u> be.

²¹ And thou shalt put the mercy seat above upon the ark; and in the ark thou shalt put the testimony that I shall give thee.

²² And there I will meet with thee, and I will commune with thee from above the mercy seat, from between the two <u>cherubims</u> which *are* upon the ark of the testimony, of all *things* which I will give thee in commandment unto the children of Israel.

Exodus 26:1-37 - Make the Tabernacle with Cherubim of Cunning Work and with Cherubim Shall it be Made

¹ Moreover thou shalt make the tabernacle *with* ten curtains *of* fine twined linen, and blue, and purple, and scarlet: *with* <u>cherubims</u> of cunning work shalt thou make them.

² The length of one curtain *shall be* eight and twenty cubits, and the breadth of one curtain four cubits: and every one of the curtains shall have one measure.

³ The five curtains shall be coupled together one to another; and *other* five curtains *shall be* coupled one to another.

⁴ And thou shalt make loops of blue upon the edge of the one curtain from the selvedge in the coupling; and likewise shalt thou make in the uttermost edge of *another* curtain, in the coupling of the second.

⁵ Fifty loops shalt thou make in the one curtain, and fifty loops shalt thou make in the edge of the curtain that *is* in the coupling of the second; that the loops may take hold one of another.

⁶ And thou shalt make fifty taches of gold, and couple the curtains together with the taches: and it shall be one tabernacle.

⁷ And thou shalt make curtains *of* goats' *hair* to be a covering upon the tabernacle: eleven curtains shalt thou make.

⁸ The length of one curtain *shall be* thirty cubits, and the breadth of one curtain four cubits: and the eleven curtains *shall be all* of one measure.

⁹ And thou shalt couple five curtains by themselves, and six curtains by themselves, and shalt double the sixth curtain in the forefront of the tabernacle.

¹⁰ And thou shalt make fifty loops on the edge of the one curtain *that is* outmost in the coupling, and fifty loops in the edge of the curtain which coupleth the second.

¹¹ And thou shalt make fifty taches of brass, and put the taches into the loops, and couple the tent together, that it may be one.

¹² And the remnant that remaineth of the curtains of the tent, the half curtain that remaineth, shall hang over the backside of the tabernacle.

¹³ And a cubit on the one side, and a cubit on the other side of that which remaineth in the length of the curtains of the tent, it shall hang over the sides of the tabernacle on this side and on that side, to cover it.

¹⁴ And thou shalt make a covering for the tent *of* rams' skins dyed red, and a covering above *of* badgers' skins.

¹⁵ And thou shalt make boards for the tabernacle *of* shittim wood standing up.

¹⁶ Ten cubits *shall be* the length of a board, and a cubit and a half *shall be* the breadth of one board.

¹⁷ Two tenons *shall there be* in one board, set in order one against another: thus shalt thou make for all the boards of the tabernacle.

¹⁸ And thou shalt make the boards for the tabernacle, twenty boards on the south side southward.

¹⁹ And thou shalt make forty sockets of silver under the twenty boards; two sockets under one board for his two tenons, and two sockets under another board for his two tenons.

[20] And for the second side of the tabernacle on the north side *there shall be* twenty boards:

[21] And their forty sockets *of* silver; two sockets under one board, and two sockets under another board.

[22] And for the sides of the tabernacle westward thou shalt make six boards.

[23] And two boards shalt thou make for the corners of the tabernacle in the two sides.

[24] And they shall be coupled together beneath, and they shall be coupled together above the head of it unto one ring: thus shall it be for them both; they shall be for the two corners.

[25] And they shall be eight boards, and their sockets *of* silver, sixteen sockets; two sockets under one board, and two sockets under another board.

[26] And thou shalt make bars *of* shittim wood; five for the boards of the one side of the tabernacle,

[27] And five bars for the boards of the other side of the tabernacle, and five bars for the boards of the side of the tabernacle, for the two sides westward.

[28] And the middle bar in the midst of the boards shall reach from end to end.

[29] And thou shalt overlay the boards with gold, and make their rings *of* gold *for* places for the bars: and thou shalt overlay the bars with gold.

[30] And thou shalt rear up the tabernacle according to the fashion thereof which was shewed thee in the mount.

[31] And thou shalt make a vail *of* blue, and purple, and scarlet, and fine twined linen of cunning work: with <u>cherubims</u> shall it be made:

[32] And thou shalt hang it upon four pillars of shittim *wood* overlaid with gold: their hooks *shall be of* gold, upon the four sockets of silver.

³³ And thou shalt hang up the vail under the taches, that thou mayest bring in thither within the vail the ark of the testimony: and the vail shall divide unto you between the holy *place* and the most holy.

³⁴ And thou shalt put the mercy seat upon the ark of the testimony in the most holy *place*.

³⁵ And thou shalt set the table without the vail, and the candlestick over against the table on the side of the tabernacle toward the south: and thou shalt put the table on the north side.

³⁶ And thou shalt make an hanging for the door of the tent, *of* blue, and purple, and scarlet, and fine twined linen, wrought with needlework.

³⁷ And thou shalt make for the hanging five pillars *of* shittim *wood*, and overlay them with gold, *and* their hooks *shall be of* gold: and thou shalt cast five sockets of brass for them.

Exodus 36:1-38 - Tabernacle Made with Cherubims of Cunning Work

¹ Then wrought Bezaleel and Aholiab, and every wise hearted man, in whom the LORD put wisdom and understanding to know how to work all manner of work for the service of the sanctuary, according to all that the LORD had commanded.

² And Moses called Bezaleel and Aholiab, and every wise hearted man, in whose heart the LORD had put wisdom, *even* every one whose heart stirred him up to come unto the work to do it:

³ And they received of Moses all the offering, which the children of Israel had brought for the work of the service of the sanctuary, to make it *withal*. And they brought yet unto him free offerings every morning.

⁴ And all the wise men, that wrought all the work of the sanctuary, came every man from his work which they made;

⁵ And they spake unto Moses, saying, The people bring much more than enough for the service of the work, which the LORD commanded to make.

⁶ And Moses gave commandment, and they caused it to be proclaimed throughout the camp, saying, Let neither man nor woman make any more work for the offering of the sanctuary. So the people were restrained from bringing.

⁷ For the stuff they had was sufficient for all the work to make it, and too much.

⁸ And every wise hearted man among them that wrought the work of the tabernacle made ten curtains *of* fine twined linen, and blue, and purple, and scarlet: *with* <u>cherubims</u> of cunning work made he them.

⁹ The length of one curtain *was* twenty and eight cubits, and the breadth of one curtain four cubits: the curtains *were* all of one size.

¹⁰ And he coupled the five curtains one unto another: and *the other* five curtains he coupled one unto another.

¹¹ And he made loops of blue on the edge of one curtain from the selvedge in the coupling: likewise he made in the uttermost side of *another* curtain, in the coupling of the second.

¹² Fifty loops made he in one curtain, and fifty loops made he in the edge of the curtain which *was* in the coupling of the second: the loops held one *curtain* to another.

¹³ And he made fifty taches of gold, and coupled the curtains one unto another with the taches: so it became one tabernacle.

¹⁴ And he made curtains *of* goats' *hair* for the tent over the tabernacle: eleven curtains he made them.

¹⁵ The length of one curtain *was* thirty cubits, and four cubits *was* the breadth of one curtain: the eleven curtains *were* of one size.

¹⁶ And he coupled five curtains by themselves, and six curtains by themselves.

¹⁷ And he made fifty loops upon the uttermost edge of the curtain in the coupling, and fifty loops made he upon the edge of the curtain which coupleth the second.

¹⁸ And he made fifty taches *of* brass to couple the tent together, that it might be one.

¹⁹ And he made a covering for the tent *of* rams' skins dyed red, and a covering *of* badgers' skins above *that*.

²⁰ And he made boards for the tabernacle *of* shittim wood, standing up.

²¹ The length of a board *was* ten cubits, and the breadth of a board one cubit and a half.

²² One board had two tenons, equally distant one from another: thus did he make for all the boards of the tabernacle.

²³ And he made boards for the tabernacle; twenty boards for the south side southward:

²⁴ And forty sockets of silver he made under the twenty boards; two sockets under one board for his two tenons, and two sockets under another board for his two tenons.

²⁵ And for the other side of the tabernacle, *which is* toward the north corner, he made twenty boards,

²⁶ And their forty sockets of silver; two sockets under one board, and two sockets under another board.

²⁷ And for the sides of the tabernacle westward he made six boards.

²⁸ And two boards made he for the corners of the tabernacle in the two sides.

²⁹ And they were coupled beneath, and coupled together at the head thereof, to one ring: thus he did to both of them in both the corners.

³⁰ And there were eight boards; and their sockets *were* sixteen sockets of silver, under every board two sockets.

³¹ And he made bars of shittim wood; five for the boards of the one side of the tabernacle,

³² And five bars for the boards of the other side of the tabernacle, and five bars for the boards of the tabernacle for the sides westward.

³³ And he made the middle bar to shoot through the boards from the one end to the other.

³⁴ And he overlaid the boards with gold, and made their rings *of* gold *to be* places for the bars, and overlaid the bars with gold.

³⁵ And he made a vail *of* blue, and purple, and scarlet, and fine twined linen: *with* <u>cherubims</u> made he it of cunning work.

³⁶ And he made thereunto four pillars *of* shittim *wood*, and overlaid them with gold: their hooks *were of* gold; and he cast for them four sockets of silver.

³⁷ And he made an hanging for the tabernacle door *of* blue, and purple, and scarlet, and fine twined linen, of needlework;

³⁸ And the five pillars of it with their hooks: and he overlaid their chapiters and their fillets with gold: but their five sockets *were of* brass.

Exodus 37:1-29 - He Made Two Cherubims of Gold, Beaten Out of One Piece at Two Ends of the Mercy Seat

¹ And Bezaleel made the ark *of* shittim wood: two cubits and a half *was* the length of it, and a cubit and a half the breadth of it, and a cubit and a half the height of it:

² And he overlaid it with pure gold within and without, and made a crown of gold to it round about.

³ And he cast for it four rings of gold, *to be set* by the four corners of it; even two rings upon the one side of it, and two rings upon the other side of it.

⁴ And he made staves *of* shittim wood, and overlaid them with gold.

⁵ And he put the staves into the rings by the sides of the ark, to bear the ark.

⁶ And he made the mercy seat *of* pure gold: two cubits and a half *was* the length thereof, and one cubit and a half the breadth thereof.

⁷ And he made two <u>cherubims</u> *of* gold, beaten out of one piece made he them, on the two ends of the mercy seat;

⁸ One <u>cherub</u> on the end on this side, and another <u>cherub</u> on the *other* end on that side: out of the mercy seat made he the <u>cherubims</u> on the two ends thereof.

⁹ And the <u>cherubims</u> spread out *their* wings on high, *and* covered with their wings over the mercy seat, with their faces one to another; *even* to the mercy seatward were the faces of the <u>cherubims</u>.

¹⁰ And he made the table *of* shittim wood: two cubits *was* the length thereof, and a cubit the breadth thereof, and a cubit and a half the height thereof:

¹¹ And he overlaid it with pure gold, and made thereunto a crown of gold round about.

¹² Also he made thereunto a border of an handbreadth round about; and made a crown of gold for the border thereof round about.

¹³ And he cast for it four rings of gold, and put the rings upon the four corners that *were* in the four feet thereof.

¹⁴ Over against the border were the rings, the places for the staves to bear the table.

¹⁵ And he made the staves *of* shittim wood, and overlaid them with gold, to bear the table.

¹⁶ And he made the vessels which *were* upon the table, his dishes, and his spoons, and his bowls, and his covers to cover withal, *of* pure gold.

¹⁷ And he made the candlestick *of* pure gold: *of* beaten work made he the candlestick; his shaft, and his branch, his bowls, his knops, and his flowers, were of the same:

¹⁸ And six branches going out of the sides thereof; three branches of the candlestick out of the one side thereof, and three branches of the candlestick out of the other side thereof:

¹⁹ Three bowls made after the fashion of almonds in one branch, a knop and a flower; and three bowls made like almonds in another branch, a knop and a flower: so throughout the six branches going out of the candlestick.

²⁰ And in the candlestick *were* four bowls made like almonds, his knops, and his flowers:

²¹ And a knop under two branches of the same, and a knop under two branches of the same, and a knop under two branches of the same, according to the six branches going out of it.

²² Their knops and their branches were of the same: all of it *was* one beaten work *of* pure gold.

²³ And he made his seven lamps, and his snuffers, and his snuffdishes, *of* pure gold.

²⁴ *Of* a talent of pure gold made he it, and all the vessels thereof.

²⁵ And he made the incense altar *of* shittim wood: the length of it *was* a cubit, and the breadth of it a cubit; *it was* foursquare; and two cubits *was* the height of it; the horns thereof were of the same.

²⁶ And he overlaid it with pure gold, *both* the top of it, and the sides thereof round about, and the horns of it: also he made unto it a crown of gold round about.

²⁷ And he made two rings of gold for it under the crown thereof, by the two corners of it, upon the two sides thereof, to be places for the staves to bear it withal.

²⁸ And he made the staves *of* shittim wood, and overlaid them with gold.

²⁹ And he made the holy anointing oil, and the pure incense of sweet spices, according to the work of the apothecary.

Numbers 7:89 - One Speaking to Moses from off the Mercy Seat from between Two Cherubims

⁸⁹ And when Moses was gone into the tabernacle of the congregation to speak with him, then he heard the voice of one speaking unto him from off the mercy seat that *was* upon the ark of testimony, from between the two <u>cherubims</u>: and he spake unto him.

1 Samuel 4:1-22 - Ark of the Covenant which Dwells between Cherubims

¹ And the word of Samuel came to all Israel. Now Israel went out against the Philistines to battle, and pitched beside Ebenezer: and the Philistines pitched in Aphek.

² And the Philistines put themselves in array against Israel: and when they joined battle, Israel was smitten before the Philistines: and they slew of the army in the field about four thousand men.

³ And when the people were come into the camp, the elders of Israel said, Wherefore hath the LORD smitten us to day before the Philistines? Let us fetch the ark of the covenant of the LORD out of Shiloh unto us, that, when it cometh among us, it may save us out of the hand of our enemies.

⁴ So the people sent to Shiloh, that they might bring from thence the ark of the covenant of the LORD of hosts, which dwelleth *between* the <u>cherubims</u>: and the two sons of Eli, Hophni and Phinehas, *were* there with the ark of the covenant of God.

⁵ And when the ark of the covenant of the LORD came into the camp, all Israel shouted with a great shout, so that the earth rang again.

⁶ And when the Philistines heard the noise of the shout, they said, What *meaneth* the noise of this great shout in the camp of the Hebrews? And they understood that the ark of the LORD was come into the camp.

⁷ And the Philistines were afraid, for they said, God is come into the camp. And they said, Woe unto us! for there hath not been such a thing heretofore.

⁸ Woe unto us! who shall deliver us out of the hand of these mighty Gods? these *are* the Gods that smote the Egyptians with all the plagues in the wilderness.

⁹ Be strong, and quit yourselves like men, O ye Philistines, that ye be not servants unto the Hebrews, as they have been to you: quit yourselves like men, and fight.

¹⁰ And the Philistines fought, and Israel was smitten, and they fled every man into his tent: and there was a very great slaughter; for there fell of Israel thirty thousand footmen.

¹¹ And the ark of God was taken; and the two sons of Eli, Hophni and Phinehas, were slain.

¹² And there ran a man of Benjamin out of the army, and came to Shiloh the same day with his clothes rent, and with earth upon his head.

¹³ And when he came, lo, Eli sat upon a seat by the wayside watching: for his heart trembled for the ark of God. And when the man came into the city, and told *it*, all the city cried out.

¹⁴ And when Eli heard the noise of the crying, he said, What *meaneth* the noise of this tumult? And the man came in hastily, and told Eli.

¹⁵ Now Eli was ninety and eight years old; and his eyes were dim, that he could not see.

¹⁶ And the man said unto Eli, I *am* he that came out of the army, and I fled to day out of the army. And he said, What is there done, my son?

¹⁷ And the messenger answered and said, Israel is fled before the Philistines, and there hath been also a great slaughter among the people, and thy two sons also, Hophni and Phinehas, are dead, and the ark of God is taken.

¹⁸ And it came to pass, when he made mention of the ark of God, that he fell from off the seat backward by the side of the gate, and his neck brake, and he died: for he was an old man, and heavy. And he had judged Israel forty years.

¹⁹ And his daughter in law, Phinehas' wife, was with child, *near* to be delivered: and when she heard the tidings that the ark of God was taken, and that her father in law and her husband were dead, she bowed herself and travailed; for her pains came upon her.

²⁰ And about the time of her death the women that stood by her said unto her, Fear not; for thou hast born a son. But she answered not, neither did she regard *it*.

²¹ And she named the child Ichabod, saying, The glory is departed from Israel: because the ark of God was taken, and because of her father in law and her husband.

²² And she said, The glory is departed from Israel: for the ark of God is taken.

2 Samuel 6:1-23 - Ark of God that Dwells between the Cherubims

¹ Again, David gathered together all *the* chosen *men* of Israel, thirty thousand.

² And David arose, and went with all the people that *were* with him from Baale of Judah, to bring up from thence the ark of God, whose name is called by the name of the LORD of hosts that dwelleth *between* the cherubims.

³ And they set the ark of God upon a new cart, and brought it out of the house of Abinadab that *was* in Gibeah: and Uzzah and Ahio, the sons of Abinadab, drave the new cart.

⁴ And they brought it out of the house of Abinadab which *was* at Gibeah, accompanying the ark of God: and Ahio went before the ark.

⁵ And David and all the house of Israel played before the LORD on all manner of *instruments made of* fir wood, even on harps, and on psalteries, and on timbrels, and on cornets, and on cymbals.

⁶ And when they came to Nachon's threshingfloor, Uzzah put forth *his hand* to the ark of God, and took hold of it; for the oxen shook *it*.

⁷ And the anger of the LORD was kindled against Uzzah; and God smote him there for *his* error; and there he died by the ark of God.

⁸ And David was displeased, because the LORD had made a breach upon Uzzah: and he called the name of the place Perezuzzah to this day.

⁹ And David was afraid of the LORD that day, and said, How shall the ark of the LORD come to me?

¹⁰ So David would not remove the ark of the LORD unto him into the city of David: but David carried it aside into the house of Obededom the Gittite.

¹¹ And the ark of the LORD continued in the house of Obededom the Gittite three months: and the LORD blessed Obededom, and all his household.

[12] And it was told king David, saying, The LORD hath blessed the house of Obededom, and all that *pertaineth* unto him, because of the ark of God. So David went and brought up the ark of God from the house of Obededom into the city of David with gladness.

[13] And it was *so*, that when they that bare the ark of the LORD had gone six paces, he sacrificed oxen and fatlings.

[14] And David danced before the LORD with all *his* might; and David *was* girded with a linen ephod.

[15] So David and all the house of Israel brought up the ark of the LORD with shouting, and with the sound of the trumpet.

[16] And as the ark of the LORD came into the city of David, Michal Saul's daughter looked through a window, and saw king David leaping and dancing before the LORD; and she despised him in her heart.

[17] And they brought in the ark of the LORD, and set it in his place, in the midst of the tabernacle that David had pitched for it: and David offered burnt offerings and peace offerings before the LORD.

[18] And as soon as David had made an end of offering burnt offerings and peace offerings, he blessed the people in the name of the LORD of hosts.

[19] And he dealt among all the people, *even* among the whole multitude of Israel, as well to the women as men, to every one a cake of bread, and a good piece *of flesh*, and a flagon *of wine*. So all the people departed every one to his house.

[20] Then David returned to bless his household. And Michal the daughter of Saul came out to meet David, and said, How glorious was the king of Israel to day, who uncovered himself to day in the eyes of the handmaids of his servants, as one of the vain fellows shamelessly uncovereth himself!

[21] And David said unto Michal, *It was* before the LORD, which chose me before thy father, and before all his house, to appoint me ruler over the people of the LORD, over Israel: therefore will I play before the LORD.

²² And I will yet be more vile than thus, and will be base in mine own sight: and of the maidservants which thou hast spoken of, of them shall I be had in honour.

²³ Therefore Michal the daughter of Saul had no child unto the day of her death.

1 Kings 6:11-38 - Two Cherubims Carved Out of Olive Wood

¹¹ And the word of the LORD came to Solomon, saying,

¹² *Concerning* this house which thou art in building, if thou wilt walk in my statutes, and execute my judgments, and keep all my commandments to walk in them; then will I perform my word with thee, which I spake unto David thy father:

¹³ And I will dwell among the children of Israel, and will not forsake my people Israel.

¹⁴ So Solomon built the house, and finished it.

¹⁵ And he built the walls of the house within with boards of cedar, both the floor of the house, and the walls of the cieling: *and* he covered *them* on the inside with wood, and covered the floor of the house with planks of fir.

¹⁶ And he built twenty cubits on the sides of the house, both the floor and the walls with boards of cedar: he even built *them* for it within, *even* for the oracle, *even* for the most holy *place*.

¹⁷ And the house, that *is*, the temple before it, was forty cubits *long*.

¹⁸ And the cedar of the house within *was* carved with knops and open flowers: all *was* cedar; there was no stone seen.

¹⁹ And the oracle he prepared in the house within, to set there the ark of the covenant of the LORD.

²⁰ And the oracle in the forepart *was* twenty cubits in length, and twenty cubits in breadth, and twenty cubits in the height thereof: and he overlaid it with pure gold; and *so* covered the altar *which was of* cedar.

²¹ So Solomon overlaid the house within with pure gold: and he made a partition by the chains of gold before the oracle; and he overlaid it with gold.

²² And the whole house he overlaid with gold, until he had finished all the house: also the whole altar that *was* by the oracle he overlaid with gold.

²³ And within the oracle he made two <u>cherubims</u> *of* olive tree, *each* ten cubits high.

²⁴ And five cubits *was* the one wing of the <u>cherub,</u> and five cubits the other wing of the <u>cherub</u>: from the uttermost part of the one wing unto the uttermost part of the other *were* ten cubits.

²⁵ And the other <u>cherub</u> *was* ten cubits: both the <u>cherubims</u> *were* of one measure and one size.

²⁶ The height of the one <u>cherub</u> *was* ten cubits, and so *was it* of the other <u>cherub</u>.

²⁷ And he set the <u>cherubims</u> within the inner house: and they stretched forth the wings of the <u>cherubims,</u> so that the wing of the one touched the *one* wall, and the wing of the other <u>cherub</u> touched the other wall; and their wings touched one another in the midst of the house.

²⁸ And he overlaid the <u>cherubims</u> with gold.

²⁹ And he carved all the walls of the house round about with carved figures of <u>cherubims</u> and palm trees and open flowers, within and without.

³⁰ And the floor of the house he overlaid with gold, within and without.

³¹ And for the entering of the oracle he made doors *of* olive tree: the lintel *and* side posts *were* a fifth part *of the wall*.

³² The two doors also *were of* olive tree; and he carved upon them carvings of <u>cherubims</u> and palm trees and open flowers, and overlaid *them* with gold, and spread gold upon the <u>cherubims,</u> and upon the palm trees.

³³ So also made he for the door of the temple posts *of* olive tree, a fourth part *of the wall*.

³⁴ And the two doors *were of* fir tree: the two leaves of the one door *were* folding, and the two leaves of the other door *were* folding.

³⁵ And he carved *thereon* cherubims and palm trees and open flowers: and covered *them* with gold fitted upon the carved work.

³⁶ And he built the inner court with three rows of hewed stone, and a row of cedar beams.

³⁷ In the fourth year was the foundation of the house of the LORD laid, in the month Zif:

³⁸ And in the eleventh year, in the month Bul, which *is* the eighth month, was the house finished throughout all the parts thereof, and according to all the fashion of it. So was he seven years in building it.

1 Kings 7:13-36 - On the Borders that were between Ledges were Cherubims and on Plates of the Border's Ledges He Graved Cherubims

¹³ And king Solomon sent and fetched Hiram out of Tyre.

¹⁴ He *was* a widow's son of the tribe of Naphtali, and his father *was* a man of Tyre, a worker in brass: and he was filled with wisdom, and understanding, and cunning to work all works in brass. And he came to king Solomon, and wrought all his work.

¹⁵ For he cast two pillars of brass, of eighteen cubits high apiece: and a line of twelve cubits did compass either of them about.

¹⁶ And he made two chapters *of* molten brass, to set upon the tops of the pillars: the height of the one chapter *was* five cubits, and the height of the other chapter *was* five cubits:

¹⁷ *And* nets of checker work, and wreaths of chain work, for the chapiters which *were* upon the top of the pillars; seven for the one chapter, and seven for the other chapter.

¹⁸ And he made the pillars, and two rows round about upon the one network, to cover the chapiters that *were* upon the top, with pomegranates: and so did he for the other chapter.

¹⁹ And the chapiters that *were* upon the top of the pillars *were* of lily work in the porch, four cubits.

²⁰ And the chapiters upon the two pillars *had pomegranates* also above, over against the belly which *was* by the network: and the pomegranates *were* two hundred in rows round about upon the other chapiter.

²¹ And he set up the pillars in the porch of the temple: and he set up the right pillar, and called the name thereof Jachin: and he set up the left pillar, and called the name thereof Boaz.

²² And upon the top of the pillars *was* lily work: so was the work of the pillars finished.

²³ And he made a molten sea, ten cubits from the one brim to the other: *it was* round all about, and his height *was* five cubits: and a line of thirty cubits did compass it round about.

²⁴ And under the brim of it round about *there were* knops compassing it, ten in a cubit, compassing the sea round about: the knops *were* cast in two rows, when it was cast.

²⁵ It stood upon twelve oxen, three looking toward the north, and three looking toward the west, and three looking toward the south, and three looking toward the east: and the sea *was set* above upon them, and all their hinder parts *were* inward.

²⁶ And it *was* an hand breadth thick, and the brim thereof was wrought like the brim of a cup, with flowers of lilies: it contained two thousand baths.

²⁷ And he made ten bases of brass; four cubits *was* the length of one base, and four cubits the breadth thereof, and three cubits the height of it.

²⁸ And the work of the bases *was* on this *manner*: they had borders, and the borders *were* between the ledges:

²⁹ And on the borders that *were* between the ledges *were* lions, oxen, and <u>cherubims</u>: and upon the ledges *there was* a base above: and beneath the lions and oxen *were* certain additions made of thin work.

⁣³⁰ And every base had four brasen wheels, and plates of brass: and the four corners thereof had undersetters: under the laver *were* undersetters molten, at the side of every addition.

³¹ And the mouth of it within the chapiter and above *was* a cubit: but the mouth thereof *was* round *after* the work of the base, a cubit and an half: and also upon the mouth of it *were* gravings with their borders, foursquare, not round.

³² And under the borders *were* four wheels; and the axletrees of the wheels *were joined* to the base: and the height of a wheel *was* a cubit and half a cubit.

³³ And the work of the wheels *was* like the work of a chariot wheel: their axletrees, and their naves, and their felloes, and their spokes, *were* all molten.

³⁴ And *there were* four undersetters to the four corners of one base: *and* the undersetters *were* of the very base itself.

³⁵ And in the top of the base *was there* a round compass of half a cubit high: and on the top of the base the ledges thereof and the borders thereof *were* of the same.

³⁶ For on the plates of the ledges thereof, and on the borders thereof, he graved <u>cherubims</u>, lions, and palm trees, according to the proportion of every one, and additions round about.

1 Kings 8:1-24 - The Most Holy Place, Even Under the Wings of Cherubims and Spread Forth their Two Wings

¹ Then Solomon assembled the elders of Israel, and all the heads of the tribes, the chief of the fathers of the children of Israel, unto king Solomon in Jerusalem, that they might bring up the ark of the covenant of the LORD out of the city of David, which *is* Zion.

² And all the men of Israel assembled themselves unto king Solomon at the feast in the month Ethanim, which *is* the seventh month.

³ And all the elders of Israel came, and the priests took up the ark.

⁴ And they brought up the ark of the LORD, and the tabernacle of the congregation, and all the holy vessels that *were* in the tabernacle, even those did the priests and the Levites bring up.

⁵ And king Solomon, and all the congregation of Israel, that were assembled unto him, *were* with him before the ark, sacrificing sheep and oxen, that could not be told nor numbered for multitude.

⁶ And the priests brought in the ark of the covenant of the LORD unto his place, into the oracle of the house, to the most holy *place, even* under the wings of the <u>cherubims</u>.

⁷ For the <u>cherubims</u> spread forth *their* two wings over the place of the ark, and the <u>cherubims</u> covered the ark and the staves thereof above.

⁸ And they drew out the staves, that the ends of the staves were seen out in the holy *place* before the oracle, and they were not seen without: and there they are unto this day.

⁹ *There was* nothing in the ark save the two tables of stone, which Moses put there at Horeb, when the LORD made *a covenant* with the children of Israel, when they came out of the land of Egypt.

¹⁰ And it came to pass, when the priests were come out of the holy *place*, that the cloud filled the house of the LORD,

¹¹ So that the priests could not stand to minister because of the cloud: for the glory of the LORD had filled the house of the LORD.

¹² Then spake Solomon, The LORD said that he would dwell in the thick darkness.

¹³ I have surely built thee an house to dwell in, a settled place for thee to abide in for ever.

¹⁴ And the king turned his face about, and blessed all the congregation of Israel: (and all the congregation of Israel stood;)

¹⁵ And he said, Blessed *be* the LORD God of Israel, which spake with his mouth unto David my father, and hath with his hand fulfilled *it*, saying,

¹⁶ Since the day that I brought forth my people Israel out of Egypt, I chose no city out of all the tribes of Israel to build an house, that my name might be therein; but I chose David to be over my people Israel.

[17] And it was in the heart of David my father to build an house for the name of the LORD God of Israel.

[18] And the LORD said unto David my father, Whereas it was in thine heart to build an house unto my name, thou didst well that it was in thine heart.

[19] Nevertheless thou shalt not build the house; but thy son that shall come forth out of thy loins, he shall build the house unto my name.

[20] And the LORD hath performed his word that he spake, and I am risen up in the room of David my father, and sit on the throne of Israel, as the LORD promised, and have built an house for the name of the LORD God of Israel.

[21] And I have set there a place for the ark, wherein *is* the covenant of the LORD, which he made with our fathers, when he brought them out of the land of Egypt.

[22] And Solomon stood before the altar of the LORD in the presence of all the congregation of Israel, and spread forth his hands toward heaven:

[23] And he said, LORD God of Israel, *there is* no God like thee, in heaven above, or on earth beneath, who keepest covenant and mercy with thy servants that walk before thee with all their heart:

[24] Who hast kept with thy servant David my father that thou promisedst him: thou spakest also with thy mouth, and hast fulfilled *it* with thine hand, as *it is* this day.

2 Kings 19:1-37 - Lord God of Israel which Dwells between Cherubims

[1] And it came to pass, when king Hezekiah heard *it*, that he rent his clothes, and covered himself with sackcloth, and went into the house of the LORD.

[2] And he sent Eliakim, which *was* over the household, and Shebna the scribe, and the elders of the priests, covered with sackcloth, to Isaiah the prophet the son of Amoz.

³ And they said unto him, Thus saith Hezekiah, This day *is* a day of trouble, and of rebuke, and blasphemy: for the children are come to the birth, and *there is* not strength to bring forth.

⁴ It may be the LORD thy God will hear all the words of Rabshakeh, whom the king of Assyria his master hath sent to reproach the living God; and will reprove the words which the LORD thy God hath heard: wherefore lift up *thy* prayer for the remnant that are left.

⁵ So the servants of king Hezekiah came to Isaiah.

⁶ And Isaiah said unto them, Thus shall ye say to your master, Thus saith the LORD, Be not afraid of the words which thou hast heard, with which the servants of the king of Assyria have blasphemed me.

⁷ Behold, I will send a blast upon him, and he shall hear a rumour, and shall return to his own land; and I will cause him to fall by the sword in his own land.

⁸ So Rabshakeh returned, and found the king of Assyria warring against Libnah: for he had heard that he was departed from Lachish.

⁹ And when he heard say of Tirhakah king of Ethiopia, Behold, he is come out to fight against thee: he sent messengers again unto Hezekiah, saying,

¹⁰ Thus shall ye speak to Hezekiah king of Judah, saying, Let not thy God in whom thou trustest deceive thee, saying, Jerusalem shall not be delivered into the hand of the king of Assyria.

¹¹ Behold, thou hast heard what the kings of Assyria have done to all lands, by destroying them utterly: and shalt thou be delivered?

¹² Have the gods of the nations delivered them which my fathers have destroyed; *as* Gozan, and Haran, and Rezeph, and the children of Eden which *were* in Thelasar?

¹³ Where *is* the king of Hamath, and the king of Arpad, and the king of the city of Sepharvaim, of Hena, and Ivah?

¹⁴ And Hezekiah received the letter of the hand of the messengers, and read it: and Hezekiah went up into the house of the LORD, and spread it before the LORD.

¹⁵ And Hezekiah prayed before the LORD, and said, O LORD God of Israel, which dwellest *between* the <u>cherubims</u>, thou art the God, *even* thou alone, of all the kingdoms of the earth; thou hast made heaven and earth.

¹⁶ LORD, bow down thine ear, and hear: open, LORD, thine eyes, and see: and hear the words of Sennacherib, which hath sent him to reproach the living God.

¹⁷ Of a truth, LORD, the kings of Assyria have destroyed the nations and their lands,

¹⁸ And have cast their gods into the fire: for they *were* no gods, but the work of men's hands, wood and stone: therefore they have destroyed them.

¹⁹ Now therefore, O LORD our God, I beseech thee, save thou us out of his hand, that all the kingdoms of the earth may know that thou *art* the LORD God, *even* thou only.

²⁰ Then Isaiah the son of Amoz sent to Hezekiah, saying, Thus saith the LORD God of Israel, *That* which thou hast prayed to me against Sennacherib king of Assyria I have heard.

²¹ This *is* the word that the LORD hath spoken concerning him; The virgin the daughter of Zion hath despised thee, *and* laughed thee to scorn; the daughter of Jerusalem hath shaken her head at thee.

²² Whom hast thou reproached and blasphemed? and against whom hast thou exalted *thy* voice, and lifted up thine eyes on high? *even* against the Holy *One* of Israel.

²³ By thy messengers thou hast reproached the Lord, and hast said, With the multitude of my chariots I am come up to the height of the mountains, to the sides of Lebanon, and will cut down the tall cedar trees thereof, *and* the choice fir trees thereof: and I will enter into the lodgings of his borders, *and into* the forest of his Carmel.

²⁴ I have digged and drunk strange waters, and with the sole of my feet have I dried up all the rivers of besieged places.

²⁵ Hast thou not heard long ago *how* I have done it, *and* of ancient times that I have formed it? now have I brought it to pass, that thou shouldest be to lay waste fenced cities *into* ruinous heaps.

²⁶ Therefore their inhabitants were of small power, they were dismayed and confounded; they were *as* the grass of the field, and *as* the green herb, *as* the grass on the housetops, and *as corn* blasted before it be grown up.

²⁷ But I know thy abode, and thy going out, and thy coming in, and thy rage against me.

²⁸ Because thy rage against me and thy tumult is come up into mine ears, therefore I will put my hook in thy nose, and my bridle in thy lips, and I will turn thee back by the way by which thou camest.

²⁹ And this *shall be* a sign unto thee, Ye shall eat this year such things as grow of themselves, and in the second year that which springeth of the same; and in the third year sow ye, and reap, and plant vineyards, and eat the fruits thereof.

³⁰ And the remnant that is escaped of the house of Judah shall yet again take root downward, and bear fruit upward.

³¹ For out of Jerusalem shall go forth a remnant, and they that escape out of mount Zion: the zeal of the LORD *of hosts* shall do this.

³² Therefore thus saith the LORD concerning the king of Assyria, He shall not come into this city, nor shoot an arrow there, nor come before it with shield, nor cast a bank against it.

³³ By the way that he came, by the same shall he return, and shall not come into this city, saith the LORD.

³⁴ For I will defend this city, to save it, for mine own sake, and for my servant David's sake.

³⁵ And it came to pass that night, that the angel of the LORD went out, and smote in the camp of the Assyrians an hundred fourscore and five thousand: and when they arose early in the morning, behold, they *were* all dead corpses.

³⁶ So Sennacherib king of Assyria departed, and went and returned, and dwelt at Nineveh.

^{37} And it came to pass, as he was worshipping in the house of Nisroch his god, that Adrammelech and Sharezer his sons smote him with the sword: and they escaped into the land of Armenia. And Esarhaddon his son reigned in his stead.

1 Chronicles 13:1-14 - Ark of God that Dwells between Cherubims

^{1} And David consulted with the captains of thousands and hundreds, *and* with every leader.

^{2} And David said unto all the congregation of Israel, If *it seem* good unto you, and *that it be* of the LORD our God, let us send abroad unto our brethren every where, *that are* left in all the land of Israel, and with them *also* to the priests and Levites *which are* in their cities *and* suburbs, that they may gather themselves unto us:

^{3} And let us bring again the ark of our God to us: for we enquired not at it in the days of Saul.

^{4} And all the congregation said that they would do so: for the thing was right in the eyes of all the people.

^{5} So David gathered all Israel together, from Shihor of Egypt even unto the entering of Hemath, to bring the ark of God from Kirjathjearim.

^{6} And David went up, and all Israel, to Baalah, *that is*, to Kirjathjearim, which *belonged* to Judah, to bring up thence the ark of God the LORD, that dwelleth *between* the <u>cherubims</u>, whose name is called *on it*.

^{7} And they carried the ark of God in a new cart out of the house of Abinadab: and Uzza and Ahio drave the cart.

^{8} And David and all Israel played before God with all *their* might, and with singing, and with harps, and with psalteries, and with timbrels, and with cymbals, and with trumpets.

^{9} And when they came unto the threshingfloor of Chidon, Uzza put forth his hand to hold the ark; for the oxen stumbled.

[10] And the anger of the LORD was kindled against Uzza, and he smote him, because he put his hand to the ark: and there he died before God.

[11] And David was displeased, because the LORD had made a breach upon Uzza: wherefore that place is called Perezuzza to this day.

[12] And David was afraid of God that day, saying, How shall I bring the ark of God *home* to me?

[13] So David brought not the ark *home* to himself to the city of David, but carried it aside into the house of Obededom the Gittite.

[14] And the ark of God remained with the family of Obededom in his house three months. And the LORD blessed the house of Obededom, and all that he had.

1 Chronicles 28:1-21 - Chariot of the Cherubims that Covered the Ark of the Covenant of the Lord

[1] And David assembled all the princes of Israel, the princes of the tribes, and the captains of the companies that ministered to the king by course, and the captains over the thousands, and captains over the hundreds, and the stewards over all the substance and possession of the king, and of his sons, with the officers, and with the mighty men, and with all the valiant men, unto Jerusalem.

[2] Then David the king stood up upon his feet, and said, Hear me, my brethren, and my people: *As for me*, I *had* in mine heart to build an house of rest for the ark of the covenant of the LORD, and for the footstool of our God, and had made ready for the building:

[3] But God said unto me, Thou shalt not build an house for my name, because thou *hast been* a man of war, and hast shed blood.

[4] Howbeit the LORD God of Israel chose me before all the house of my father to be king over Israel for ever: for he hath chosen Judah *to be* the ruler; and of the house of Judah, the house of my father; and among the sons of my father he liked me to make *me* king over all Israel:

⁵ And of all my sons, (for the LORD hath given me many sons,) he hath chosen Solomon my son to sit upon the throne of the kingdom of the LORD over Israel.

⁶ And he said unto me, Solomon thy son, he shall build my house and my courts: for I have chosen him *to be* my son, and I will be his father.

⁷ Moreover I will establish his kingdom for ever, if he be constant to do my commandments and my judgments, as at this day.

⁸ Now therefore in the sight of all Israel the congregation of the LORD, and in the audience of our God, keep and seek for all the commandments of the LORD your God: that ye may possess this good land, and leave *it* for an inheritance for your children after you for ever.

⁹ And thou, Solomon my son, know thou the God of thy father, and serve him with a perfect heart and with a willing mind: for the LORD searcheth all hearts, and understandeth all the imaginations of the thoughts: if thou seek him, he will be found of thee; but if thou forsake him, he will cast thee off for ever.

¹⁰ Take heed now; for the LORD hath chosen thee to build an house for the sanctuary: be strong, and do *it*.

¹¹ Then David gave to Solomon his son the pattern of the porch, and of the houses thereof, and of the treasuries thereof, and of the upper chambers thereof, and of the inner parlours thereof, and of the place of the mercy seat,

¹² And the pattern of all that he had by the spirit, of the courts of the house of the LORD, and of all the chambers round about, of the treasuries of the house of God, and of the treasuries of the dedicated things:

¹³ Also for the courses of the priests and the Levites, and for all the work of the service of the house of the LORD, and for all the vessels of service in the house of the LORD.

¹⁴ *He gave* of gold by weight for *things* of gold, for all instruments of all manner of service; *silver also* for all instruments of silver by weight, for all instruments of every kind of service:

¹⁵ Even the weight for the candlesticks of gold, and for their lamps of gold, by weight for every candlestick, and for the lamps thereof: and for the candlesticks of silver by weight, *both* for the candlestick, and *also* for the lamps thereof, according to the use of every candlestick.

¹⁶ And by weight *he gave* gold for the tables of shewbread, for every table; and *likewise* silver for the tables of silver:

¹⁷ Also pure gold for the fleshhooks, and the bowls, and the cups: and for the golden basons *he gave gold* by weight for every bason; and *likewise silver* by weight for every bason of silver:

¹⁸ And for the altar of incense refined gold by weight; and gold for the pattern of the chariot of the <u>cherubims</u>, that spread out *their wings*, and covered the ark of the covenant of the LORD.

¹⁹ All *this, said David*, the LORD made me understand in writing by *his* hand upon me, *even* all the works of this pattern.

²⁰ And David said to Solomon his son, Be strong and of good courage, and do *it*: fear not, nor be dismayed: for the LORD God, *even* my God, *will be* with thee; he will not fail thee, nor forsake thee, until thou hast finished all the work for the service of the house of the LORD.

²¹ And, behold, the courses of the priests and the Levites, *even they shall be with thee* for all the service of the house of God: and *there shall be* with thee for all manner of workmanship every willing skilful man, for any manner of service: also the princes and all the people *will be* wholly at thy commandment.

2 Chronicles 3:1-17 - Graved Cherubims on the Walls and Most Holy House, Two Cherubims Description

¹ Then Solomon began to build the house of the LORD at Jerusalem in mount Moriah, where *the LORD* appeared unto David his father, in the place that David had prepared in the threshingfloor of Ornan the Jebusite.

² And he began to build in the second *day* of the second month, in the fourth year of his reign.

³ Now these *are the things wherein* Solomon was instructed for the building of the house of God. The length by cubits after the first measure *was* threescore cubits, and the breadth twenty cubits.

⁴ And the porch that *was* in the front *of the house*, the length *of it was* according to the breadth of the house, twenty cubits, and the height *was* an hundred and twenty: and he overlaid it within with pure gold.

⁵ And the greater house he cieled with fir tree, which he overlaid with fine gold, and set thereon palm trees and chains.

⁶ And he garnished the house with precious stones for beauty: and the gold *was* gold of Parvaim.

⁷ He overlaid also the house, the beams, the posts, and the walls thereof, and the doors thereof, with gold; and graved cherubims on the walls.

⁸ And he made the most holy house, the length whereof *was* according to the breadth of the house, twenty cubits, and the breadth thereof twenty cubits: and he overlaid it with fine gold, *amounting* to six hundred talents.

⁹ And the weight of the nails *was* fifty shekels of gold. And he overlaid the upper chambers with gold.

¹⁰ And in the most holy house he made two cherubims of image work, and overlaid them with gold.

¹¹ And the wings of the cherubims *were* twenty cubits long: one wing *of the one cherub* was five cubits, reaching to the wall of the house: and the other wing *was likewise* five cubits, reaching to the wing of the other cherub.

¹² And *one* wing of the other cherub *was* five cubits, reaching to the wall of the house: and the other wing *was* five cubits *also*, joining to the wing of the other cherub.

¹³ The wings of these cherubims spread themselves forth twenty cubits: and they stood on their feet, and their faces *were* inward.

¹⁴ And he made the vail *of* blue, and purple, and crimson, and fine linen, and wrought cherubims thereon.

[15] Also he made before the house two pillars of thirty and five cubits high, and the chapter that *was* on the top of each of them *was* five cubits.

[16] And he made chains, *as* in the oracle, and put *them* on the heads of the pillars; and made an hundred pomegranates, and put *them* on the chains.

[17] And he reared up the pillars before the temple, one on the right hand, and the other on the left; and called the name of that on the right hand Jachin, and the name of that on the left Boaz.

2 Chronicles 5:1-14 - Cherubims Spread their Wings over the Ark

[1] Thus all the work that Solomon made for the house of the LORD was finished: and Solomon brought in *all* the things that David his father had dedicated; and the silver, and the gold, and all the instruments, put he among the treasures of the house of God.

[2] Then Solomon assembled the elders of Israel, and all the heads of the tribes, the chief of the fathers of the children of Israel, unto Jerusalem, to bring up the ark of the covenant of the LORD out of the city of David, which *is* Zion.

[3] Wherefore all the men of Israel assembled themselves unto the king in the feast which *was* in the seventh month.

[4] And all the elders of Israel came; and the Levites took up the ark.

[5] And they brought up the ark, and the tabernacle of the congregation, and all the holy vessels that *were* in the tabernacle, these did the priests *and* the Levites bring up.

[6] Also king Solomon, and all the congregation of Israel that were assembled unto him before the ark, sacrificed sheep and oxen, which could not be told nor numbered for multitude.

[7] And the priests brought in the ark of the covenant of the LORD unto his place, to the oracle of the house, into the most holy *place, even* under the wings of the cherubims:

⁸ For the <u>cherubims</u> spread forth *their* wings over the place of the ark, and the <u>cherubims</u> covered the ark and the staves thereof above.

⁹ And they drew out the staves *of the ark*, that the ends of the staves were seen from the ark before the oracle; but they were not seen without. And there it is unto this day.

¹⁰ *There was* nothing in the ark save the two tables which Moses put *therein* at Horeb, when the LORD made *a covenant* with the children of Israel, when they came out of Egypt.

¹¹ And it came to pass, when the priests were come out of the holy *place*: (for all the priests *that were* present were sanctified, *and* did not *then* wait by course:

¹² Also the Levites *which were* the singers, all of them of Asaph, of Heman, of Jeduthun, with their sons and their brethren, *being* arrayed in white linen, having cymbals and psalteries and harps, stood at the east end of the altar, and with them an hundred and twenty priests sounding with trumpets:)

¹³ It came even to pass, as the trumpeters and singers *were* as one, to make one sound to be heard in praising and thanking the LORD; and when they lifted up *their* voice with the trumpets and cymbals and instruments of musick, and praised the LORD, *saying*, For *he is* good; for his mercy *endureth* for ever: that *then* the house was filled with a cloud, *even* the house of the LORD;

¹⁴ So that the priests could not stand to minister by reason of the cloud: for the glory of the LORD had filled the house of God.

Psalms 80 - Shepherd of Israel, Thou that Dwells between Cherubims

¹ (To the chief Musician upon Shoshannimeduth, A Psalm of Asaph.) Give ear, O Shepherd of Israel, thou that leadest Joseph like a flock; thou that dwellest *between* the <u>cherubims</u>, shine forth.

² Before Ephraim and Benjamin and Manasseh stir up thy strength, and come *and* save us.

³ Turn us again, O God, and cause thy face to shine; and we shall be saved.

⁴ O LORD God of hosts, how long wilt thou be angry against the prayer of thy people?

⁵ Thou feedest them with the bread of tears; and givest them tears to drink in great measure.

⁶ Thou makest us a strife unto our neighbours: and our enemies laugh among themselves.

⁷ Turn us again, O God of hosts, and cause thy face to shine; and we shall be saved.

⁸ Thou hast brought a vine out of Egypt: thou hast cast out the heathen, and planted it.

⁹ Thou preparedst *room* before it, and didst cause it to take deep root, and it filled the land.

¹⁰ The hills were covered with the shadow of it, and the boughs thereof *were like* the goodly cedars.

¹¹ She sent out her boughs unto the sea, and her branches unto the river.

¹² Why hast thou *then* broken down her hedges, so that all they which pass by the way do pluck her?

¹³ The boar out of the wood doth waste it, and the wild beast of the field doth devour it.

¹⁴ Return, we beseech thee, O God of hosts: look down from heaven, and behold, and visit this vine;

¹⁵ And the vineyard which thy right hand hath planted, and the branch *that* thou madest strong for thyself.

¹⁶ *It is* burned with fire, *it is* cut down: they perish at the rebuke of thy countenance.

¹⁷ Let thy hand be upon the man of thy right hand, upon the son of man *whom* thou madest strong for thyself.

[18] So will not we go back from thee: quicken us, and we will call upon thy name.

[19] Turn us again, O LORD God of hosts, cause thy face to shine; and we shall be saved.

Psalms 99 - Lord Reigns and Sits between the Cherubims

[1] The LORD reigneth; let the people tremble: he sitteth *between* the cherubims; let the earth be moved.

[2] The LORD *is* great in Zion; and he *is* high above all the people.

[3] Let them praise thy great and terrible name; *for* it *is* holy.

[4] The king's strength also loveth judgment; thou dost establish equity, thou executest judgment and righteousness in Jacob.

[5] Exalt ye the LORD our God, and worship at his footstool; *for* he *is* holy.

[6] Moses and Aaron among his priests, and Samuel among them that call upon his name; they called upon the LORD, and he answered them.

[7] He spake unto them in the cloudy pillar: they kept his testimonies, and the ordinance *that* he gave them.

[8] Thou answeredst them, O LORD our God: thou wast a God that forgavest them, though thou tookest vengeance of their inventions.

[9] Exalt the LORD our God, and worship at his holy hill; for the LORD our God *is* holy.

Isaiah 37:1-38 - Lord of Hosts, God of Israel that Dwells between Cherubims

[1] And it came to pass, when king Hezekiah heard *it*, that he rent his clothes, and covered himself with sackcloth, and went into the house of the LORD.

² And he sent Eliakim, who *was* over the household, and Shebna the scribe, and the elders of the priests covered with sackcloth, unto Isaiah the prophet the son of Amoz.

³ And they said unto him, Thus saith Hezekiah, This day *is* a day of trouble, and of rebuke, and of blasphemy: for the children are come to the birth, and *there is* not strength to bring forth.

⁴ It may be the LORD thy God will hear the words of Rabshakeh, whom the king of Assyria his master hath sent to reproach the living God, and will reprove the words which the LORD thy God hath heard: wherefore lift up *thy* prayer for the remnant that is left.

⁵ So the servants of king Hezekiah came to Isaiah.

⁶ And Isaiah said unto them, Thus shall ye say unto your master, Thus saith the LORD, Be not afraid of the words that thou hast heard, wherewith the servants of the king of Assyria have blasphemed me.

⁷ Behold, I will send a blast upon him, and he shall hear a rumour, and return to his own land; and I will cause him to fall by the sword in his own land.

⁸ So Rabshakeh returned, and found the king of Assyria warring against Libnah: for he had heard that he was departed from Lachish.

⁹ And he heard say concerning Tirhakah king of Ethiopia, He is come forth to make war with thee. And when he heard *it*, he sent messengers to Hezekiah, saying,

¹⁰ Thus shall ye speak to Hezekiah king of Judah, saying, Let not thy God, in whom thou trustest, deceive thee, saying, Jerusalem shall not be given into the hand of the king of Assyria.

¹¹ Behold, thou hast heard what the kings of Assyria have done to all lands by destroying them utterly; and shalt thou be delivered?

¹² Have the gods of the nations delivered them which my fathers have destroyed, *as* Gozan, and Haran, and Rezeph, and the children of Eden which *were* in Telassar?

¹³ Where *is* the king of Hamath, and the king of Arphad, and the king of the city of Sepharvaim, Hena, and Ivah?

[14] And Hezekiah received the letter from the hand of the messengers, and read it: and Hezekiah went up unto the house of the LORD, and spread it before the LORD.

[15] And Hezekiah prayed unto the LORD, saying,

[16] O LORD of hosts, God of Israel, that dwellest *between* the cherubims, thou *art* the God, *even* thou alone, of all the kingdoms of the earth: thou hast made heaven and earth.

[17] Incline thine ear, O LORD, and hear; open thine eyes, O LORD, and see: and hear all the words of Sennacherib, which hath sent to reproach the living God.

[18] Of a truth, LORD, the kings of Assyria have laid waste all the nations, and their countries,

[19] And have cast their gods into the fire: for they *were* no gods, but the work of men's hands, wood and stone: therefore they have destroyed them.

[20] Now therefore, O LORD our God, save us from his hand, that all the kingdoms of the earth may know that thou *art* the LORD, *even* thou only.

[21] Then Isaiah the son of Amoz sent unto Hezekiah, saying, Thus saith the LORD God of Israel, Whereas thou hast prayed to me against Sennacherib king of Assyria:

[22] This *is* the word which the LORD hath spoken concerning him; The virgin, the daughter of Zion, hath despised thee, *and* laughed thee to scorn; the daughter of Jerusalem hath shaken her head at thee.

[23] Whom hast thou reproached and blasphemed? and against whom hast thou exalted *thy* voice, and lifted up thine eyes on high? *even* against the Holy One of Israel.

[24] By thy servants hast thou reproached the Lord, and hast said, By the multitude of my chariots am I come up to the height of the mountains, to the sides of Lebanon; and I will cut down the tall cedars thereof, *and* the choice fir trees thereof: and I will enter into the height of his border, *and* the forest of his Carmel.

²⁵ I have digged, and drunk water; and with the sole of my feet have I dried up all the rivers of the besieged places.

²⁶ Hast thou not heard long ago, *how* I have done it; *and* of ancient times, that I have formed it? now have I brought it to pass, that thou shouldest be to lay waste defenced cities *into* ruinous heaps.

²⁷ Therefore their inhabitants *were* of small power, they were dismayed and confounded: they were *as* the grass of the field, and *as* the green herb, *as* the grass on the housetops, and *as corn* blasted before it be grown up.

²⁸ But I know thy abode, and thy going out, and thy coming in, and thy rage against me.

²⁹ Because thy rage against me, and thy tumult, is come up into mine ears, therefore will I put my hook in thy nose, and my bridle in thy lips, and I will turn thee back by the way by which thou camest.

³⁰ And this *shall be* a sign unto thee, Ye shall eat *this* year such as groweth of itself; and the second year that which springeth of the same: and in the third year sow ye, and reap, and plant vineyards, and eat the fruit thereof.

³¹ And the remnant that is escaped of the house of Judah shall again take root downward, and bear fruit upward:

³² For out of Jerusalem shall go forth a remnant, and they that escape out of mount Zion: the zeal of the LORD of hosts shall do this.

³³ Therefore thus saith the LORD concerning the king of Assyria, He shall not come into this city, nor shoot an arrow there, nor come before it with shields, nor cast a bank against it.

³⁴ By the way that he came, by the same shall he return, and shall not come into this city, saith the LORD.

³⁵ For I will defend this city to save it for mine own sake, and for my servant David's sake.

³⁶ Then the angel of the LORD went forth, and smote in the camp of the Assyrians a hundred and fourscore and five thousand: and when they arose early in the morning, behold, they *were* all dead corpses.

⁣³⁷ So Sennacherib king of Assyria departed, and went and returned, and dwelt at Nineveh.

³⁸ And it came to pass, as he was worshipping in the house of Nisroch his god, that Adrammelech and Sharezer his sons smote him with the sword; and they escaped into the land of Armenia: and Esarhaddon his son reigned in his stead.

Ezekiel 10:1-22 - Position, Appearance and Duties of the Cherubims

¹ Then I looked, and, behold, in the firmament that was above the head of the cherubims there appeared over them as it were a sapphire stone, as the appearance of the likeness of a throne.

² And he spake unto the man clothed with linen, and said, Go in between the wheels, *even* under the cherub, and fill thine hand with coals of fire from between the cherubims, and scatter *them* over the city. And he went in in my sight.

³ Now the cherubims stood on the right side of the house, when the man went in; and the cloud filled the inner court.

⁴ Then the glory of the LORD went up from the cherub, *and stood* over the threshold of the house; and the house was filled with the cloud, and the court was full of the brightness of the LORD'S glory.

⁵ And the sound of the cherubims' wings was heard *even* to the outer court, as the voice of the Almighty God when he speaketh.

⁶ And it came to pass, *that* when he had commanded the man clothed with linen, saying, Take fire from between the wheels, from between the cherubims; then he went in, and stood beside the wheels.

⁷ And *one* cherub stretched forth his hand from between the cherubims unto the fire that *was* between the cherubims, and took *thereof*, and put *it* into the hands of *him that was* clothed with linen: who took *it*, and went out.

⁸ And there appeared in the cherubims the form of a man's hand under their wings.

⁹ And when I looked, behold the four wheels by the cherubims, one wheel by one cherub, and another wheel by another cherub: and the appearance of the wheels *was* as the colour of a beryl stone.

¹⁰ And *as for* their appearances, they four had one likeness, as if a wheel had been in the midst of a wheel.

¹¹ When they went, they went upon their four sides; they turned not as they went, but to the place whither the head looked they followed it; they turned not as they went.

¹² And their whole body, and their backs, and their hands, and their wings, and the wheels, *were* full of eyes round about, *even* the wheels that they four had.

¹³ As for the wheels, it was cried unto them in my hearing, O wheel.

¹⁴ And every one had four faces: the first face *was* the face of a cherub, and the second face *was* the face of a man, and the third the face of a lion, and the fourth the face of an eagle.

¹⁵ And the cherubims were lifted up. This *is* the living creature that I saw by the river of Chebar.

¹⁶ And when the cherubims went, the wheels went by them: and when the cherubims lifted up their wings to mount up from the earth, the same wheels also turned not from beside them.

¹⁷ When they stood, *these* stood; and when they were lifted up, *these* lifted up themselves *also*: for the spirit of the living creature *was* in them.

¹⁸ Then the glory of the LORD departed from off the threshold of the house, and stood over the cherubims.

¹⁹ And the cherubims lifted up their wings, and mounted up from the earth in my sight: when they went out, the wheels also *were* beside them, and *every one* stood at the door of the east gate of the LORD'S house; and the glory of the God of Israel *was* over them above.

²⁰ This *is* the living creature that I saw under the God of Israel by the river of Chebar; and I knew that they *were* the cherubims.

²¹ Every one had four faces apiece, and every one four wings; and the likeness of the hands of a man *was* under their wings.

²² And the likeness of their faces *was* the same faces which I saw by the river of Chebar, their appearances and themselves: they went every one straight forward.

Ezekiel 11:14-25 - The Cherubims Lift up their Wings

¹⁴ Again the word of the LORD came unto me, saying,

¹⁵ Son of man, thy brethren, *even* thy brethren, the men of thy kindred, and all the house of Israel wholly, *are* they unto whom the inhabitants of Jerusalem have said, Get you far from the LORD: unto us is this land given in possession.

¹⁶ Therefore say, Thus saith the Lord GOD; Although I have cast them far off among the heathen, and although I have scattered them among the countries, yet will I be to them as a little sanctuary in the countries where they shall come.

¹⁷ Therefore say, Thus saith the Lord GOD; I will even gather you from the people, and assemble you out of the countries where ye have been scattered, and I will give you the land of Israel.

¹⁸ And they shall come thither, and they shall take away all the detestable things thereof and all the abominations thereof from thence.

¹⁹ And I will give them one heart, and I will put a new spirit within you; and I will take the stony heart out of their flesh, and will give them an heart of flesh:

²⁰ That they may walk in my statutes, and keep mine ordinances, and do them: and they shall be my people, and I will be their God.

²¹ But *as for them* whose heart walketh after the heart of their detestable things and their abominations, I will recompense their way upon their own heads, saith the Lord GOD.

²² Then did the cherubims lift up their wings, and the wheels beside them; and the glory of the God of Israel *was* over them above.

²³ And the glory of the LORD went up from the midst of the city, and stood upon the mountain which *is* on the east side of the city.

²⁴ Afterwards the spirit took me up, and brought me in a vision by the Spirit of God into Chaldea, to them of the captivity. So the vision that I had seen went up from me.

²⁵ Then I spake unto them of the captivity all the things that the LORD had shewed me.

Ezekiel 41:1-26 - Cherubims and Palm Trees with Every Cherub had Two Faces

¹ Afterward he brought me to the temple, and measured the posts, six cubits broad on the one side, and six cubits broad on the other side, *which was* the breadth of the tabernacle.

² And the breadth of the door *was* ten cubits; and the sides of the door *were* five cubits on the one side, and five cubits on the other side: and he measured the length thereof, forty cubits: and the breadth, twenty cubits.

³ Then went he inward, and measured the post of the door, two cubits; and the door, six cubits; and the breadth of the door, seven cubits.

⁴ So he measured the length thereof, twenty cubits; and the breadth, twenty cubits, before the temple: and he said unto me, This *is* the most holy *place*.

⁵ After he measured the wall of the house, six cubits; and the breadth of *every* side chamber, four cubits, round about the house on every side.

⁶ And the side chambers *were* three, one over another, and thirty in order; and they entered into the wall which *was* of the house for the side chambers round about, that they might have hold, but they had not hold in the wall of the house.

⁷ And *there was* an enlarging, and a winding about still upward to the side chambers: for the winding about of the house went still upward round about the house: therefore the breadth of the house *was still* upward, and so increased *from* the lowest *chamber* to the highest by the midst.

⁸ I saw also the height of the house round about: the foundations of the side chambers *were* a full reed of six great cubits.

⁹ The thickness of the wall, which *was* for the side chamber without, *was* five cubits: and *that* which *was* left *was* the place of the side chambers that *were* within.

¹⁰ And between the chambers *was* the wideness of twenty cubits round about the house on every side.

¹¹ And the doors of the side chambers *were* toward *the place that was* left, one door toward the north, and another door toward the south: and the breadth of the place that was left *was* five cubits round about.

¹² Now the building that *was* before the separate place at the end toward the west *was* seventy cubits broad; and the wall of the building *was* five cubits thick round about, and the length thereof ninety cubits.

¹³ So he measured the house, an hundred cubits long; and the separate place, and the building, with the walls thereof, an hundred cubits long;

¹⁴ Also the breadth of the face of the house, and of the separate place toward the east, an hundred cubits.

¹⁵ And he measured the length of the building over against the separate place which *was* behind it, and the galleries thereof on the one side and on the other side, an hundred cubits, with the inner temple, and the porches of the court;

¹⁶ The door posts, and the narrow windows, and the galleries round about on their three stories, over against the door, cieled with wood round about, and from the ground up to the windows, and the windows *were* covered;

¹⁷ To that above the door, even unto the inner house, and without, and by all the wall round about within and without, by measure.

¹⁸ And *it was* made with <u>cherubims</u> and palm trees, so that a palm tree *was* between a <u>cherub</u> and a <u>cherub</u>; and *every* <u>cherub</u> had two faces;

¹⁹ So that the face of a man *was* toward the palm tree on the one side, and the face of a young lion toward the palm tree on the other side: *it was* made through all the house round about.

²⁰ From the ground unto above the door *were* <u>cherubims</u> and palm trees made, and *on* the wall of the temple.

²¹ The posts of the temple *were* squared, *and* the face of the sanctuary; the appearance *of the one* as the appearance *of the other*.

²² The altar of wood *was* three cubits high, and the length thereof two cubits; and the corners thereof, and the length thereof, and the walls thereof, *were* of wood: and he said unto me, This *is* the table that *is* before the LORD.

²³ And the temple and the sanctuary had two doors.

²⁴ And the doors had two leaves *apiece*, two turning leaves; two *leaves* for the one door, and two leaves for the other *door*.

²⁵ And *there were* made on them, on the doors of the temple, <u>cherubims</u> and palm trees, like as *were* made upon the walls; and *there were* thick planks upon the face of the porch without.

²⁶ And *there were* narrow windows and palm trees on the one side and on the other side, on the sides of the porch, and *upon* the side chambers of the house, and thick planks.

Hebrews 9:1-28 - Cherubims of Glory Shadowing the Mercy Seat

¹ Then verily the first *covenant* had also ordinances of divine service, and a worldly sanctuary.

² For there was a tabernacle made; the first, wherein *was* the candlestick, and the table, and the shewbread; which is called the sanctuary.

³ And after the second veil, the tabernacle which is called the Holiest of all;

⁴ Which had the golden censer, and the ark of the covenant overlaid round about with gold, wherein *was* the golden pot that had manna, and Aaron's rod that budded, and the tables of the covenant;

⁵ And over it the <u>cherubims</u> of glory shadowing the mercyseat; of which we cannot now speak particularly.

⁶ Now when these things were thus ordained, the priests went always into the first tabernacle, accomplishing the service *of God*.

⁷ But into the second *went* the high priest alone once every year, not without blood, which he offered for himself, and *for* the errors of the people:

⁸ The Holy Ghost this signifying, that the way into the holiest of all was not yet made manifest, while as the first tabernacle was yet standing:

⁹ Which *was* a figure for the time then present, in which were offered both gifts and sacrifices, that could not make him that did the service perfect, as pertaining to the conscience;

¹⁰ *Which stood* only in meats and drinks, and divers washings, and carnal ordinances, imposed *on them* until the time of reformation.

¹¹ But Christ being come an high priest of good things to come, by a greater and more perfect tabernacle, not made with hands, that is to say, not of this building;

¹² Neither by the blood of goats and calves, but by his own blood he entered in once into the holy place, having obtained eternal redemption *for us*.

¹³ For if the blood of bulls and of goats, and the ashes of an heifer sprinkling the unclean, sanctifieth to the purifying of the flesh:

¹⁴ How much more shall the blood of Christ, who through the eternal Spirit offered himself without spot to God, purge your conscience from dead works to serve the living God?

[15] And for this cause he is the mediator of the new testament, that by means of death, for the redemption of the transgressions *that were* under the first testament, they which are called might receive the promise of eternal inheritance.

[16] For where a testament *is*, there must also of necessity be the death of the testator.

[17] For a testament *is* of force after men are dead: otherwise it is of no strength at all while the testator liveth.

[18] Whereupon neither the first *testament* was dedicated without blood.

[19] For when Moses had spoken every precept to all the people according to the law, he took the blood of calves and of goats, with water, and scarlet wool, and hyssop, and sprinkled both the book, and all the people,

[20] Saying, This *is* the blood of the testament which God hath enjoined unto you.

[21] Moreover he sprinkled with blood both the tabernacle, and all the vessels of the ministry.

[22] And almost all things are by the law purged with blood; and without shedding of blood is no remission.

[23] *It was* therefore necessary that the patterns of things in the heavens should be purified with these; but the heavenly things themselves with better sacrifices than these.

[24] For Christ is not entered into the holy places made with hands, *which are* the figures of the true; but into heaven itself, now to appear in the presence of God for us:

[25] Nor yet that he should offer himself often, as the high priest entereth into the holy place every year with blood of others;

[26] For then must he often have suffered since the foundation of the world: but now once in the end of the world hath he appeared to put away sin by the sacrifice of himself.

[27] And as it is appointed unto men once to die, but after this the judgment:

²⁸ So Christ was once offered to bear the sins of many; and unto them that look for him shall he appear the second time without sin unto salvation.

Thrones

Ezekiel 1:1-28 - Description of Thrones in a Vision of Enoch

¹ Now it came to pass in the thirtieth year, in the fourth *month*, in the fifth *day* of the month, as I *was* among the captives by the river of Chebar, *that* the heavens were opened, and I saw visions of God.

² In the fifth *day* of the month, which *was* the fifth year of king Jehoiachin's captivity,

³ The word of the LORD came expressly unto Ezekiel the priest, the son of Buzi, in the land of the Chaldeans by the river Chebar; and the hand of the LORD was there upon him.

⁴ And I looked, and, behold, a whirlwind came out of the north, a great cloud, and a fire infolding itself, and a brightness *was* about it, and out of the midst thereof as the colour of amber, out of the midst of the fire.

⁵ Also out of the midst thereof *came* the likeness of four living creatures. And this *was* their appearance; they had the likeness of a man.

⁶ And every one had four faces, and every one had four wings.

⁷ And their feet *were* straight feet; and the sole of their feet *was* like the sole of a calf's foot: and they sparkled like the colour of burnished brass.

⁸ And *they had* the hands of a man under their wings on their four sides; and they four had their faces and their wings.

⁹ Their wings *were* joined one to another; they turned not when they went; they went every one straight forward.

¹⁰ As for the likeness of their faces, they four had the face of a man, and the face of a lion, on the right side: and they four had the face of an ox on the left side; they four also had the face of an eagle.

¹¹ Thus *were* their faces: and their wings *were* stretched upward; two *wings* of every one *were* joined one to another, and two covered their bodies.

¹² And they went every one straight forward: whither the spirit was to go, they went; *and* they turned not when they went.

¹³ As for the likeness of the living creatures, their appearance *was* like burning coals of fire, *and* like the appearance of lamps: it went up and down among the living creatures; and the fire was bright, and out of the fire went forth lightning.

¹⁴ And the living creatures ran and returned as the appearance of a flash of lightning.

¹⁵ Now as I beheld the living creatures, behold one wheel upon the earth by the living creatures, with his four faces.

¹⁶ The appearance of the wheels and their work *was* like unto the colour of a beryl: and they four had one likeness: and their appearance and their work *was* as it were a wheel in the middle of a wheel.

¹⁷ When they went, they went upon their four sides: *and* they turned not when they went.

¹⁸ As for their rings, they were so high that they were dreadful; and their rings *were* full of eyes round about them four.

¹⁹ And when the living creatures went, the wheels went by them: and when the living creatures were lifted up from the earth, the wheels were lifted up.

²⁰ Whithersoever the spirit was to go, they went, thither *was their* spirit to go; and the wheels were lifted up over against them: for the spirit of the living creature *was* in the wheels.

²¹ When those went, *these* went; and when those stood, *these* stood; and when those were lifted up from the earth, the wheels were lifted up over against them: for the spirit of the living creature *was* in the wheels.

²² And the likeness of the firmament upon the heads of the living creature *was* as the colour of the terrible crystal, stretched forth over their heads above.

²³ And under the firmament *were* their wings straight, the one toward the other: every one had two, which covered on this side, and every one had two, which covered on that side, their bodies.

²⁴ And when they went, I heard the noise of their wings, like the noise of great waters, as the voice of the Almighty, the voice of speech, as the noise of an host: when they stood, they let down their wings.

²⁵ And there was a voice from the firmament that *was* over their heads, when they stood, *and* had let down their wings.

²⁶ And above the firmament that *was* over their heads *was* the likeness of a throne, as the appearance of a sapphire stone: and upon the likeness of the throne *was* the likeness as the appearance of a man above upon it.

²⁷ And I saw as the colour of amber, as the appearance of fire round about within it, from the appearance of his loins even upward, and from the appearance of his loins even downward, I saw as it were the appearance of fire, and it had brightness round about.

²⁸ As the appearance of the bow that is in the cloud in the day of rain, so *was* the appearance of the brightness round about. This *was* the appearance of the likeness of the glory of the LORD. And when I saw *it*, I fell upon my face, and I heard a voice of one that spake.

Daniel 7:1-28 - Daniel Beheld till the Thrones were Cast Down

¹ In the first year of Belshazzar king of Babylon Daniel had a dream and visions of his head upon his bed: then he wrote the dream, *and* told the sum of the matters.

² Daniel spake and said, I saw in my vision by night, and, behold, the four winds of the heaven strove upon the great sea.

³ And four great beasts came up from the sea, diverse one from another.

⁴ The first *was* like a lion, and had eagle's wings: I beheld till the wings thereof were plucked, and it was lifted up from the earth, and made stand upon the feet as a man, and a man's heart was given to it.

⁵ And behold another beast, a second, like to a bear, and it raised up itself on one side, and *it had* three ribs in the mouth of it between the teeth of it: and they said thus unto it, Arise, devour much flesh.

⁶ After this I beheld, and lo another, like a leopard, which had upon the back of it four wings of a fowl; the beast had also four heads; and dominion was given to it.

⁷ After this I saw in the night visions, and behold a fourth beast, dreadful and terrible, and strong exceedingly; and it had great iron teeth: it devoured and brake in pieces, and stamped the residue with the feet of it: and it *was* diverse from all the beasts that *were* before it; and it had ten horns.

⁸ I considered the horns, and, behold, there came up among them another little horn, before whom there were three of the first horns plucked up by the roots: and, behold, in this horn *were* eyes like the eyes of man, and a mouth speaking great things.

⁹ I beheld till the <u>thrones</u> were cast down, and the Ancient of days did sit, whose garment *was* white as snow, and the hair of his head like the pure wool: his <u>throne</u> *was like* the fiery flame, *and* his wheels *as* burning fire.

¹⁰ A fiery stream issued and came forth from before him: thousand thousands ministered unto him, and ten thousand times ten thousand stood before him: the judgment was set, and the books were opened.

¹¹ I beheld then because of the voice of the great words which the horn spake: I beheld *even* till the beast was slain, and his body destroyed, and given to the burning flame.

¹² As concerning the rest of the beasts, they had their dominion taken away: yet their lives were prolonged for a season and time.

¹³ I saw in the night visions, and, behold, *one* like the Son of man came with the clouds of heaven, and came to the Ancient of days, and they brought him near before him.

¹⁴ And there was given him dominion, and glory, and a kingdom, that all people, nations, and languages, should serve him: his dominion *is* an everlasting dominion, which shall not pass away, and his kingdom *that* which shall not be destroyed.

¹⁵ I Daniel was grieved in my spirit in the midst of *my* body, and the visions of my head troubled me.

¹⁶ I came near unto one of them that stood by, and asked him the truth of all this. So he told me, and made me know the interpretation of the things.

¹⁷ These great beasts, which are four, *are* four kings, *which* shall arise out of the earth.

¹⁸ But the saints of the most High shall take the kingdom, and possess the kingdom for ever, even for ever and ever.

¹⁹ Then I would know the truth of the fourth beast, which was diverse from all the others, exceeding dreadful, whose teeth *were of* iron, and his nails *of* brass; *which* devoured, brake in pieces, and stamped the residue with his feet;

²⁰ And of the ten horns that *were* in his head, and *of* the other which came up, and before whom three fell; even *of* that horn that had eyes, and a mouth that spake very great things, whose look *was* more stout than his fellows.

²¹ I beheld, and the same horn made war with the saints, and prevailed against them;

²² Until the Ancient of days came, and judgment was given to the saints of the most High; and the time came that the saints possessed the kingdom.

²³ Thus he said, The fourth beast shall be the fourth kingdom upon earth, which shall be diverse from all kingdoms, and shall devour the whole earth, and shall tread it down, and break it in pieces.

24 And the ten horns out of this kingdom *are* ten kings *that* shall arise: and another shall rise after them; and he shall be diverse from the first, and he shall subdue three kings.

25 And he shall speak *great* words against the most High, and shall wear out the saints of the most High, and think to change times and laws: and they shall be given into his hand until a time and times and the dividing of time.

26 But the judgment shall sit, and they shall take away his dominion, to consume and to destroy *it* unto the end.

27 And the kingdom and dominion, and the greatness of the kingdom under the whole heaven, shall be given to the people of the saints of the most High, whose kingdom *is* an everlasting kingdom, and all dominions shall serve and obey him.

28 Hitherto *is* the end of the matter. As for me Daniel, my cogitations much troubled me, and my countenance changed in me: but I kept the matter in my heart.

Colossians 1:9-18 - All Things Created, Thrones, Dominions or Principalities

9 For this cause we also, since the day we heard *it*, do not cease to pray for you, and to desire that ye might be filled with the knowledge of his will in all wisdom and spiritual understanding;

10 That ye might walk worthy of the Lord unto all pleasing, being fruitful in every good work, and increasing in the knowledge of God;

11 Strengthened with all might, according to his glorious power, unto all patience and longsuffering with joyfulness;

12 Giving thanks unto the Father, which hath made us meet to be partakers of the inheritance of the saints in light:

13 Who hath delivered us from the power of darkness, and hath translated *us* into the kingdom of his dear Son:

¹⁴ In whom we have redemption through his blood, *even* the forgiveness of sins:

¹⁵ Who is the image of the invisible God, the firstborn of every creature:

¹⁶ For by him were all things created, that are in heaven, and that are in earth, visible and invisible, whether *they be* thrones, or dominions, or principalities, or powers: all things were created by him, and for him:

¹⁷ And he is before all things, and by him all things consist.

¹⁸ And he is the head of the body, the church: who is the beginning, the firstborn from the dead; that in all *things* he might have the preeminence.

Dominions

Daniel 7:1-28 - The Kingdom and Dominion

¹ In the first year of Belshazzar king of Babylon Daniel had a dream and visions of his head upon his bed: then he wrote the dream, *and* told the sum of the matters.

² Daniel spake and said, I saw in my vision by night, and, behold, the four winds of the heaven strove upon the great sea.

³ And four great beasts came up from the sea, diverse one from another.

⁴ The first *was* like a lion, and had eagle's wings: I beheld till the wings thereof were plucked, and it was lifted up from the earth, and made stand upon the feet as a man, and a man's heart was given to it.

⁵ And behold another beast, a second, like to a bear, and it raised up itself on one side, and *it had* three ribs in the mouth of it between the teeth of it: and they said thus unto it, Arise, devour much flesh.

⁶ After this I beheld, and lo another, like a leopard, which had upon the back of it four wings of a fowl; the beast had also four heads; and dominion was given to it.

⁷ After this I saw in the night visions, and behold a fourth beast, dreadful and terrible, and strong exceedingly; and it had great iron teeth: it devoured and brake in pieces, and stamped the residue with the feet of it: and it *was* diverse from all the beasts that *were* before it; and it had ten horns.

⁸ I considered the horns, and, behold, there came up among them another little horn, before whom there were three of the first horns plucked up by the roots: and, behold, in this horn *were* eyes like the eyes of man, and a mouth speaking great things.

⁹ I beheld till the thrones were cast down, and the Ancient of days did sit, whose garment *was* white as snow, and the hair of his head like the pure wool: his throne *was like* the fiery flame, *and* his wheels *as* burning fire.

¹⁰ A fiery stream issued and came forth from before him: thousand thousands ministered unto him, and ten thousand times ten thousand stood before him: the judgment was set, and the books were opened.

¹¹ I beheld then because of the voice of the great words which the horn spake: I beheld *even* till the beast was slain, and his body destroyed, and given to the burning flame.

¹² As concerning the rest of the beasts, they had their <u>dominion</u> taken away: yet their lives were prolonged for a season and time.

¹³ I saw in the night visions, and, behold, *one* like the Son of man came with the clouds of heaven, and came to the Ancient of days, and they brought him near before him.

¹⁴ And there was given him <u>dominion</u>, and glory, and a kingdom, that all people, nations, and languages, should serve him: his <u>dominion</u> *is* an everlasting <u>dominion</u>, which shall not pass away, and his kingdom *that* which shall not be destroyed.

¹⁵ I Daniel was grieved in my spirit in the midst of *my* body, and the visions of my head troubled me.

¹⁶ I came near unto one of them that stood by, and asked him the truth of all this. So he told me, and made me know the interpretation of the things.

¹⁷ These great beasts, which are four, *are* four kings, *which* shall arise out of the earth.

¹⁸ But the saints of the most High shall take the kingdom, and possess the kingdom for ever, even for ever and ever.

¹⁹ Then I would know the truth of the fourth beast, which was diverse from all the others, exceeding dreadful, whose teeth *were of* iron, and his nails *of* brass; *which* devoured, brake in pieces, and stamped the residue with his feet;

²⁰ And of the ten horns that *were* in his head, and *of* the other which came up, and before whom three fell; even *of* that horn that had eyes, and a mouth that spake very great things, whose look *was* more stout than his fellows.

²¹ I beheld, and the same horn made war with the saints, and prevailed against them;

²² Until the Ancient of days came, and judgment was given to the saints of the most High; and the time came that the saints possessed the kingdom.

²³ Thus he said, The fourth beast shall be the fourth kingdom upon earth, which shall be diverse from all kingdoms, and shall devour the whole earth, and shall tread it down, and break it in pieces.

²⁴ And the ten horns out of this kingdom *are* ten kings *that* shall arise: and another shall rise after them; and he shall be diverse from the first, and he shall subdue three kings.

²⁵ And he shall speak *great* words against the most High, and shall wear out the saints of the most High, and think to change times and laws: and they shall be given into his hand until a time and times and the dividing of time.

²⁶ But the judgment shall sit, and they shall take away his <u>dominion</u>, to consume and to destroy *it* unto the end.

²⁷ And the kingdom and <u>dominion</u>, and the greatness of the kingdom under the whole heaven, shall be given to the people of the saints of the most High, whose kingdom *is* an everlasting kingdom, and all <u>dominions</u> shall serve and obey him.

[28] Hitherto *is* the end of the matter. As for me Daniel, my cogitations much troubled me, and my countenance changed in me: but I kept the matter in my heart.

Colossians 1:9-18 - All Things Created, Thrones, Dominions or Principalities

[9] For this cause we also, since the day we heard *it*, do not cease to pray for you, and to desire that ye might be filled with the knowledge of his will in all wisdom and spiritual understanding;

[10] That ye might walk worthy of the Lord unto all pleasing, being fruitful in every good work, and increasing in the knowledge of God;

[11] Strengthened with all might, according to his glorious power, unto all patience and longsuffering with joyfulness;

[12] Giving thanks unto the Father, which hath made us meet to be partakers of the inheritance of the saints in light:

[13] Who hath delivered us from the power of darkness, and hath translated *us* into the kingdom of his dear Son:

[14] In whom we have redemption through his blood, *even* the forgiveness of sins:

[15] Who is the image of the invisible God, the firstborn of every creature:

[16] For by him were all things created, that are in heaven, and that are in earth, visible and invisible, whether *they be* thrones, or <u>dominions</u>, or principalities, or powers: all things were created by him, and for him:

[17] And he is before all things, and by him all things consist.

[18] And he is the head of the body, the church: who is the beginning, the firstborn from the dead; that in all *things* he might have the preeminence.

Powers

Matthew 24:1-37 - Immediately after the Tribulation . . . the Powers of Heavens shall be Shaken

[1] And Jesus went out, and departed from the temple: and his disciples came to *him* for to shew him the buildings of the temple.

[2] And Jesus said unto them, See ye not all these things? verily I say unto you, There shall not be left here one stone upon another, that shall not be thrown down.

[3] And as he sat upon the mount of Olives, the disciples came unto him privately, saying, Tell us, when shall these things be? and what *shall be* the sign of thy coming, and of the end of the world?

[4] And Jesus answered and said unto them, Take heed that no man deceive you.

[5] For many shall come in my name, saying, I am Christ; and shall deceive many.

[6] And ye shall hear of wars and rumours of wars: see that ye be not troubled: for all *these things* must come to pass, but the end is not yet.

[7] For nation shall rise against nation, and kingdom against kingdom: and there shall be famines, and pestilences, and earthquakes, in divers places.

[8] All these *are* the beginning of sorrows.

[9] Then shall they deliver you up to be afflicted, and shall kill you: and ye shall be hated of all nations for my name's sake.

[10] And then shall many be offended, and shall betray one another, and shall hate one another.

[11] And many false prophets shall rise, and shall deceive many.

[12] And because iniquity shall abound, the love of many shall wax cold.

[13] But he that shall endure unto the end, the same shall be saved.

¹⁴ And this gospel of the kingdom shall be preached in all the world for a witness unto all nations; and then shall the end come.

¹⁵ When ye therefore shall see the abomination of desolation, spoken of by Daniel the prophet, stand in the holy place, (whoso readeth, let him understand:)

¹⁶ Then let them which be in Judaea flee into the mountains:

¹⁷ Let him which is on the housetop not come down to take any thing out of his house:

¹⁸ Neither let him which is in the field return back to take his clothes.

¹⁹ And woe unto them that are with child, and to them that give suck in those days!

²⁰ But pray ye that your flight be not in the winter, neither on the sabbath day:

²¹ For then shall be great tribulation, such as was not since the beginning of the world to this time, no, nor ever shall be.

²² And except those days should be shortened, there should no flesh be saved: but for the elect's sake those days shall be shortened.

²³ Then if any man shall say unto you, Lo, here *is* Christ, or there; believe *it* not.

²⁴ For there shall arise false Christs, and false prophets, and shall shew great signs and wonders; insomuch that, if *it were* possible, they shall deceive the very elect.

²⁵ Behold, I have told you before.

²⁶ Wherefore if they shall say unto you, Behold, he is in the desert; go not forth: behold, *he is* in the secret chambers; believe *it* not.

²⁷ For as the lightning cometh out of the east, and shineth even unto the west; so shall also the coming of the Son of man be.

²⁸ For wheresoever the carcase is, there will the eagles be gathered together.

²⁹ Immediately after the tribulation of those days shall the sun be darkened, and the moon shall not give her light, and the stars shall fall from heaven, and the <u>powers</u> of the heavens shall be shaken:

³⁰ And then shall appear the sign of the Son of man in heaven: and then shall all the tribes of the earth mourn, and they shall see the Son of man coming in the clouds of heaven with <u>power</u> and great glory.

³¹ And he shall send his angels with a great sound of a trumpet, and they shall gather together his elect from the four winds, from one end of heaven to the other.

³² Now learn a parable of the fig tree; When his branch is yet tender, and putteth forth leaves, ye know that summer *is* nigh:

³³ So likewise ye, when ye shall see all these things, know that it is near, *even* at the doors.

³⁴ Verily I say unto you, This generation shall not pass, till all these things be fulfilled.

³⁵ Heaven and earth shall pass away, but my words shall not pass away.

³⁶ But of that day and hour knoweth no *man*, no, not the angels of heaven, but my Father only.

³⁷ But as the days of Noe *were*, so shall also the coming of the Son of man be.

Mark 13:1-37 - The Stars of Heaven shall Fall and the Powers that are in Heaven shall be Shaken

¹ And as he went out of the temple, one of his disciples saith unto him, Master, see what manner of stones and what buildings *are here*!

² And Jesus answering said unto him, Seest thou these great buildings? there shall not be left one stone upon another, that shall not be thrown down.

³ And as he sat upon the mount of Olives over against the temple, Peter and James and John and Andrew asked him privately,

⁴ Tell us, when shall these things be? and what *shall be* the sign when all these things shall be fulfilled?

⁵ And Jesus answering them began to say, Take heed lest any *man* deceive you:

⁶ For many shall come in my name, saying, I am *Christ*; and shall deceive many.

⁷ And when ye shall hear of wars and rumours of wars, be ye not troubled: for *such things* must needs be; but the end *shall* not *be* yet.

⁸ For nation shall rise against nation, and kingdom against kingdom: and there shall be earthquakes in divers places, and there shall be famines and troubles: these *are* the beginnings of sorrows.

⁹ But take heed to yourselves: for they shall deliver you up to councils; and in the synagogues ye shall be beaten: and ye shall be brought before rulers and kings for my sake, for a testimony against them.

¹⁰ And the gospel must first be published among all nations.

¹¹ But when they shall lead *you*, and deliver you up, take no thought beforehand what ye shall speak, neither do ye premeditate: but whatsoever shall be given you in that hour, that speak ye: for it is not ye that speak, but the Holy Ghost.

¹² Now the brother shall betray the brother to death, and the father the son; and children shall rise up against *their* parents, and shall cause them to be put to death.

¹³ And ye shall be hated of all *men* for my name's sake: but he that shall endure unto the end, the same shall be saved.

¹⁴ But when ye shall see the abomination of desolation, spoken of by Daniel the prophet, standing where it ought not, (let him that readeth understand,) then let them that be in Judaea flee to the mountains:

¹⁵ And let him that is on the housetop not go down into the house, neither enter *therein*, to take any thing out of his house:

¹⁶ And let him that is in the field not turn back again for to take up his garment.

[17] But woe to them that are with child, and to them that give suck in those days!

[18] And pray ye that your flight be not in the winter.

[19] For *in* those days shall be affliction, such as was not from the beginning of the creation which God created unto this time, neither shall be.

[20] And except that the Lord had shortened those days, no flesh should be saved: but for the elect's sake, whom he hath chosen, he hath shortened the days.

[21] And then if any man shall say to you, Lo, here *is* Christ; or, lo, *he is* there; believe *him* not:

[22] For false Christs and false prophets shall rise, and shall shew signs and wonders, to seduce, if *it were* possible, even the elect.

[23] But take ye heed: behold, I have foretold you all things.

[24] But in those days, after that tribulation, the sun shall be darkened, and the moon shall not give her light,

[25] And the stars of heaven shall fall, and the <u>powers</u> that are in heaven shall be shaken.

[26] And then shall they see the Son of man coming in the clouds with great <u>power</u> and glory.

[27] And then shall he send his angels, and shall gather together his elect from the four winds, from the uttermost part of the earth to the uttermost part of heaven.

[28] Now learn a parable of the fig tree; When her branch is yet tender, and putteth forth leaves, ye know that summer is near:

[29] So ye in like manner, when ye shall see these things come to pass, know that it is nigh, *even* at the doors.

[30] Verily I say unto you, that this generation shall not pass, till all these things be done.

[31] Heaven and earth shall pass away: but my words shall not pass away.

³² But of that day and *that* hour knoweth no man, no, not the angels which are in heaven, neither the Son, but the Father.

³³ Take ye heed, watch and pray: for ye know not when the time is.

³⁴ *For the Son of man is* as a man taking a far journey, who left his house, and gave authority to his servants, and to every man his work, and commanded the porter to watch.

³⁵ Watch ye therefore: for ye know not when the master of the house cometh, at even, or at midnight, or at the cockcrowing, or in the morning:

³⁶ Lest coming suddenly he find you sleeping.

³⁷ And what I say unto you I say unto all, Watch.

Romans 8:35-39 - For I am Persuaded, that neither Death . . . nor Powers

³⁵ Who shall separate us from the love of Christ? *shall* tribulation, or distress, or persecution, or famine, or nakedness, or peril, or sword?

³⁶ As it is written, For thy sake we are killed all the day long; we are accounted as sheep for the slaughter.

³⁷ Nay, in all these things we are more than conquerors through him that loved us.

³⁸ For I am persuaded, that neither death, nor life, nor angels, nor principalities, nor <u>powers</u>, nor things present, nor things to come,

³⁹ Nor height, nor depth, nor any other creature, shall be able to separate us from the love of God, which is in Christ Jesus our Lord.

Romans 13:1-8 - Let Every Soul be Subject unto the Higher Powers

¹ Let every soul be subject unto the higher <u>powers</u>. For there is no <u>power</u> but of God: the <u>powers</u> that be are ordained of God.

² Whosoever therefore resisteth the <u>power</u>, resisteth the ordinance of God: and they that resist shall receive to themselves damnation.

³ For rulers are not a terror to good works, but to the evil. Wilt thou then not be afraid of the <u>power</u>? do that which is good, and thou shalt have praise of the same:

⁴ For he is the minister of God to thee for good. But if thou do that which is evil, be afraid; for he beareth not the sword in vain: for he is the minister of God, a revenger to *execute* wrath upon him that doeth evil.

⁵ Wherefore *ye* must needs be subject, not only for wrath, but also for conscience sake.

⁶ For for this cause pay ye tribute also: for they are God's ministers, attending continually upon this very thing.

⁷ Render therefore to all their dues: tribute to whom tribute *is due*; custom to whom custom; fear to whom fear; honour to whom honour.

⁸ Owe no man any thing, but to love one another: for he that loveth another hath fulfilled the law.

Ephesians 3:1-12 - To the Intent that now unto the Principalities and Powers in Heavenly Places might be known . . .

¹ For this cause I Paul, the prisoner of Jesus Christ for you Gentiles,

² If ye have heard of the dispensation of the grace of God which is given me to you-ward:

³ How that by revelation he made known unto me the mystery; (as I wrote afore in few words,

⁴ Whereby, when ye read, ye may understand my knowledge in the mystery of Christ)

⁵ Which in other ages was not made known unto the sons of men, as it is now revealed unto his holy apostles and prophets by the Spirit;

⁶ That the Gentiles should be fellowheirs, and of the same body, and partakers of his promise in Christ by the gospel:

⁷ Whereof I was made a minister, according to the gift of the grace of God given unto me by the effectual working of his power.

⁸ Unto me, who am less than the least of all saints, is this grace given, that I should preach among the Gentiles the unsearchable riches of Christ;

⁹ And to make all *men* see what *is* the fellowship of the mystery, which from the beginning of the world hath been hid in God, who created all things by Jesus Christ:

¹⁰ To the intent that now unto the principalities and powers in heavenly *places* might be known by the church the manifold wisdom of God,

¹¹ According to the eternal purpose which he purposed in Christ Jesus our Lord:

¹² In whom we have boldness and access with confidence by the faith of him.

Ephesians 6:10-13 - For we Wrestle not against Flesh and Blood but against Powers

¹⁰ Finally, my brethren, be strong in the Lord, and in the power of his might.

¹¹ Put on the whole armour of God, that ye may be able to stand against the wiles of the devil.

¹² For we wrestle not against flesh and blood, but against principalities, against powers, against the rulers of the darkness of this world, against spiritual wickedness in high *places*.

¹³ Wherefore take unto you the whole armour of God, that ye may be able to withstand in the evil day, and having done all, to stand.

Colossians 1:9-17 - For by Him were All Things Created, that are in Heaven . . . whether they be . . . or Powers

[9] For this cause we also, since the day we heard *it*, do not cease to pray for you, and to desire that ye might be filled with the knowledge of his will in all wisdom and spiritual understanding;

[10] That ye might walk worthy of the Lord unto all pleasing, being fruitful in every good work, and increasing in the knowledge of God;

[11] Strengthened with all might, according to his glorious <u>power</u>, unto all patience and longsuffering with joyfulness;

[12] Giving thanks unto the Father, which hath made us meet to be partakers of the inheritance of the saints in light:

[13] Who hath delivered us from the <u>power</u> of darkness, and hath translated *us* into the kingdom of his dear Son:

[14] In whom we have redemption through his blood, *even* the forgiveness of sins:

[15] Who is the image of the invisible God, the firstborn of every creature:

[16] For by him were all things created, that are in heaven, and that are in earth, visible and invisible, whether *they be* thrones, or dominions, or principalities, or <u>powers</u>: all things were created by him, and for him:

[17] And he is before all things, and by him all things consist.

Colossians 2:8-17 - And Having Spoiled Principalities and Powers

[8] Beware lest any man spoil you through philosophy and vain deceit, after the tradition of men, after the rudiments of the world, and not after Christ.

[9] For in him dwelleth all the fulness of the Godhead bodily.

¹⁰ And ye are complete in him, which is the head of all principality and <u>power</u>:

¹¹ In whom also ye are circumcised with the circumcision made without hands, in putting off the body of the sins of the flesh by the circumcision of Christ:

¹² Buried with him in baptism, wherein also ye are risen with *him* through the faith of the operation of God, who hath raised him from the dead.

¹³ And you, being dead in your sins and the uncircumcision of your flesh, hath he quickened together with him, having forgiven you all trespasses;

¹⁴ Blotting out the handwriting of ordinances that was against us, which was contrary to us, and took it out of the way, nailing it to his cross;

¹⁵ *And* having spoiled principalities and <u>powers</u>, he made a shew of them openly, triumphing over them in it.

¹⁶ Let no man therefore judge you in meat, or in drink, or in respect of an holyday, or of the new moon, or of the sabbath *days*:

¹⁷ Which are a shadow of things to come; but the body *is* of Christ.

Titus 3:1-7 - To be Subject to Principalities and Powers

¹ Put them in mind to be subject to principalities and <u>powers</u>, to obey magistrates, to be ready to every good work,

² To speak evil of no man, to be no brawlers, *but* gentle, shewing all meekness unto all men.

³ For we ourselves also were sometimes foolish, disobedient, deceived, serving divers lusts and pleasures, living in malice and envy, hateful, *and* hating one another.

⁴ But after that the kindness and love of God our Saviour toward man appeared,

⁵ Not by works of righteousness which we have done, but according to his mercy he saved us, by the washing of regeneration, and renewing of the Holy Ghost;

⁶ Which he shed on us abundantly through Jesus Christ our Saviour;

⁷ That being justified by his grace, we should be made heirs according to the hope of eternal life.

Hebrews 6:1-6 - Have Tasted the Good Word of God and the Powers of the World

¹ Therefore leaving the principles of the doctrine of Christ, let us go on unto perfection; not laying again the foundation of repentance from dead works, and of faith toward God,

² Of the doctrine of baptisms, and of laying on of hands, and of resurrection of the dead, and of eternal judgment.

³ And this will we do, if God permit.

⁴ For *it is* impossible for those who were once enlightened, and have tasted of the heavenly gift, and were made partakers of the Holy Ghost,

⁵ And have tasted the good word of God, and the <u>powers</u> of the world to come,

⁶ If they shall fall away, to renew them again unto repentance; seeing they crucify to themselves the Son of God afresh, and put *him* to an open shame.

1 Peter 3:18-22 - Powers being Made Subject unto Him

¹⁸ For Christ also hath once suffered for sins, the just for the unjust, that he might bring us to God, being put to death in the flesh, but quickened by the Spirit:

¹⁹ By which also he went and preached unto the spirits in prison;

²⁰ Which sometime were disobedient, when once the longsuffering of God waited in the days of Noah, while the ark was a preparing, wherein few, that is, eight souls were saved by water.

²¹ The like figure whereunto *even* baptism doth also now save us (not the putting away of the filth of the flesh, but the answer of a good conscience toward God,) by the resurrection of Jesus Christ:

²² Who is gone into heaven, and is on the right hand of God; angels and authorities and <u>powers</u> being made subject unto him.

Principalities

Jeremiah 13:16-18 - Your Principalities shall Come Down, even the Crown of Your Glory

¹⁶ Give glory to the LORD your God, before he cause darkness, and before your feet stumble upon the dark mountains, and, while ye look for light, he turn it into the shadow of death, *and* make *it* gross darkness.

¹⁷ But if ye will not hear it, my soul shall weep in secret places for *your* pride; and mine eye shall weep sore, and run down with tears, because the LORD'S flock is carried away captive.

¹⁸ Say unto the king and to the queen, Humble yourselves, sit down: for your <u>principalities</u> shall come down, *even* the crown of your glory.

Romans 8:35-39 - For I am Persuaded that neither Death nor Principalities

³⁵ Who shall separate us from the love of Christ? *shall* tribulation, or distress, or persecution, or famine, or nakedness, or peril, or sword?

³⁶ As it is written, For thy sake we are killed all the day long; we are accounted as sheep for the slaughter.

[37] Nay, in all these things we are more than conquerors through him that loved us.

[38] For I am persuaded, that neither death, nor life, nor angels, nor <u>principalities</u>, nor powers, nor things present, nor things to come,

[39] Nor height, nor depth, nor any other creature, shall be able to separate us from the love of God, which is in Christ Jesus our Lord.

Ephesians 3:1-12 - Now unto the Principalities and Powers in Heavenly Places be Known by the Church, the Manifold Wisdom

[1] For this cause I Paul, the prisoner of Jesus Christ for you Gentiles,

[2] If ye have heard of the dispensation of the grace of God which is given me to you-ward:

[3] How that by revelation he made known unto me the mystery; (as I wrote afore in few words,

[4] Whereby, when ye read, ye may understand my knowledge in the mystery of Christ)

[5] Which in other ages was not made known unto the sons of men, as it is now revealed unto his holy apostles and prophets by the Spirit;

[6] That the Gentiles should be fellowheirs, and of the same body, and partakers of his promise in Christ by the gospel:

[7] Whereof I was made a minister, according to the gift of the grace of God given unto me by the effectual working of his power.

[8] Unto me, who am less than the least of all saints, is this grace given, that I should preach among the Gentiles the unsearchable riches of Christ;

[9] And to make all *men* see what *is* the fellowship of the mystery, which from the beginning of the world hath been hid in God, who created all things by Jesus Christ:

[10] To the intent that now unto the <u>principalities</u> and powers in heavenly *places* might be known by the church the manifold wisdom of God,

¹¹ According to the eternal purpose which he purposed in Christ Jesus our Lord:

¹² In whom we have boldness and access with confidence by the faith of him.

Ephesians 6:10-13 - For we Wrestle not against Flesh and Blood but against Principalities

¹⁰ Finally, my brethren, be strong in the Lord, and in the power of his might.

¹¹ Put on the whole armour of God, that ye may be able to stand against the wiles of the devil.

¹² For we wrestle not against flesh and blood, but against <u>principalities</u>, against powers, against the rulers of the darkness of this world, against spiritual wickedness in high *places*.

¹³ Wherefore take unto you the whole armour of God, that ye may be able to withstand in the evil day, and having done all, to stand.

Colossians 1:9-17 - All Things Created whether they be Principalities

⁹ For this cause we also, since the day we heard *it*, do not cease to pray for you, and to desire that ye might be filled with the knowledge of his will in all wisdom and spiritual understanding;

¹⁰ That ye might walk worthy of the Lord unto all pleasing, being fruitful in every good work, and increasing in the knowledge of God;

¹¹ Strengthened with all might, according to his glorious power, unto all patience and longsuffering with joyfulness;

¹² Giving thanks unto the Father, which hath made us meet to be partakers of the inheritance of the saints in light:

¹³ Who hath delivered us from the power of darkness, and hath translated *us* into the kingdom of his dear Son:

¹⁴ In whom we have redemption through his blood, *even* the forgiveness of sins:

¹⁵ Who is the image of the invisible God, the firstborn of every creature:

¹⁶ For by him were all things created, that are in heaven, and that are in earth, visible and invisible, whether *they be* thrones, or dominions, or principalities, or powers: all things were created by him, and for him:

¹⁷ And he is before all things, and by him all things consist.

Colossians 2:8-17 - Having Spoiled Principalities

⁸ Beware lest any man spoil you through philosophy and vain deceit, after the tradition of men, after the rudiments of the world, and not after Christ.

⁹ For in him dwelleth all the fulness of the Godhead bodily.

¹⁰ And ye are complete in him, which is the head of all principality and power:

¹¹ In whom also ye are circumcised with the circumcision made without hands, in putting off the body of the sins of the flesh by the circumcision of Christ:

¹² Buried with him in baptism, wherein also ye are risen with *him* through the faith of the operation of God, who hath raised him from the dead.

¹³ And you, being dead in your sins and the uncircumcision of your flesh, hath he quickened together with him, having forgiven you all trespasses;

¹⁴ Blotting out the handwriting of ordinances that was against us, which was contrary to us, and took it out of the way, nailing it to his cross;

¹⁵ *And* having spoiled principalities and powers, he made a shew of them openly, triumphing over them in it.

¹⁶ Let no man therefore judge you in meat, or in drink, or in respect of an holyday, or of the new moon, or of the sabbath *days*:

¹⁷ Which are a shadow of things to come; but the body *is* of Christ.

Titus 3:1-7 - To be Subject to Principalities and Powers

¹ Put them in mind to be subject to principalities and powers, to obey magistrates, to be ready to every good work,

² To speak evil of no man, to be no brawlers, *but* gentle, shewing all meekness unto all men.

³ For we ourselves also were sometimes foolish, disobedient, deceived, serving divers lusts and pleasures, living in malice and envy, hateful, *and* hating one another.

⁴ But after that the kindness and love of God our Saviour toward man appeared,

⁵ Not by works of righteousness which we have done, but according to his mercy he saved us, by the washing of regeneration, and renewing of the Holy Ghost;

⁶ Which he shed on us abundantly through Jesus Christ our Saviour;

⁷ That being justified by his grace, we should be made heirs according to the hope of eternal life.

Archangels

1 Thessalonians 4:13-18 - The Lord shall Descend from Heaven with the Voice of the Archangel

¹³ But I would not have you to be ignorant, brethren, concerning them which are asleep, that ye sorrow not, even as others which have no hope.

[14] For if we believe that Jesus died and rose again, even so them also which sleep in Jesus will God bring with him.

[15] For this we say unto you by the word of the Lord, that we which are alive *and* remain unto the coming of the Lord shall not prevent them which are asleep.

[16] For the Lord himself shall descend from heaven with a shout, with the voice of the archangel, and with the trump of God: and the dead in Christ shall rise first:

[17] Then we which are alive *and* remain shall be caught up together with them in the clouds, to meet the Lord in the air: and so shall we ever be with the Lord.

[18] Wherefore comfort one another with these words.

Revelation 8:1-2 - I Saw Seven Angels which Stood before God (Commonly thought that these were the Seven Archangels in Christian Theology)

[1] And when he had opened the seventh seal, there was silence in heaven about the space of half an hour.

[2] And I saw the seven angels which stood before God; and to them were given seven trumpets.

Michael

Daniel 10:1-21 - Michael shall Stand Up and none that Hold with Me these Things but Michael your Prince

[1] In the third year of Cyrus king of Persia a thing was revealed unto Daniel, whose name was called Belteshazzar; and the thing *was* true, but the time appointed *was* long: and he understood the thing, and had understanding of the vision.

² In those days I Daniel was mourning three full weeks.

³ I ate no pleasant bread, neither came flesh nor wine in my mouth, neither did I anoint myself at all, till three whole weeks were fulfilled.

⁴ And in the four and twentieth day of the first month, as I was by the side of the great river, which *is* Hiddekel;

⁵ Then I lifted up mine eyes, and looked, and behold a certain man clothed in linen, whose loins *were* girded with fine gold of Uphaz:

⁶ His body also *was* like the beryl, and his face as the appearance of lightning, and his eyes as lamps of fire, and his arms and his feet like in colour to polished brass, and the voice of his words like the voice of a multitude.

⁷ And I Daniel alone saw the vision: for the men that were with me saw not the vision; but a great quaking fell upon them, so that they fled to hide themselves.

⁸ Therefore I was left alone, and saw this great vision, and there remained no strength in me: for my comeliness was turned in me into corruption, and I retained no strength.

⁹ Yet heard I the voice of his words: and when I heard the voice of his words, then was I in a deep sleep on my face, and my face toward the ground.

¹⁰ And, behold, an hand touched me, which set me upon my knees and *upon* the palms of my hands.

¹¹ And he said unto me, O Daniel, a man greatly beloved, understand the words that I speak unto thee, and stand upright: for unto thee am I now sent. And when he had spoken this word unto me, I stood trembling.

¹² Then said he unto me, Fear not, Daniel: for from the first day that thou didst set thine heart to understand, and to chasten thyself before thy God, thy words were heard, and I am come for thy words.

¹³ But the prince of the kingdom of Persia withstood me one and twenty days: but, lo, <u>Michael</u>, one of the chief princes, came to help me; and I remained there with the kings of Persia.

[14] Now I am come to make thee understand what shall befall thy people in the latter days: for yet the vision *is* for *many* days.

[15] And when he had spoken such words unto me, I set my face toward the ground, and I became dumb.

[16] And, behold, *one* like the similitude of the sons of men touched my lips: then I opened my mouth, and spake, and said unto him that stood before me, O my lord, by the vision my sorrows are turned upon me, and I have retained no strength.

[17] For how can the servant of this my lord talk with this my lord? for as for me, straightway there remained no strength in me, neither is there breath left in me.

[18] Then there came again and touched me *one* like the appearance of a man, and he strengthened me,

[19] And said, O man greatly beloved, fear not: peace *be* unto thee, be strong, yea, be strong. And when he had spoken unto me, I was strengthened, and said, Let my lord speak; for thou hast strengthened me.

[20] Then said he, Knowest thou wherefore I come unto thee? and now will I return to fight with the prince of Persia: and when I am gone forth, lo, the prince of Grecia shall come.

[21] But I will shew thee that which is noted in the scripture of truth: and *there is* none that holdeth with me in these things, but Michael your prince.

Daniel 12:1-3 - Michael Stand Up, the Great Prince

[1] And at that time shall Michael stand up, the great prince which standeth for the children of thy people: and there shall be a time of trouble, such as never was since there was a nation *even* to that same time: and at that time thy people shall be delivered, every one that shall be found written in the book.

² And many of them that sleep in the dust of the earth shall awake, some to everlasting life, and some to shame *and* everlasting contempt.

³ And they that be wise shall shine as the brightness of the firmament; and they that turn many to righteousness as the stars for ever and ever.

Jude 1:1- 9 - Michael the Archangel Disputed about the Body of Moses

¹ Jude, the servant of Jesus Christ, and brother of James, to them that are sanctified by God the Father, and preserved in Jesus Christ, *and* called:

² Mercy unto you, and peace, and love, be multiplied.

³ Beloved, when I gave all diligence to write unto you of the common salvation, it was needful for me to write unto you, and exhort *you* that ye should earnestly contend for the faith which was once delivered unto the saints.

⁴ For there are certain men crept in unawares, who were before of old ordained to this condemnation, ungodly men, turning the grace of our God into lasciviousness, and denying the only Lord God, and our Lord Jesus Christ.

⁵ I will therefore put you in remembrance, though ye once knew this, how that the Lord, having saved the people out of the land of Egypt, afterward destroyed them that believed not.

⁶ And the angels which kept not their first estate, but left their own habitation, he hath reserved in everlasting chains under darkness unto the judgment of the great day.

⁷ Even as Sodom and Gomorrha, and the cities about them in like manner, giving themselves over to fornication, and going after strange flesh, are set forth for an example, suffering the vengeance of eternal fire.

⁸ Likewise also these *filthy* dreamers defile the flesh, despise dominion, and speak evil of dignities.

⁹ Yet <u>Michael the archangel</u>, when contending with the devil he disputed about the body of Moses, durst not bring against him a railing accusation, but said, The Lord rebuke thee.

Revelation 12:1-10 - Michael and his Angels Fought against the Dragon

¹ And there appeared a great wonder in heaven; a woman clothed with the sun, and the moon under her feet, and upon her head a crown of twelve stars:

² And she being with child cried, travailing in birth, and pained to be delivered.

³ And there appeared another wonder in heaven; and behold a great red dragon, having seven heads and ten horns, and seven crowns upon his heads.

⁴ And his tail drew the third part of the stars of heaven, and did cast them to the earth: and the dragon stood before the woman which was ready to be delivered, for to devour her child as soon as it was born.

⁵ And she brought forth a man child, who was to rule all nations with a rod of iron: and her child was caught up unto God, and *to* his throne.

⁶ And the woman fled into the wilderness, where she hath a place prepared of God, that they should feed her there a thousand two hundred *and* threescore days.

⁷ And there was war in heaven: <u>Michael and his angels</u> fought against the dragon; and the dragon fought and his angels,

⁸ And prevailed not; neither was their place found any more in heaven.

⁹ And the great dragon was cast out, that old serpent, called the Devil, and Satan, which deceiveth the whole world: he was cast out into the earth, and his angels were cast out with him.

¹⁰ And I heard a loud voice saying in heaven, Now is come salvation, and strength, and the kingdom of our God, and the power of his Christ: for the accuser of our brethren is cast down, which accused them before our God day and night.

Gabriel

Daniel 8:1-27 - Gabriel, Make this Man Understand the Vision

¹ In the third year of the reign of king Belshazzar a vision appeared unto me, *even unto* me Daniel, after that which appeared unto me at the first.

² And I saw in a vision; and it came to pass, when I saw, that I *was* at Shushan *in* the palace, which *is* in the province of Elam; and I saw in a vision, and I was by the river of Ulai.

³ Then I lifted up mine eyes, and saw, and, behold, there stood before the river a ram which had *two* horns: and the *two* horns *were* high; but one *was* higher than the other, and the higher came up last.

⁴ I saw the ram pushing westward, and northward, and southward; so that no beasts might stand before him, neither *was there any* that could deliver out of his hand; but he did according to his will, and became great.

⁵ And as I was considering, behold, an he goat came from the west on the face of the whole earth, and touched not the ground: and the goat *had* a notable horn between his eyes.

⁶ And he came to the ram that had *two* horns, which I had seen standing before the river, and ran unto him in the fury of his power.

⁷ And I saw him come close unto the ram, and he was moved with choler against him, and smote the ram, and brake his two horns: and there was no power in the ram to stand before him, but he cast him down to the ground, and stamped upon him: and there was none that could deliver the ram out of his hand.

⁸ Therefore the he goat waxed very great: and when he was strong, the great horn was broken; and for it came up four notable ones toward the four winds of heaven.

⁹ And out of one of them came forth a little horn, which waxed exceeding great, toward the south, and toward the east, and toward the pleasant *land*.

¹⁰ And it waxed great, *even* to the host of heaven; and it cast down *some* of the host and of the stars to the ground, and stamped upon them.

¹¹ Yea, he magnified *himself* even to the prince of the host, and by him the daily *sacrifice* was taken away, and the place of his sanctuary was cast down.

¹² And an host was given *him* against the daily *sacrifice* by reason of transgression, and it cast down the truth to the ground; and it practised, and prospered.

¹³ Then I heard one saint speaking, and another saint said unto that certain *saint* which spake, How long *shall be* the vision *concerning* the daily *sacrifice*, and the transgression of desolation, to give both the sanctuary and the host to be trodden under foot?

¹⁴ And he said unto me, Unto two thousand and three hundred days; then shall the sanctuary be cleansed.

¹⁵ And it came to pass, when I, *even* I Daniel, had seen the vision, and sought for the meaning, then, behold, there stood before me as the appearance of a man.

¹⁶ And I heard a man's voice between *the banks of* Ulai, which called, and said, <u>Gabriel</u>, make this *man* to understand the vision.

¹⁷ So he came near where I stood: and when he came, I was afraid, and fell upon my face: but he said unto me, Understand, O son of man: for at the time of the end *shall be* the vision.

¹⁸ Now as he was speaking with me, I was in a deep sleep on my face toward the ground: but he touched me, and set me upright.

¹⁹ And he said, Behold, I will make thee know what shall be in the last end of the indignation: for at the time appointed the end *shall be*.

²⁰ The ram which thou sawest having *two* horns *are* the kings of Media and Persia.

²¹ And the rough goat *is* the king of Grecia: and the great horn that *is* between his eyes *is* the first king.

²² Now that being broken, whereas four stood up for it, four kingdoms shall stand up out of the nation, but not in his power.

²³ And in the latter time of their kingdom, when the transgressors are come to the full, a king of fierce countenance, and understanding dark sentences, shall stand up.

²⁴ And his power shall be mighty, but not by his own power: and he shall destroy wonderfully, and shall prosper, and practise, and shall destroy the mighty and the holy people.

²⁵ And through his policy also he shall cause craft to prosper in his hand; and he shall magnify *himself* in his heart, and by peace shall destroy many: he shall also stand up against the Prince of princes; but he shall be broken without hand.

²⁶ And the vision of the evening and the morning which was told *is* true: wherefore shut thou up the vision; for it *shall be* for many days.

²⁷ And I Daniel fainted, and was sick *certain* days; afterward I rose up, and did the king's business; and I was astonished at the vision, but none understood *it*.

Daniel 9:20-27 - Gabriel being Caused to Fly Swiftly and Touched Me

²⁰ And whiles I *was* speaking, and praying, and confessing my sin and the sin of my people Israel, and presenting my supplication before the LORD my God for the holy mountain of my God;

²¹ Yea, whiles I *was* speaking in prayer, even the man Gabriel, whom I had seen in the vision at the beginning, being caused to fly swiftly, touched me about the time of the evening oblation.

²² And he informed *me*, and talked with me, and said, O Daniel, I am now come forth to give thee skill and understanding.

²³ At the beginning of thy supplications the commandment came forth, and I am come to shew *thee*; for thou *art* greatly beloved: therefore understand the matter, and consider the vision.

²⁴ Seventy weeks are determined upon thy people and upon thy holy city, to finish the transgression, and to make an end of sins, and to make reconciliation for iniquity, and to bring in everlasting righteousness, and to seal up the vision and prophecy, and to anoint the most Holy.

²⁵ Know therefore and understand, *that* from the going forth of the commandment to restore and to build Jerusalem unto the Messiah the Prince *shall be* seven weeks, and threescore and two weeks: the street shall be built again, and the wall, even in troublous times.

²⁶ And after threescore and two weeks shall Messiah be cut off, but not for himself: and the people of the prince that shall come shall destroy the city and the sanctuary; and the end thereof *shall be* with a flood, and unto the end of the war desolations are determined.

²⁷ And he shall confirm the covenant with many for one week: and in the midst of the week he shall cause the sacrifice and the oblation to cease, and for the overspreading of abominations he shall make *it* desolate, even until the consummation, and that determined shall be poured upon the desolate.

Luke 1:1-38 - Gabriel Speaking to Zachariah about Birth of Son John and Gabriel Proclaiming the Birth of Jesus to Mary

¹ Forasmuch as many have taken in hand to set forth in order a declaration of those things which are most surely believed among us,

² Even as they delivered them unto us, which from the beginning were eyewitnesses, and ministers of the word;

³ It seemed good to me also, having had perfect understanding of all things from the very first, to write unto thee in order, most excellent Theophilus,

⁴ That thou mightest know the certainty of those things, wherein thou hast been instructed.

⁵ There was in the days of Herod, the king of Judaea, a certain priest named Zacharias, of the course of Abia: and his wife *was* of the daughters of Aaron, and her name *was* Elisabeth.

⁶ And they were both righteous before God, walking in all the commandments and ordinances of the Lord blameless.

⁷ And they had no child, because that Elisabeth was barren, and they both were *now* well stricken in years.

⁸ And it came to pass, that while he executed the priest's office before God in the order of his course,

⁹ According to the custom of the priest's office, his lot was to burn incense when he went into the temple of the Lord.

¹⁰ And the whole multitude of the people were praying without at the time of incense.

¹¹ And there appeared unto him an <u>angel of the Lord</u> standing on the right side of the altar of incense.

¹² And when Zacharias saw *him*, he was troubled, and fear fell upon him.

¹³ But the <u>angel</u> said unto him, Fear not, Zacharias: for thy prayer is heard; and thy wife Elisabeth shall bear thee a son, and thou shalt call his name John.

¹⁴ And thou shalt have joy and gladness; and many shall rejoice at his birth.

¹⁵ For he shall be great in the sight of the Lord, and shall drink neither wine nor strong drink; and he shall be filled with the Holy Ghost, even from his mother's womb.

¹⁶ And many of the children of Israel shall he turn to the Lord their God.

¹⁷ And he shall go before him in the spirit and power of Elias, to turn the hearts of the fathers to the children, and the disobedient to the wisdom of the just; to make ready a people prepared for the Lord.

¹⁸ And Zacharias said unto the <u>angel</u>, Whereby shall I know this? for I am an old man, and my wife well stricken in years.

¹⁹ And the <u>angel</u> answering said unto him, I am <u>Gabriel</u>, that stand in the presence of God; and am sent to speak unto thee, and to shew thee these glad tidings.

²⁰ And, behold, thou shalt be dumb, and not able to speak, until the day that these things shall be performed, because thou believest not my words, which shall be fulfilled in their season.

²¹ And the people waited for Zacharias, and marvelled that he tarried so long in the temple.

²² And when he came out, he could not speak unto them: and they perceived that he had seen a vision in the temple: for he beckoned unto them, and remained speechless.

²³ And it came to pass, that, as soon as the days of his ministration were accomplished, he departed to his own house.

²⁴ And after those days his wife Elisabeth conceived, and hid herself five months, saying,

²⁵ Thus hath the Lord dealt with me in the days wherein he looked on *me*, to take away my reproach among men.

²⁶ And in the sixth month the <u>angel</u> <u>Gabriel</u> was sent from God unto a city of Galilee, named Nazareth,

²⁷ To a virgin espoused to a man whose name was Joseph, of the house of David; and the virgin's name *was* Mary.

²⁸ And the <u>angel</u> came in unto her, and said, Hail, *thou that art* highly favoured, the Lord *is* with thee: blessed *art* thou among women.

²⁹ And when she saw *him*, she was troubled at his saying, and cast in her mind what manner of salutation this should be.

³⁰ And the <u>angel</u> said unto her, Fear not, Mary: for thou hast found favour with God.

³¹ And, behold, thou shalt conceive in thy womb, and bring forth a son, and shalt call his name JESUS.

[32] He shall be great, and shall be called the Son of the Highest: and the Lord God shall give unto him the throne of his father David:

[33] And he shall reign over the house of Jacob for ever; and of his kingdom there shall be no end.

[34] Then said Mary unto the <u>angel</u>, How shall this be, seeing I know not a man?

[35] And the <u>angel</u> answered and said unto her, The Holy Ghost shall come upon thee, and the power of the Highest shall overshadow thee: therefore also that holy thing which shall be born of thee shall be called the Son of God.

[36] And, behold, thy cousin Elisabeth, she hath also conceived a son in her old age: and this is the sixth month with her, who was called barren.

[37] For with God nothing shall be impossible.

[38] And Mary said, Behold the handmaid of the Lord; be it unto me according to thy word. And the <u>angel</u> departed from her.

The Complete Reference to Angels in the Bible

Angels in the Old Testament

Genesis 16:1-16 - Angel of the Lord Aiding Hagar and Ishmael

¹ Now Sarai Abram's wife bare him no children: and she had an handmaid, an Egyptian, whose name *was* Hagar.

² And Sarai said unto Abram, Behold now, the LORD hath restrained me from bearing: I pray thee, go in unto my maid; it may be that I may obtain children by her. And Abram hearkened to the voice of Sarai.

³ And Sarai Abram's wife took Hagar her maid the Egyptian, after Abram had dwelt ten years in the land of Canaan, and gave her to her husband Abram to be his wife.

⁴ And he went in unto Hagar, and she conceived: and when she saw that she had conceived, her mistress was despised in her eyes.

⁵ And Sarai said unto Abram, My wrong *be* upon thee: I have given my maid into thy bosom; and when she saw that she had conceived, I was despised in her eyes: the LORD judge between me and thee.

⁶ But Abram said unto Sarai, Behold, thy maid *is* in thy hand; do to her as it pleaseth thee. And when Sarai dealt hardly with her, she fled from her face.

⁷ And the angel of the LORD found her by a fountain of water in the wilderness, by the fountain in the way to Shur.

⁸ And he said, Hagar, Sarai's maid, whence camest thou? and whither wilt thou go? And she said, I flee from the face of my mistress Sarai.

⁹ And the <u>angel of the LORD</u> said unto her, Return to thy mistress, and submit thyself under her hands.

¹⁰ And the <u>angel of the LORD</u> said unto her, I will multiply thy seed exceedingly, that it shall not be numbered for multitude.

¹¹ And the <u>angel of the LORD</u> said unto her, Behold, thou *art* with child, and shalt bear a son, and shalt call his name Ishmael; because the LORD hath heard thy affliction.

¹² And he will be a wild man; his hand *will be* against every man, and every man's hand against him; and he shall dwell in the presence of all his brethren.

¹³ And she called the name of the LORD that spake unto her, Thou God seest me: for she said, Have I also here looked after him that seeth me?

¹⁴ Wherefore the well was called Beerlahairoi; behold, *it is* between Kadesh and Bered.

¹⁵ And Hagar bare Abram a son: and Abram called his son's name, which Hagar bare, Ishmael.

¹⁶ And Abram *was* fourscore and six years old, when Hagar bare Ishmael to Abram.

Genesis 19:1-28 - Two Angels to Sodom and Gomorrah

¹ And there came two <u>angels</u> to Sodom at even; and Lot sat in the gate of Sodom: and Lot seeing *them* rose up to meet them; and he bowed himself with his face toward the ground;

² And he said, Behold now, my lords, turn in, I pray you, into your servant's house, and tarry all night, and wash your feet, and ye shall rise up early, and go on your ways. And they said, Nay; but we will abide in the street all night.

³ And he pressed upon them greatly; and they turned in unto him, and entered into his house; and he made them a feast, and did bake unleavened bread, and they did eat.

⁴ But before they lay down, the men of the city, *even* the men of Sodom, compassed the house round, both old and young, all the people from every quarter:

⁵ And they called unto Lot, and said unto him, Where *are* the men which came in to thee this night? bring them out unto us, that we may know them.

⁶ And Lot went out at the door unto them, and shut the door after him,

⁷ And said, I pray you, brethren, do not so wickedly.

⁸ Behold now, I have two daughters which have not known man; let me, I pray you, bring them out unto you, and do ye to them as *is* good in your eyes: only unto these men do nothing; for therefore came they under the shadow of my roof.

⁹ And they said, Stand back. And they said *again*, This one *fellow* came in to sojourn, and he will needs be a judge: now will we deal worse with thee, than with them. And they pressed sore upon the man, *even* Lot, and came near to break the door.

¹⁰ But the men put forth their hand, and pulled Lot into the house to them, and shut to the door.

¹¹ And they smote the men that *were* at the door of the house with blindness, both small and great: so that they wearied themselves to find the door.

¹² And the men said unto Lot, Hast thou here any besides? son in law, and thy sons, and thy daughters, and whatsoever thou hast in the city, bring *them* out of this place:

¹³ For we will destroy this place, because the cry of them is waxen great before the face of the LORD; and the LORD hath sent us to destroy it.

¹⁴ And Lot went out, and spake unto his sons in law, which married his daughters, and said, Up, get you out of this place; for the LORD will destroy this city. But he seemed as one that mocked unto his sons in law.

¹⁵ And when the morning arose, then the <u>angels</u> hastened Lot, saying, Arise, take thy wife, and thy two daughters, which are here; lest thou be consumed in the iniquity of the city.

¹⁶ And while he lingered, the men laid hold upon his hand, and upon the hand of his wife, and upon the hand of his two daughters; the LORD being merciful unto him: and they brought him forth, and set him without the city.

¹⁷ And it came to pass, when they had brought them forth abroad, that he said, Escape for thy life; look not behind thee, neither stay thou in all the plain; escape to the mountain, lest thou be consumed.

¹⁸ And Lot said unto them, Oh, not so, my Lord:

¹⁹ Behold now, thy servant hath found grace in thy sight, and thou hast magnified thy mercy, which thou hast shewed unto me in saving my life; and I cannot escape to the mountain, lest some evil take me, and I die:

²⁰ Behold now, this city *is* near to flee unto, and it *is* a little one: Oh, let me escape thither, (*is* it not a little one?) and my soul shall live.

²¹ And he said unto him, See, I have accepted thee concerning this thing also, that I will not overthrow this city, for the which thou hast spoken.

²² Haste thee, escape thither; for I cannot do any thing till thou be come thither. Therefore the name of the city was called Zoar.

²³ The sun was risen upon the earth when Lot entered into Zoar.

²⁴ Then the LORD rained upon Sodom and upon Gomorrah brimstone and fire from the LORD out of heaven;

²⁵ And he overthrew those cities, and all the plain, and all the inhabitants of the cities, and that which grew upon the ground.

²⁶ But his wife looked back from behind him, and she became a pillar of salt.

²⁷ And Abraham gat up early in the morning to the place where he stood before the LORD:

28 And he looked toward Sodom and Gomorrah, and toward all the land of the plain, and beheld, and, lo, the smoke of the country went up as the smoke of a furnace.

Genesis 21:1-21 - Angel of God Rescues Hagar and Ishmael

1 And the LORD visited Sarah as he had said, and the LORD did unto Sarah as he had spoken.

2 For Sarah conceived, and bare Abraham a son in his old age, at the set time of which God had spoken to him.

3 And Abraham called the name of his son that was born unto him, whom Sarah bare to him, Isaac.

4 And Abraham circumcised his son Isaac being eight days old, as God had commanded him.

5 And Abraham was an hundred years old, when his son Isaac was born unto him.

6 And Sarah said, God hath made me to laugh, *so that* all that hear will laugh with me.

7 And she said, Who would have said unto Abraham, that Sarah should have given children suck? for I have born *him* a son in his old age.

8 And the child grew, and was weaned: and Abraham made a great feast the *same* day that Isaac was weaned.

9 And Sarah saw the son of Hagar the Egyptian, which she had born unto Abraham, mocking.

10 Wherefore she said unto Abraham, Cast out this bondwoman and her son: for the son of this bondwoman shall not be heir with my son, *even* with Isaac.

11 And the thing was very grievous in Abraham's sight because of his son.

¹² And God said unto Abraham, Let it not be grievous in thy sight because of the lad, and because of thy bondwoman; in all that Sarah hath said unto thee, hearken unto her voice; for in Isaac shall thy seed be called.

¹³ And also of the son of the bondwoman will I make a nation, because he *is* thy seed.

¹⁴ And Abraham rose up early in the morning, and took bread, and a bottle of water, and gave *it* unto Hagar, putting *it* on her shoulder, and the child, and sent her away: and she departed, and wandered in the wilderness of Beersheba.

¹⁵ And the water was spent in the bottle, and she cast the child under one of the shrubs.

¹⁶ And she went, and sat her down over against *him* a good way off, as it were a bowshot: for she said, Let me not see the death of the child. And she sat over against *him*, and lift up her voice, and wept.

¹⁷ And God heard the voice of the lad; and the angel of God called to Hagar out of heaven, and said unto her, What aileth thee, Hagar? fear not; for God hath heard the voice of the lad where he *is*.

¹⁸ Arise, lift up the lad, and hold him in thine hand; for I will make him a great nation.

¹⁹ And God opened her eyes, and she saw a well of water; and she went, and filled the bottle with water, and gave the lad drink.

²⁰ And God was with the lad; and he grew, and dwelt in the wilderness, and became an archer.

²¹ And he dwelt in the wilderness of Paran: and his mother took him a wife out of the land of Egypt.

Genesis 22:1-18 - Angel of the Lord Stops Abraham from Slaying Isaac

¹ And it came to pass after these things, that God did tempt Abraham, and said unto him, Abraham: and he said, Behold, *here* I *am*.

² And he said, Take now thy son, thine only *son* Isaac, whom thou lovest, and get thee into the land of Moriah; and offer him there for a burnt offering upon one of the mountains which I will tell thee of.

³ And Abraham rose up early in the morning, and saddled his ass, and took two of his young men with him, and Isaac his son, and clave the wood for the burnt offering, and rose up, and went unto the place of which God had told him.

⁴ Then on the third day Abraham lifted up his eyes, and saw the place afar off.

⁵ And Abraham said unto his young men, Abide ye here with the ass; and I and the lad will go yonder and worship, and come again to you.

⁶ And Abraham took the wood of the burnt offering, and laid *it* upon Isaac his son; and he took the fire in his hand, and a knife; and they went both of them together.

⁷ And Isaac spake unto Abraham his father, and said, My father: and he said, Here *am* I, my son. And he said, Behold the fire and the wood: but where *is* the lamb for a burnt offering?

⁸ And Abraham said, My son, God will provide himself a lamb for a burnt offering: so they went both of them together.

⁹ And they came to the place which God had told him of; and Abraham built an altar there, and laid the wood in order, and bound Isaac his son, and laid him on the altar upon the wood.

¹⁰ And Abraham stretched forth his hand, and took the knife to slay his son.

¹¹ And the <u>angel of the LORD</u> called unto him out of heaven, and said, Abraham, Abraham: and he said, Here *am* I.

¹² And he said, Lay not thine hand upon the lad, neither do thou any thing unto him: for now I know that thou fearest God, seeing thou hast not withheld thy son, thine only *son* from me.

¹³ And Abraham lifted up his eyes, and looked, and behold behind *him* a ram caught in a thicket by his horns: and Abraham went and took the ram, and offered him up for a burnt offering in the stead of his son.

¹⁴ And Abraham called the name of that place Jehovahjireh: as it is said *to* this day, In the mount of the LORD it shall be seen.

¹⁵ And the <u>angel of the LORD</u> called unto Abraham out of heaven the second time,

¹⁶ And said, By myself have I sworn, saith the LORD, for because thou hast done this thing, and hast not withheld thy son, thine only *son*:

¹⁷ That in blessing I will bless thee, and in multiplying I will multiply thy seed as the stars of the heaven, and as the sand which *is* upon the sea shore; and thy seed shall possess the gate of his enemies;

¹⁸ And in thy seed shall all the nations of the earth be blessed; because thou hast obeyed my voice.

Genesis 24:1-67 - Angel Finds Isaac's Wife

¹ And Abraham was old, *and* well stricken in age: and the LORD had blessed Abraham in all things.

² And Abraham said unto his eldest servant of his house, that ruled over all that he had, Put, I pray thee, thy hand under my thigh:

³ And I will make thee swear by the LORD, the God of heaven, and the God of the earth, that thou shalt not take a wife unto my son of the daughters of the Canaanites, among whom I dwell:

⁴ But thou shalt go unto my country, and to my kindred, and take a wife unto my son Isaac.

⁵ And the servant said unto him, Peradventure the woman will not be willing to follow me unto this land: must I needs bring thy son again unto the land from whence thou camest?

⁶ And Abraham said unto him, Beware thou that thou bring not my son thither again.

⁷ The LORD God of heaven, which took me from my father's house, and from the land of my kindred, and which spake unto me, and that sware unto me, saying, Unto thy seed will I give this land; he shall send his <u>angel</u> before thee, and thou shalt take a wife unto my son from thence.

⁸ And if the woman will not be willing to follow thee, then thou shalt be clear from this my oath: only bring not my son thither again.

⁹ And the servant put his hand under the thigh of Abraham his master, and sware to him concerning that matter.

¹⁰ And the servant took ten camels of the camels of his master, and departed; for all the goods of his master *were* in his hand: and he arose, and went to Mesopotamia, unto the city of Nahor.

¹¹ And he made his camels to kneel down without the city by a well of water at the time of the evening, *even* the time that women go out to draw *water*.

¹² And he said, O LORD God of my master Abraham, I pray thee, send me good speed this day, and shew kindness unto my master Abraham.

¹³ Behold, I stand *here* by the well of water; and the daughters of the men of the city come out to draw water:

¹⁴ And let it come to pass, that the damsel to whom I shall say, Let down thy pitcher, I pray thee, that I may drink; and she shall say, Drink, and I will give thy camels drink also: *let the same be* she *that* thou hast appointed for thy servant Isaac; and thereby shall I know that thou hast shewed kindness unto my master.

¹⁵ And it came to pass, before he had done speaking, that, behold, Rebekah came out, who was born to Bethuel, son of Milcah, the wife of Nahor, Abraham's brother, with her pitcher upon her shoulder.

¹⁶ And the damsel *was* very fair to look upon, a virgin, neither had any man known her: and she went down to the well, and filled her pitcher, and came up.

¹⁷ And the servant ran to meet her, and said, Let me, I pray thee, drink a little water of thy pitcher.

¹⁸ And she said, Drink, my lord: and she hasted, and let down her pitcher upon her hand, and gave him drink.

¹⁹ And when she had done giving him drink, she said, I will draw *water* for thy camels also, until they have done drinking.

²⁰ And she hasted, and emptied her pitcher into the trough, and ran again unto the well to draw *water*, and drew for all his camels.

²¹ And the man wondering at her held his peace, to wit whether the LORD had made his journey prosperous or not.

²² And it came to pass, as the camels had done drinking, that the man took a golden earring of half a shekel weight, and two bracelets for her hands of ten *shekels* weight of gold;

²³ And said, Whose daughter *art* thou? tell me, I pray thee: is there room *in* thy father's house for us to lodge in?

²⁴ And she said unto him, I *am* the daughter of Bethuel the son of Milcah, which she bare unto Nahor.

²⁵ She said moreover unto him, We have both straw and provender enough, and room to lodge in.

²⁶ And the man bowed down his head, and worshipped the LORD.

²⁷ And he said, Blessed *be* the LORD God of my master Abraham, who hath not left destitute my master of his mercy and his truth: I *being* in the way, the LORD led me to the house of my master's brethren.

²⁸ And the damsel ran, and told *them of* her mother's house these things.

²⁹ And Rebekah had a brother, and his name *was* Laban: and Laban ran out unto the man, unto the well.

³⁰ And it came to pass, when he saw the earring and bracelets upon his sister's hands, and when he heard the words of Rebekah his sister, saying, Thus spake the man unto me; that he came unto the man; and, behold, he stood by the camels at the well.

³¹ And he said, Come in, thou blessed of the LORD; wherefore standest thou without? for I have prepared the house, and room for the camels.

³² And the man came into the house: and he ungirded his camels, and gave straw and provender for the camels, and water to wash his feet, and the men's feet that *were* with him.

³³ And there was set *meat* before him to eat: but he said, I will not eat, until I have told mine errand. And he said, Speak on.

⁴⁴ And he said, I *am* Abraham's servant.

³⁵ And the LORD hath blessed my master greatly; and he is become great: and he hath given him flocks, and herds, and silver, and gold, and menservants, and maidservants, and camels, and asses.

³⁶ And Sarah my master's wife bare a son to my master when she was old: and unto him hath he given all that he hath.

³⁷ And my master made me swear, saying, Thou shalt not take a wife to my son of the daughters of the Canaanites, in whose land I dwell:

³⁸ But thou shalt go unto my father's house, and to my kindred, and take a wife unto my son.

³⁹ And I said unto my master, Peradventure the woman will not follow me.

⁴⁰ And he said unto me, The LORD, before whom I walk, will send his <u>angel</u> with thee, and prosper thy way; and thou shalt take a wife for my son of my kindred, and of my father's house:

⁴¹ Then shalt thou be clear from *this* my oath, when thou comest to my kindred; and if they give not thee *one*, thou shalt be clear from my oath.

⁴² And I came this day unto the well, and said, O LORD God of my master Abraham, if now thou do prosper my way which I go:

⁴³ Behold, I stand by the well of water; and it shall come to pass, that when the virgin cometh forth to draw *water*, and I say to her, Give me, I pray thee, a little water of thy pitcher to drink;

⁴⁴ And she say to me, Both drink thou, and I will also draw for thy camels: *let* the same *be* the woman whom the LORD hath appointed out for my master's son.

⁴⁵ And before I had done speaking in mine heart, behold, Rebekah came forth with her pitcher on her shoulder; and she went down unto the well, and drew *water*: and I said unto her, Let me drink, I pray thee.

⁴⁶ And she made haste, and let down her pitcher from her *shoulder*, and said, Drink, and I will give thy camels drink also: so I drank, and she made the camels drink also.

⁴⁷ And I asked her, and said, Whose daughter *art* thou? And she said, The daughter of Bethuel, Nahor's son, whom Milcah bare unto him: and I put the earring upon her face, and the bracelets upon her hands.

⁴⁸ And I bowed down my head, and worshipped the LORD, and blessed the LORD God of my master Abraham, which had led me in the right way to take my master's brother's daughter unto his son.

⁴⁹ And now if ye will deal kindly and truly with my master, tell me: and if not, tell me; that I may turn to the right hand, or to the left.

⁵⁰ Then Laban and Bethuel answered and said, The thing proceedeth from the LORD: we cannot speak unto thee bad or good.

⁵¹ Behold, Rebekah *is* before thee, take *her*, and go, and let her be thy master's son's wife, as the LORD hath spoken.

⁵² And it came to pass, that, when Abraham's servant heard their words, he worshipped the LORD, *bowing himself* to the earth.

⁵³ And the servant brought forth jewels of silver, and jewels of gold, and raiment, and gave *them* to Rebekah: he gave also to her brother and to her mother precious things.

⁵⁴ And they did eat and drink, he and the men that *were* with him, and tarried all night; and they rose up in the morning, and he said, Send me away unto my master.

⁵⁵ And her brother and her mother said, Let the damsel abide with us *a few* days, at the least ten; after that she shall go.

⁵⁶ And he said unto them, Hinder me not, seeing the LORD hath prospered my way; send me away that I may go to my master.

⁵⁷ And they said, We will call the damsel, and enquire at her mouth.

⁵⁸ And they called Rebekah, and said unto her, Wilt thou go with this man? And she said, I will go.

⁵⁹ And they sent away Rebekah their sister, and her nurse, and Abraham's servant, and his men.

⁶⁰ And they blessed Rebekah, and said unto her, Thou *art* our sister, be thou *the mother* of thousands of millions, and let thy seed possess the gate of those which hate them.

⁶¹ And Rebekah arose, and her damsels, and they rode upon the camels, and followed the man: and the servant took Rebekah, and went his way.

⁶² And Isaac came from the way of the well Lahairoi; for he dwelt in the south country.

⁶³ And Isaac went out to meditate in the field at the eventide: and he lifted up his eyes, and saw, and, behold, the camels *were* coming.

⁶⁴ And Rebekah lifted up her eyes, and when she saw Isaac, she lighted off the camel.

⁶⁵ For she *had* said unto the servant, What man *is* this that walketh in the field to meet us? And the servant *had* said, It *is* my master: therefore she took a vail, and covered herself.

⁶⁶ And the servant told Isaac all things that he had done.

⁶⁷ And Isaac brought her into his mother Sarah's tent, and took Rebekah, and she became his wife; and he loved her: and Isaac was comforted after his mother's *death*.

Genesis 28:1-22 - Angels of God Descending and Ascending on Jacob's Ladder

¹ And Isaac called Jacob, and blessed him, and charged him, and said unto him, Thou shalt not take a wife of the daughters of Canaan.

² Arise, go to Padanaram, to the house of Bethuel thy mother's father; and take thee a wife from thence of the daughters of Laban thy mother's brother.

³ And God Almighty bless thee, and make thee fruitful, and multiply thee, that thou mayest be a multitude of people;

⁴ And give thee the blessing of Abraham, to thee, and to thy seed with thee; that thou mayest inherit the land wherein thou art a stranger, which God gave unto Abraham.

⁵ And Isaac sent away Jacob: and he went to Padanaram unto Laban, son of Bethuel the Syrian, the brother of Rebekah, Jacob's and Esau's mother.

⁶ When Esau saw that Isaac had blessed Jacob, and sent him away to Padanaram, to take him a wife from thence; and that as he blessed him he gave him a charge, saying, Thou shalt not take a wife of the daughters of Canaan;

⁷ And that Jacob obeyed his father and his mother, and was gone to Padanaram;

⁸ And Esau seeing that the daughters of Canaan pleased not Isaac his father;

⁹ Then went Esau unto Ishmael, and took unto the wives which he had Mahalath the daughter of Ishmael Abraham's son, the sister of Nebajoth, to be his wife.

¹⁰ And Jacob went out from Beersheba, and went toward Haran.

¹¹ And he lighted upon a certain place, and tarried there all night, because the sun was set; and he took of the stones of that place, and put *them for* his pillows, and lay down in that place to sleep.

¹² And he dreamed, and behold a ladder set up on the earth, and the top of it reached to heaven: and behold the <u>angels of God</u> ascending and descending on it.

¹³ And, behold, the LORD stood above it, and said, I *am* the LORD God of Abraham thy father, and the God of Isaac: the land whereon thou liest, to thee will I give it, and to thy seed;

¹⁴ And thy seed shall be as the dust of the earth, and thou shalt spread abroad to the west, and to the east, and to the north, and to the south: and in thee and in thy seed shall all the families of the earth be blessed.

¹⁵ And, behold, I *am* with thee, and will keep thee in all *places* whither thou goest, and will bring thee again into this land; for I will not leave thee, until I have done *that* which I have spoken to thee of.

¹⁶ And Jacob awaked out of his sleep, and he said, Surely the LORD is in this place; and I knew *it* not.

17 And he was afraid, and said, How dreadful *is* this place! this *is* none other but the house of God, and this *is* the gate of heaven.

18 And Jacob rose up early in the morning, and took the stone that he had put *for* his pillows, and set it up *for* a pillar, and poured oil upon the top of it.

19 And he called the name of that place Bethel: but the name of that city *was called* Luz at the first.

20 And Jacob vowed a vow, saying, If God will be with me, and will keep me in this way that I go, and will give me bread to eat, and raiment to put on,

21 So that I come again to my father's house in peace; then shall the LORD be my God:

22 And this stone, which I have set *for* a pillar, shall be God's house: and of all that thou shalt give me I will surely give the tenth unto thee.

Genesis 31:1-13 - Jacob Explaining Dream from the Angel of God

1 And he heard the words of Laban's sons, saying, Jacob hath taken away all that *was* our father's; and of *that* which *was* our father's hath he gotten all this glory.

2 And Jacob beheld the countenance of Laban, and, behold, it *was* not toward him as before.

3 And the LORD said unto Jacob, Return unto the land of thy fathers, and to thy kindred; and I will be with thee.

4 And Jacob sent and called Rachel and Leah to the field unto his flock,

5 And said unto them, I see your father's countenance, that it *is* not toward me as before; but the God of my father hath been with me.

6 And ye know that with all my power I have served your father.

7 And your father hath deceived me, and changed my wages ten times; but God suffered him not to hurt me.

[8] If he said thus, The speckled shall be thy wages; then all the cattle bare speckled: and if he said thus, The ringstraked shall be thy hire; then bare all the cattle ringstraked.

[9] Thus God hath taken away the cattle of your father, and given *them* to me.

[10] And it came to pass at the time that the cattle conceived, that I lifted up mine eyes, and saw in a dream, and, behold, the rams which leaped upon the cattle *were* ringstraked, speckled, and grisled.

[11] And the <u>angel of God</u> spake unto me in a dream, *saying*, Jacob: And I said, Here *am* I.

[12] And he said, Lift up now thine eyes, and see, all the rams which leap upon the cattle *are* ringstraked, speckled, and grisled: for I have seen all that Laban doeth unto thee.

[13] I *am* the God of Bethel, where thou anointedst the pillar, *and* where thou vowedst a vow unto me: now arise, get thee out from this land, and return unto the land of thy kindred.

Genesis 32:1-3 - Jacob Met Angels of God

[1] And Jacob went on his way, and the <u>angels of God</u> met him.

[2] And when Jacob saw them, he said, This *is* God's host: and he called the name of that place Mahanaim.

[3] And Jacob sent messengers before him to Esau his brother unto the land of Seir, the country of Edom.

Genesis 48:1-22 - Israel (Jacob) Asking Angel Blessing for Joseph

[1] And it came to pass after these things, that *one* told Joseph, Behold, thy father *is* sick: and he took with him his two sons, Manasseh and Ephraim.

² And *one* told Jacob, and said, Behold, thy son Joseph cometh unto thee: and Israel strengthened himself, and sat upon the bed.

³ And Jacob said unto Joseph, God Almighty appeared unto me at Luz in the land of Canaan, and blessed me,

⁴ And said unto me, Behold, I will make thee fruitful, and multiply thee, and I will make of thee a multitude of people; and will give this land to thy seed after thee *for* an everlasting possession.

⁵ And now thy two sons, Ephraim and Manasseh, which were born unto thee in the land of Egypt before I came unto thee into Egypt, *are* mine; as Reuben and Simeon, they shall be mine.

⁶ And thy issue, which thou begettest after them, shall be thine, *and* shall be called after the name of their brethren in their inheritance.

⁷ And as for me, when I came from Padan, Rachel died by me in the land of Canaan in the way, when yet *there was* but a little way to come unto Ephrath: and I buried her there in the way of Ephrath; the same *is* Bethlehem.

⁸ And Israel beheld Joseph's sons, and said, Who *are* these?

⁹ And Joseph said unto his father, They *are* my sons, whom God hath given me in this *place*. And he said, Bring them, I pray thee, unto me, and I will bless them.

¹⁰ Now the eyes of Israel were dim for age, *so that* he could not see. And he brought them near unto him; and he kissed them, and embraced them.

¹¹ And Israel said unto Joseph, I had not thought to see thy face: and, lo, God hath shewed me also thy seed.

¹² And Joseph brought them out from between his knees, and he bowed himself with his face to the earth.

¹³ And Joseph took them both, Ephraim in his right hand toward Israel's left hand, and Manasseh in his left hand toward Israel's right hand, and brought *them* near unto him.

¹⁴ And Israel stretched out his right hand, and laid *it* upon Ephraim's head, who *was* the younger, and his left hand upon Manasseh's head, guiding his hands wittingly; for Manasseh *was* the firstborn.

¹⁵ And he blessed Joseph, and said, God, before whom my fathers Abraham and Isaac did walk, the God which fed me all my life long unto this day,

¹⁶ The <u>Angel</u> which redeemed me from all evil, bless the lads; and let my name be named on them, and the name of my fathers Abraham and Isaac; and let them grow into a multitude in the midst of the earth.

¹⁷ And when Joseph saw that his father laid his right hand upon the head of Ephraim, it displeased him: and he held up his father's hand, to remove it from Ephraim's head unto Manasseh's head.

¹⁸ And Joseph said unto his father, Not so, my father: for this *is* the firstborn; put thy right hand upon his head.

¹⁹ And his father refused, and said, I know *it*, my son, I know *it*: he also shall become a people, and he also shall be great: but truly his younger brother shall be greater than he, and his seed shall become a multitude of nations.

²⁰ And he blessed them that day, saying, In thee shall Israel bless, saying, God make thee as Ephraim and as Manasseh: and he set Ephraim before Manasseh.

²¹ And Israel said unto Joseph, Behold, I die: but God shall be with you, and bring you again unto the land of your fathers.

²² Moreover I have given to thee one portion above thy brethren, which I took out of the hand of the Amorite with my sword and with my bow.

Exodus 3:1-22 - Moses and Angel of the Lord in Burning Bush

¹ Now Moses kept the flock of Jethro his father in law, the priest of Midian: and he led the flock to the backside of the desert, and came to the mountain of God, *even* to Horeb.

² And the <u>angel of the LORD</u> appeared unto him in a flame of fire out of the midst of a bush: and he looked, and, behold, the bush burned with fire, and the bush *was* not consumed.

³ And Moses said, I will now turn aside, and see this great sight, why the bush is not burnt.

⁴ And when the LORD saw that he turned aside to see, God called unto him out of the midst of the bush, and said, Moses, Moses. And he said, Here *am* I.

⁵ And he said, Draw not nigh hither: put off thy shoes from off thy feet, for the place whereon thou standest *is* holy ground.

⁶ Moreover he said, I *am* the God of thy father, the God of Abraham, the God of Isaac, and the God of Jacob. And Moses hid his face; for he was afraid to look upon God.

⁷ And the LORD said, I have surely seen the affliction of my people which *are* in Egypt, and have heard their cry by reason of their taskmasters; for I know their sorrows;

⁸ And I am come down to deliver them out of the hand of the Egyptians, and to bring them up out of that land unto a good land and a large, unto a land flowing with milk and honey; unto the place of the Canaanites, and the Hittites, and the Amorites, and the Perizzites, and the Hivites, and the Jebusites.

⁹ Now therefore, behold, the cry of the children of Israel is come unto me: and I have also seen the oppression wherewith the Egyptians oppress them.

¹⁰ Come now therefore, and I will send thee unto Pharaoh, that thou mayest bring forth my people the children of Israel out of Egypt.

¹¹ And Moses said unto God, Who *am* I, that I should go unto Pharaoh, and that I should bring forth the children of Israel out of Egypt?

¹² And he said, Certainly I will be with thee; and this *shall be* a token unto thee, that I have sent thee: When thou hast brought forth the people out of Egypt, ye shall serve God upon this mountain.

¹³ And Moses said unto God, Behold, *when* I come unto the children of Israel, and shall say unto them, The God of your fathers hath sent me unto you; and they shall say to me, What *is* his name? what shall I say unto them?

¹⁴ And God said unto Moses, I AM THAT I AM: and he said, Thus shalt thou say unto the children of Israel, I AM hath sent me unto you.

¹⁵ And God said moreover unto Moses, Thus shalt thou say unto the children of Israel, The LORD God of your fathers, the God of Abraham, the God of Isaac, and the God of Jacob, hath sent me unto you: this *is* my name for ever, and this *is* my memorial unto all generations.

¹⁶ Go, and gather the elders of Israel together, and say unto them, The LORD God of your fathers, the God of Abraham, of Isaac, and of Jacob, appeared unto me, saying, I have surely visited you, and *seen* that which is done to you in Egypt:

¹⁷ And I have said, I will bring you up out of the affliction of Egypt unto the land of the Canaanites, and the Hittites, and the Amorites, and the Perizzites, and the Hivites, and the Jebusites, unto a land flowing with milk and honey.

¹⁸ And they shall hearken to thy voice: and thou shalt come, thou and the elders of Israel, unto the king of Egypt, and ye shall say unto him, The LORD God of the Hebrews hath met with us: and now let us go, we beseech thee, three days' journey into the wilderness, that we may sacrifice to the LORD our God.

¹⁹ And I am sure that the king of Egypt will not let you go, no, not by a mighty hand.

²⁰ And I will stretch out my hand, and smite Egypt with all my wonders which I will do in the midst thereof: and after that he will let you go.

²¹ And I will give this people favour in the sight of the Egyptians: and it shall come to pass, that, when ye go, ye shall not go empty:

²² But every woman shall borrow of her neighbour, and of her that sojourneth in her house, jewels of silver, and jewels of gold, and raiment: and ye shall put *them* upon your sons, and upon your daughters; and ye shall spoil the Egyptians.

Exodus 14:1-31 - Angel of God Went before the Camp of Israel

¹ And the LORD spake unto Moses, saying,

² Speak unto the children of Israel, that they turn and encamp before Pihahiroth, between Migdol and the sea, over against Baalzephon: before it shall ye encamp by the sea.

³ For Pharaoh will say of the children of Israel, They *are* entangled in the land, the wilderness hath shut them in.

⁴ And I will harden Pharaoh's heart, that he shall follow after them; and I will be honoured upon Pharaoh, and upon all his host; that the Egyptians may know that I *am* the LORD. And they did so.

⁵ And it was told the king of Egypt that the people fled: and the heart of Pharaoh and of his servants was turned against the people, and they said, Why have we done this, that we have let Israel go from serving us?

⁶ And he made ready his chariot, and took his people with him:

⁷ And he took six hundred chosen chariots, and all the chariots of Egypt, and captains over every one of them.

⁸ And the LORD hardened the heart of Pharaoh king of Egypt, and he pursued after the children of Israel: and the children of Israel went out with an high hand.

⁹ But the Egyptians pursued after them, all the horses *and* chariots of Pharaoh, and his horsemen, and his army, and overtook them encamping by the sea, beside Pihahiroth, before Baalzephon.

¹⁰ And when Pharaoh drew nigh, the children of Israel lifted up their eyes, and, behold, the Egyptians marched after them; and they were sore afraid: and the children of Israel cried out unto the LORD.

¹¹ And they said unto Moses, Because *there were* no graves in Egypt, hast thou taken us away to die in the wilderness? wherefore hast thou dealt thus with us, to carry us forth out of Egypt?

¹² *Is* not this the word that we did tell thee in Egypt, saying, Let us alone, that we may serve the Egyptians? For *it had been* better for us to serve the Egyptians, than that we should die in the wilderness.

¹³ And Moses said unto the people, Fear ye not, stand still, and see the salvation of the LORD, which he will shew to you to day: for the Egyptians whom ye have seen to day, ye shall see them again no more for ever.

¹⁴ The LORD shall fight for you, and ye shall hold your peace.

¹⁵ And the LORD said unto Moses, Wherefore criest thou unto me? speak unto the children of Israel, that they go forward:

¹⁶ But lift thou up thy rod, and stretch out thine hand over the sea, and divide it: and the children of Israel shall go on dry *ground* through the midst of the sea.

¹⁷ And I, behold, I will harden the hearts of the Egyptians, and they shall follow them: and I will get me honour upon Pharaoh, and upon all his host, upon his chariots, and upon his horsemen.

¹⁸ And the Egyptians shall know that I *am* the LORD, when I have gotten me honour upon Pharaoh, upon his chariots, and upon his horsemen.

¹⁹ And the <u>angel of God</u>, which went before the camp of Israel, removed and went behind them; and the pillar of the cloud went from before their face, and stood behind them:

²⁰ And it came between the camp of the Egyptians and the camp of Israel; and it was a cloud and darkness *to them*, but it gave light by night *to these*: so that the one came not near the other all the night.

²¹ And Moses stretched out his hand over the sea; and the LORD caused the sea to go *back* by a strong east wind all that night, and made the sea dry *land*, and the waters were divided.

²² And the children of Israel went into the midst of the sea upon the dry *ground*: and the waters *were* a wall unto them on their right hand, and on their left.

²³ And the Egyptians pursued, and went in after them to the midst of the sea, *even* all Pharaoh's horses, his chariots, and his horsemen.

²⁴ And it came to pass, that in the morning watch the LORD looked unto the host of the Egyptians through the pillar of fire and of the cloud, and troubled the host of the Egyptians,

²⁵ And took off their chariot wheels, that they drave them heavily: so that the Egyptians said, Let us flee from the face of Israel; for the LORD fighteth for them against the Egyptians.

²⁶ And the LORD said unto Moses, Stretch out thine hand over the sea, that the waters may come again upon the Egyptians, upon their chariots, and upon their horsemen.

²⁷ And Moses stretched forth his hand over the sea, and the sea returned to his strength when the morning appeared; and the Egyptians fled against it; and the LORD overthrew the Egyptians in the midst of the sea.

²⁸ And the waters returned, and covered the chariots, and the horsemen, *and* all the host of Pharaoh that came into the sea after them; there remained not so much as one of them.

²⁹ But the children of Israel walked upon dry *land* in the midst of the sea; and the waters *were* a wall unto them on their right hand, and on their left.

³⁰ Thus the LORD saved Israel that day out of the hand of the Egyptians; and Israel saw the Egyptians dead upon the sea shore.

³¹ And Israel saw that great work which the LORD did upon the Egyptians: and the people feared the LORD, and believed the LORD, and his servant Moses.

Exodus 23:19-33 - God Sending an Angel before Moses and Israel

¹⁹ The first of the firstfruits of thy land thou shalt bring into the house of the LORD thy God. Thou shalt not seethe a kid in his mother's milk.

²⁰ Behold, I send an Angel before thee, to keep thee in the way, and to bring thee into the place which I have prepared.

²¹ Beware of him, and obey his voice, provoke him not; for he will not pardon your transgressions: for my name *is* in him.

²² But if thou shalt indeed obey his voice, and do all that I speak; then I will be an enemy unto thine enemies, and an adversary unto thine adversaries.

²³ For mine <u>Angel</u> shall go before thee, and bring thee in unto the Amorites, and the Hittites, and the Perizzites, and the Canaanites, the Hivites, and the Jebusites: and I will cut them off.

²⁴ Thou shalt not bow down to their gods, nor serve them, nor do after their works: but thou shalt utterly overthrow them, and quite break down their images.

²⁵ And ye shall serve the LORD your God, and he shall bless thy bread, and thy water; and I will take sickness away from the midst of thee.

²⁶ There shall nothing cast their young, nor be barren, in thy land: the number of thy days I will fulfil.

²⁷ I will send my fear before thee, and will destroy all the people to whom thou shalt come, and I will make all thine enemies turn their backs unto thee.

²⁸ And I will send hornets before thee, which shall drive out the Hivite, the Canaanite, and the Hittite, from before thee.

²⁹ I will not drive them out from before thee in one year; lest the land become desolate, and the beast of the field multiply against thee.

³⁰ By little and little I will drive them out from before thee, until thou be increased, and inherit the land.

³¹ And I will set thy bounds from the Red sea even unto the sea of the Philistines, and from the desert unto the river: for I will deliver the inhabitants of the land into your hand; and thou shalt drive them out before thee.

³² Thou shalt make no covenant with them, nor with their gods.

³³ They shall not dwell in thy land, lest they make thee sin against me: for if thou serve their gods, it will surely be a snare unto thee.

Exodus 32:1-35 - God Sending an Angel before Moses and Israel

¹ And when the people saw that Moses delayed to come down out of the mount, the people gathered themselves together unto Aaron, and said unto him, Up, make us gods, which shall go before us; for *as for* this Moses, the man that brought us up out of the land of Egypt, we wot not what is become of him.

² And Aaron said unto them, Break off the golden earrings, which *are* in the ears of your wives, of your sons, and of your daughters, and bring *them* unto me.

³ And all the people brake off the golden earrings which *were* in their ears, and brought *them* unto Aaron.

⁴ And he received *them* at their hand, and fashioned it with a graving tool, after he had made it a molten calf: and they said, These *be* thy gods, O Israel, which brought thee up out of the land of Egypt.

⁵ And when Aaron saw *it*, he built an altar before it; and Aaron made proclamation, and said, To morrow *is* a feast to the LORD.

⁶ And they rose up early on the morrow, and offered burnt offerings, and brought peace offerings; and the people sat down to eat and to drink, and rose up to play.

⁷ And the LORD said unto Moses, Go, get thee down; for thy people, which thou broughtest out of the land of Egypt, have corrupted *themselves*:

⁸ They have turned aside quickly out of the way which I commanded them: they have made them a molten calf, and have worshipped it, and have sacrificed thereunto, and said, These *be* thy gods, O Israel, which have brought thee up out of the land of Egypt.

⁹ And the LORD said unto Moses, I have seen this people, and, behold, it *is* a stiffnecked people:

¹⁰ Now therefore let me alone, that my wrath may wax hot against them, and that I may consume them: and I will make of thee a great nation.

¹¹ And Moses besought the LORD his God, and said, LORD, why doth thy wrath wax hot against thy people, which thou hast brought forth out of the land of Egypt with great power, and with a mighty hand?

¹² Wherefore should the Egyptians speak, and say, For mischief did he bring them out, to slay them in the mountains, and to consume them from the face of the earth? Turn from thy fierce wrath, and repent of this evil against thy people.

¹³ Remember Abraham, Isaac, and Israel, thy servants, to whom thou swarest by thine own self, and saidst unto them, I will multiply your seed as the stars of heaven, and all this land that I have spoken of will I give unto your seed, and they shall inherit *it* for ever.

¹⁴ And the LORD repented of the evil which he thought to do unto his people.

¹⁵ And Moses turned, and went down from the mount, and the two tables of the testimony *were* in his hand: the tables *were* written on both their sides; on the one side and on the other *were* they written.

¹⁶ And the tables *were* the work of God, and the writing *was* the writing of God, graven upon the tables.

¹⁷ And when Joshua heard the noise of the people as they shouted, he said unto Moses, *There is* a noise of war in the camp.

¹⁸ And he said, *It is* not the voice of *them that* shout for mastery, neither *is it* the voice of *them that* cry for being overcome: *but* the noise of *them that* sing do I hear.

¹⁹ And it came to pass, as soon as he came nigh unto the camp, that he saw the calf, and the dancing: and Moses' anger waxed hot, and he cast the tables out of his hands, and brake them beneath the mount.

²⁰ And he took the calf which they had made, and burnt *it* in the fire, and ground *it* to powder, and strawed *it* upon the water, and made the children of Israel drink *of it*.

²¹ And Moses said unto Aaron, What did this people unto thee, that thou hast brought so great a sin upon them?

²² And Aaron said, Let not the anger of my lord wax hot: thou knowest the people, that they *are set* on mischief.

²³ For they said unto me, Make us gods, which shall go before us: for *as for* this Moses, the man that brought us up out of the land of Egypt, we wot not what is become of him.

²⁴ And I said unto them, Whosoever hath any gold, let them break *it* off. So they gave *it* me: then I cast it into the fire, and there came out this calf.

²⁵ And when Moses saw that the people *were* naked; (for Aaron had made them naked unto *their* shame among their enemies:)

²⁶ Then Moses stood in the gate of the camp, and said, Who *is* on the LORD'S side? *let him come* unto me. And all the sons of Levi gathered themselves together unto him.

²⁷ And he said unto them, Thus saith the LORD God of Israel, Put every man his sword by his side, *and* go in and out from gate to gate throughout the camp, and slay every man his brother, and every man his companion, and every man his neighbour.

²⁸ And the children of Levi did according to the word of Moses: and there fell of the people that day about three thousand men.

²⁹ For Moses had said, Consecrate yourselves to day to the LORD, even every man upon his son, and upon his brother; that he may bestow upon you a blessing this day.

³⁰ And it came to pass on the morrow, that Moses said unto the people, Ye have sinned a great sin: and now I will go up unto the LORD; peradventure I shall make an atonement for your sin.

³¹ And Moses returned unto the LORD, and said, Oh, this people have sinned a great sin, and have made them gods of gold.

³² Yet now, if thou wilt forgive their sin--; and if not, blot me, I pray thee, out of thy book which thou hast written.

³³ And the LORD said unto Moses, Whosoever hath sinned against me, him will I blot out of my book.

³⁴ Therefore now go, lead the people unto *the place* of which I have spoken unto thee: behold, mine <u>Angel</u> shall go before thee: nevertheless in the day when I visit I will visit their sin upon them.

[35] And the LORD plagued the people, because they made the calf, which Aaron made.

Exodus 33:1-3 - God Sending an Angel to Drive Out the Inhabitants of the Promised Land

[1] And the LORD said unto Moses, Depart, *and* go up hence, thou and the people which thou hast brought up out of the land of Egypt, unto the land which I sware unto Abraham, to Isaac, and to Jacob, saying, Unto thy seed will I give it:

[2] And I will send an <u>angel</u> before thee; and I will drive out the Canaanite, the Amorite, and the Hittite, and the Perizzite, the Hivite, and the Jebusite:

[3] Unto a land flowing with milk and honey: for I will not go up in the midst of thee; for thou *art* a stiffnecked people: lest I consume thee in the way.

Numbers 20:1-17 - Moses' Messengers Retelling Story of God Sending an Angel Leading Israel out of Egypt

[1] Then came the children of Israel, *even* the whole congregation, into the desert of Zin in the first month: and the people abode in Kadesh; and Miriam died there, and was buried there.

[2] And there was no water for the congregation: and they gathered themselves together against Moses and against Aaron.

[3] And the people chode with Moses, and spake, saying, Would God that we had died when our brethren died before the LORD!

[4] And why have ye brought up the congregation of the LORD into this wilderness, that we and our cattle should die there?

[5] And wherefore have ye made us to come up out of Egypt, to bring us in unto this evil place? it *is* no place of seed, or of figs, or of vines, or of pomegranates; neither *is* there any water to drink.

⁶ And Moses and Aaron went from the presence of the assembly unto the door of the tabernacle of the congregation, and they fell upon their faces: and the glory of the LORD appeared unto them.

⁷ And the LORD spake unto Moses, saying,

⁸ Take the rod, and gather thou the assembly together, thou, and Aaron thy brother, and speak ye unto the rock before their eyes; and it shall give forth his water, and thou shalt bring forth to them water out of the rock: so thou shalt give the congregation and their beasts drink.

⁹ And Moses took the rod from before the LORD, as he commanded him.

¹⁰ And Moses and Aaron gathered the congregation together before the rock, and he said unto them, Hear now, ye rebels; must we fetch you water out of this rock?

¹¹ And Moses lifted up his hand, and with his rod he smote the rock twice: and the water came out abundantly, and the congregation drank, and their beasts *also*.

¹² And the LORD spake unto Moses and Aaron, Because ye believed me not, to sanctify me in the eyes of the children of Israel, therefore ye shall not bring this congregation into the land which I have given them.

¹³ This *is* the water of Meribah; because the children of Israel strove with the LORD, and he was sanctified in them.

¹⁴ And Moses sent messengers from Kadesh unto the king of Edom, Thus saith thy brother Israel, Thou knowest all the travail that hath befallen us:

¹⁵ How our fathers went down into Egypt, and we have dwelt in Egypt a long time; and the Egyptians vexed us, and our fathers:

¹⁶ And when we cried unto the LORD, he heard our voice, and sent an <u>angel</u>, and hath brought us forth out of Egypt: and, behold, we *are* in Kadesh, a city in the uttermost of thy border:

[17] Let us pass, I pray thee, through thy country: we will not pass through the fields, or through the vineyards, neither will we drink *of* the water of the wells: we will go by the king's *high* way, we will not turn to the right hand nor to the left, until we have passed thy borders.

Numbers 22:1-41 - Balaam and the Angel of the Lord

[1] And the children of Israel set forward, and pitched in the plains of Moab on this side Jordan *by* Jericho.

[2] And Balak the son of Zippor saw all that Israel had done to the Amorites.

[3] And Moab was sore afraid of the people, because they *were* many: and Moab was distressed because of the children of Israel.

[4] And Moab said unto the elders of Midian, Now shall this company lick up all *that are* round about us, as the ox licketh up the grass of the field. And Balak the son of Zippor *was* king of the Moabites at that time.

[5] He sent messengers therefore unto Balaam the son of Beor to Pethor, which *is* by the river of the land of the children of his people, to call him, saying, Behold, there is a people come out from Egypt: behold, they cover the face of the earth, and they abide over against me:

[6] Come now therefore, I pray thee, curse me this people; for they *are* too mighty for me: peradventure I shall prevail, *that* we may smite them, and *that* I may drive them out of the land: for I wot that he whom thou blessest *is* blessed, and he whom thou cursest is cursed.

[7] And the elders of Moab and the elders of Midian departed with the rewards of divination in their hand; and they came unto Balaam, and spake unto him the words of Balak.

[8] And he said unto them, Lodge here this night, and I will bring you word again, as the LORD shall speak unto me: and the princes of Moab abode with Balaam.

⁹ And God came unto Balaam, and said, What men *are* these with thee?

¹⁰ And Balaam said unto God, Balak the son of Zippor, king of Moab, hath sent unto me, *saying*,

¹¹ Behold, *there is* a people come out of Egypt, which covereth the face of the earth: come now, curse me them; peradventure I shall be able to overcome them, and drive them out.

¹² And God said unto Balaam, Thou shalt not go with them; thou shalt not curse the people: for they *are* blessed.

¹³ And Balaam rose up in the morning, and said unto the princes of Balak, Get you into your land: for the LORD refuseth to give me leave to go with you.

¹⁴ And the princes of Moab rose up, and they went unto Balak, and said, Balaam refuseth to come with us.

¹⁵ And Balak sent yet again princes, more, and more honourable than they.

¹⁶ And they came to Balaam, and said to him, Thus saith Balak the son of Zippor, Let nothing, I pray thee, hinder thee from coming unto me:

¹⁷ For I will promote thee unto very great honour, and I will do whatsoever thou sayest unto me: come therefore, I pray thee, curse me this people.

¹⁸ And Balaam answered and said unto the servants of Balak, If Balak would give me his house full of silver and gold, I cannot go beyond the word of the LORD my God, to do less or more.

¹⁹ Now therefore, I pray you, tarry ye also here this night, that I may know what the LORD will say unto me more.

²⁰ And God came unto Balaam at night, and said unto him, If the men come to call thee, rise up, *and* go with them; but yet the word which I shall say unto thee, that shalt thou do.

²¹ And Balaam rose up in the morning, and saddled his ass, and went with the princes of Moab.

²² And God's anger was kindled because he went: and the <u>angel of the LORD</u> stood in the way for an adversary against him. Now he was riding upon his ass, and his two servants *were* with him.

²³ And the ass saw the <u>angel of the LORD</u> standing in the way, and his sword drawn in his hand: and the ass turned aside out of the way, and went into the field: and Balaam smote the ass, to turn her into the way.

²⁴ But the <u>angel of the LORD</u> stood in a path of the vineyards, a wall *being* on this side, and a wall on that side.

²⁵ And when the ass saw the <u>angel of the LORD</u>, she thrust herself unto the wall, and crushed Balaam's foot against the wall: and he smote her again.

²⁶ And the <u>angel of the LORD</u> went further, and stood in a narrow place, where *was* no way to turn either to the right hand or to the left.

²⁷ And when the ass saw the <u>angel of the LORD</u>, she fell down under Balaam: and Balaam's anger was kindled, and he smote the ass with a staff.

²⁸ And the LORD opened the mouth of the ass, and she said unto Balaam, What have I done unto thee, that thou hast smitten me these three times?

²⁹ And Balaam said unto the ass, Because thou hast mocked me: I would there were a sword in mine hand, for now would I kill thee.

³⁰ And the ass said unto Balaam, *Am* not I thine ass, upon which thou hast ridden ever since *I was* thine unto this day? was I ever wont to do so unto thee? And he said, Nay.

³¹ Then the LORD opened the eyes of Balaam, and he saw the <u>angel of the LORD</u> standing in the way, and his sword drawn in his hand: and he bowed down his head, and fell flat on his face.

³² And the <u>angel of the LORD</u> said unto him, Wherefore hast thou smitten thine ass these three times? behold, I went out to withstand thee, because *thy* way is perverse before me:

³³ And the ass saw me, and turned from me these three times: unless she had turned from me, surely now also I had slain thee, and saved her alive.

³⁴ And Balaam said unto the angel of the LORD, I have sinned; for I knew not that thou stoodest in the way against me: now therefore, if it displease thee, I will get me back again.

³⁵ And the angel of the LORD said unto Balaam, Go with the men: but only the word that I shall speak unto thee, that thou shalt speak. So Balaam went with the princes of Balak.

³⁶ And when Balak heard that Balaam was come, he went out to meet him unto a city of Moab, which *is* in the border of Arnon, which *is* in the utmost coast.

³⁷ And Balak said unto Balaam, Did I not earnestly send unto thee to call thee? wherefore camest thou not unto me? am I not able indeed to promote thee to honour?

³⁸ And Balaam said unto Balak, Lo, I am come unto thee: have I now any power at all to say any thing? the word that God putteth in my mouth, that shall I speak.

³⁹ And Balaam went with Balak, and they came unto Kirjathhuzoth.

⁴⁰ And Balak offered oxen and sheep, and sent to Balaam, and to the princes that *were* with him.

⁴¹ And it came to pass on the morrow, that Balak took Balaam, and brought him up into the high places of Baal, that thence he might see the utmost *part* of the people.

Judges 2:1-7 - Angel of the Lord Prophesying about Israel's Disobedience to Joshua and Israelites

¹ And an angel of the LORD came up from Gilgal to Bochim, and said, I made you to go up out of Egypt, and have brought you unto the land which I sware unto your fathers; and I said, I will never break my covenant with you.

² And ye shall make no league with the inhabitants of this land; ye shall throw down their altars: but ye have not obeyed my voice: why have ye done this?

³ Wherefore I also said, I will not drive them out from before you; but they shall be *as thorns* in your sides, and their gods shall be a snare unto you.

⁴ And it came to pass, when the <u>angel of the LORD</u> spake these words unto all the children of Israel, that the people lifted up their voice, and wept.

⁵ And they called the name of that place Bochim: and they sacrificed there unto the LORD.

⁶ And when Joshua had let the people go, the children of Israel went every man unto his inheritance to possess the land.

⁷ And the people served the LORD all the days of Joshua, and all the days of the elders that outlived Joshua, who had seen all the great works of the LORD, that he did for Israel.

Judges 5:1-31 - Deborah's Song Including a Verse about the Angel of the Lord

¹ Then sang Deborah and Barak the son of Abinoam on that day, saying,

² Praise ye the LORD for the avenging of Israel, when the people willingly offered themselves.

³ Hear, O ye kings; give ear, O ye princes; I, *even* I, will sing unto the LORD; I will sing *praise* to the LORD God of Israel.

⁴ LORD, when thou wentest out of Seir, when thou marchedst out of the field of Edom, the earth trembled, and the heavens dropped, the clouds also dropped water.

⁵ The mountains melted from before the LORD, *even* that Sinai from before the LORD God of Israel.

⁶ In the days of Shamgar the son of Anath, in the days of Jael, the highways were unoccupied, and the travellers walked through byways.

⁷ *The inhabitants of* the villages ceased, they ceased in Israel, until that I Deborah arose, that I arose a mother in Israel.

⁸ They chose new gods; then *was* war in the gates: was there a shield or spear seen among forty thousand in Israel?

⁹ My heart *is* toward the governors of Israel, that offered themselves willingly among the people. Bless ye the LORD.

¹⁰ Speak, ye that ride on white asses, ye that sit in judgment, and walk by the way.

¹¹ *They that are delivered* from the noise of archers in the places of drawing water, there shall they rehearse the righteous acts of the LORD, *even* the righteous acts *toward the inhabitants* of his villages in Israel: then shall the people of the LORD go down to the gates.

¹² Awake, awake, Deborah: awake, awake, utter a song: arise, Barak, and lead thy captivity captive, thou son of Abinoam.

¹³ Then he made him that remaineth have dominion over the nobles among the people: the LORD made me have dominion over the mighty.

¹⁴ Out of Ephraim *was there* a root of them against Amalek; after thee, Benjamin, among thy people; out of Machir came down governors, and out of Zebulun they that handle the pen of the writer.

¹⁵ And the princes of Issachar *were* with Deborah; even Issachar, and also Barak: he was sent on foot into the valley. For the divisions of Reuben *there were* great thoughts of heart.

¹⁶ Why abodest thou among the sheepfolds, to hear the bleatings of the flocks? For the divisions of Reuben *there were* great searchings of heart.

¹⁷ Gilead abode beyond Jordan: and why did Dan remain in ships? Asher continued on the sea shore, and abode in his breaches.

¹⁸ Zebulun and Naphtali *were* a people *that* jeoparded their lives unto the death in the high places of the field.

¹⁹ The kings came *and* fought, then fought the kings of Canaan in Taanach by the waters of Megiddo; they took no gain of money.

²⁰ They fought from heaven; the stars in their courses fought against Sisera.

²¹ The river of Kishon swept them away, that ancient river, the river Kishon. O my soul, thou hast trodden down strength.

²² Then were the horsehoofs broken by the means of the pransings, the pransings of their mighty ones.

²³ Curse ye Meroz, said the <u>angel of the LORD</u>, curse ye bitterly the inhabitants thereof; because they came not to the help of the LORD, to the help of the LORD against the mighty.

²⁴ Blessed above women shall Jael the wife of Heber the Kenite be, blessed shall she be above women in the tent.

²⁵ He asked water, *and* she gave *him* milk; she brought forth butter in a lordly dish.

²⁶ She put her hand to the nail, and her right hand to the workmen's hammer; and with the hammer she smote Sisera, she smote off his head, when she had pierced and stricken through his temples.

²⁷ At her feet he bowed, he fell, he lay down: at her feet he bowed, he fell: where he bowed, there he fell down dead.

²⁸ The mother of Sisera looked out at a window, and cried through the lattice, Why is his chariot *so* long in coming? why tarry the wheels of his chariots?

²⁹ Her wise ladies answered her, yea, she returned answer to herself,

³⁰ Have they not sped? have they *not* divided the prey; to every man a damsel *or* two; to Sisera a prey of divers colours, a prey of divers colours of needlework, of divers colours of needlework on both sides, *meet* for the necks of *them that take* the spoil?

³¹ So let all thine enemies perish, O LORD: but *let* them that love him *be* as the sun when he goeth forth in his might. And the land had rest forty years.

Judges 6:1-40 - Gideon and the Angel of the Lord

¹ And the children of Israel did evil in the sight of the LORD: and the LORD delivered them into the hand of Midian seven years.

² And the hand of Midian prevailed against Israel: *and* because of the Midianites the children of Israel made them the dens which *are* in the mountains, and caves, and strong holds.

³ And *so* it was, when Israel had sown, that the Midianites came up, and the Amalekites, and the children of the east, even they came up against them;

⁴ And they encamped against them, and destroyed the increase of the earth, till thou come unto Gaza, and left no sustenance for Israel, neither sheep, nor ox, nor ass.

⁵ For they came up with their cattle and their tents, and they came as grasshoppers for multitude; *for* both they and their camels were without number: and they entered into the land to destroy it.

⁶ And Israel was greatly impoverished because of the Midianites; and the children of Israel cried unto the LORD.

⁷ And it came to pass, when the children of Israel cried unto the LORD because of the Midianites,

⁸ That the LORD sent a prophet unto the children of Israel, which said unto them, Thus saith the LORD God of Israel, I brought you up from Egypt, and brought you forth out of the house of bondage;

⁹ And I delivered you out of the hand of the Egyptians, and out of the hand of all that oppressed you, and drave them out from before you, and gave you their land;

¹⁰ And I said unto you, I *am* the LORD your God; fear not the gods of the Amorites, in whose land ye dwell: but ye have not obeyed my voice.

¹¹ And there came an angel of the LORD, and sat under an oak which *was* in Ophrah, that *pertained* unto Joash the Abiezrite: and his son Gideon threshed wheat by the winepress, to hide *it* from the Midianites.

¹² And the angel of the LORD appeared unto him, and said unto him, The LORD *is* with thee, thou mighty man of valour.

¹³ And Gideon said unto him, Oh my Lord, if the LORD be with us, why then is all this befallen us? and where *be* all his miracles which our fathers told us of, saying, Did not the LORD bring us up from Egypt? but now the LORD hath forsaken us, and delivered us into the hands of the Midianites.

¹⁴ And the LORD looked upon him, and said, Go in this thy might, and thou shalt save Israel from the hand of the Midianites: have not I sent thee?

¹⁵ And he said unto him, Oh my Lord, wherewith shall I save Israel? behold, my family *is* poor in Manasseh, and I *am* the least in my father's house.

¹⁶ And the LORD said unto him, Surely I will be with thee, and thou shalt smite the Midianites as one man.

¹⁷ And he said unto him, If now I have found grace in thy sight, then shew me a sign that thou talkest with me.

¹⁸ Depart not hence, I pray thee, until I come unto thee, and bring forth my present, and set *it* before thee. And he said, I will tarry until thou come again.

¹⁹ And Gideon went in, and made ready a kid, and unleavened cakes of an ephah of flour: the flesh he put in a basket, and he put the broth in a pot, and brought *it* out unto him under the oak, and presented *it*.

²⁰ And the angel of God said unto him, Take the flesh and the unleavened cakes, and lay *them* upon this rock, and pour out the broth. And he did so.

²¹ Then the angel of the LORD put forth the end of the staff that *was* in his hand, and touched the flesh and the unleavened cakes; and there rose up fire out of the rock, and consumed the flesh and the unleavened cakes. Then the angel of the LORD departed out of his sight.

²² And when Gideon perceived that he *was* an angel of the LORD, Gideon said, Alas, O Lord GOD! for because I have seen an angel of the LORD face to face.

²³ And the LORD said unto him, Peace *be* unto thee; fear not: thou shalt not die.

²⁴ Then Gideon built an altar there unto the LORD, and called it Jehovahshalom: unto this day it *is* yet in Ophrah of the Abiezrites.

²⁵ And it came to pass the same night, that the LORD said unto him, Take thy father's young bullock, even the second bullock of seven years old, and throw down the altar of Baal that thy father hath, and cut down the grove that *is* by it:

²⁶ And build an altar unto the LORD thy God upon the top of this rock, in the ordered place, and take the second bullock, and offer a burnt sacrifice with the wood of the grove which thou shalt cut down.

²⁷ Then Gideon took ten men of his servants, and did as the LORD had said unto him: and *so* it was, because he feared his father's household, and the men of the city, that he could not do *it* by day, that he did *it* by night.

²⁸ And when the men of the city arose early in the morning, behold, the altar of Baal was cast down, and the grove was cut down that *was* by it, and the second bullock was offered upon the altar *that was* built.

²⁹ And they said one to another, Who hath done this thing? And when they enquired and asked, they said, Gideon the son of Joash hath done this thing.

³⁰ Then the men of the city said unto Joash, Bring out thy son, that he may die: because he hath cast down the altar of Baal, and because he hath cut down the grove that *was* by it.

³¹ And Joash said unto all that stood against him, Will ye plead for Baal? will ye save him? he that will plead for him, let him be put to death whilst *it is yet* morning: if he *be* a god, let him plead for himself, because *one* hath cast down his altar.

³² Therefore on that day he called him Jerubbaal, saying, Let Baal plead against him, because he hath thrown down his altar.

³³ Then all the Midianites and the Amalekites and the children of the east were gathered together, and went over, and pitched in the valley of Jezreel.

³⁴ But the Spirit of the LORD came upon Gideon, and he blew a trumpet; and Abiezer was gathered after him.

³⁵ And he sent messengers throughout all Manasseh; who also was gathered after him: and he sent messengers unto Asher, and unto Zebulun, and unto Naphtali; and they came up to meet them.

³⁶ And Gideon said unto God, If thou wilt save Israel by mine hand, as thou hast said,

³⁷ Behold, I will put a fleece of wool in the floor; *and* if the dew be on the fleece only, and *it be* dry upon all the earth *beside*, then shall I know that thou wilt save Israel by mine hand, as thou hast said.

³⁸ And it was so: for he rose up early on the morrow, and thrust the fleece together, and wringed the dew out of the fleece, a bowl full of water.

³⁹ And Gideon said unto God, Let not thine anger be hot against me, and I will speak but this once: let me prove, I pray thee, but this once with the fleece; let it now be dry only upon the fleece, and upon all the ground let there be dew.

⁴⁰ And God did so that night: for it was dry upon the fleece only, and there was dew on all the ground.

Judges 13:1-25 - Angel of the Lord Prophesying Samson's Birth

¹ And the children of Israel did evil again in the sight of the LORD; and the LORD delivered them into the hand of the Philistines forty years.

² And there was a certain man of Zorah, of the family of the Danites, whose name *was* Manoah; and his wife *was* barren, and bare not.

³ And the <u>angel of the LORD</u> appeared unto the woman, and said unto her, Behold now, thou *art* barren, and bearest not: but thou shalt conceive, and bear a son.

⁴ Now therefore beware, I pray thee, and drink not wine nor strong drink, and eat not any unclean *thing*:

⁵ For, lo, thou shalt conceive, and bear a son; and no razor shall come on his head: for the child shall be a Nazarite unto God from the womb: and he shall begin to deliver Israel out of the hand of the Philistines.

⁶ Then the woman came and told her husband, saying, A man of God came unto me, and his countenance *was* like the countenance of an <u>angel of God</u>, very terrible: but I asked him not whence he *was*, neither told he me his name:

⁷ But he said unto me, Behold, thou shalt conceive, and bear a son; and now drink no wine nor strong drink, neither eat any unclean *thing*: for the child shall be a Nazarite to God from the womb to the day of his death.

⁸ Then Manoah intreated the LORD, and said, O my Lord, let the man of God which thou didst send come again unto us, and teach us what we shall do unto the child that shall be born.

⁹ And God hearkened to the voice of Manoah; and the <u>angel of God</u> came again unto the woman as she sat in the field: but Manoah her husband *was* not with her.

¹⁰ And the woman made haste, and ran, and shewed her husband, and said unto him, Behold, the man hath appeared unto me, that came unto me the *other* day.

¹¹ And Manoah arose, and went after his wife, and came to the man, and said unto him, *Art* thou the man that spakest unto the woman? And he said, I *am*.

¹² And Manoah said, Now let thy words come to pass. How shall we order the child, and *how* shall we do unto him?

¹³ And the <u>angel of the LORD</u> said unto Manoah, Of all that I said unto the woman let her beware.

¹⁴ She may not eat of any *thing* that cometh of the vine, neither let her drink wine or strong drink, nor eat any unclean *thing*: all that I commanded her let her observe.

¹⁵ And Manoah said unto the <u>angel of the LORD</u>, I pray thee, let us detain thee, until we shall have made ready a kid for thee.

¹⁶ And the <u>angel of the LORD</u> said unto Manoah, Though thou detain me, I will not eat of thy bread: and if thou wilt offer a burnt offering, thou must offer it unto the LORD. For Manoah knew not that he *was* an <u>angel of the LORD</u>.

¹⁷ And Manoah said unto the <u>angel of the LORD</u>, What *is* thy name, that when thy sayings come to pass we may do thee honour?

¹⁸ And the <u>angel of the LORD</u> said unto him, Why askest thou thus after my name, seeing it *is* secret?

¹⁹ So Manoah took a kid with a meat offering, and offered *it* upon a rock unto the LORD: and *the angel* did wondrously; and Manoah and his wife looked on.

²⁰ For it came to pass, when the flame went up toward heaven from off the altar, that the <u>angel of the LORD</u> ascended in the flame of the altar. And Manoah and his wife looked on *it*, and fell on their faces to the ground.

²¹ But the <u>angel of the LORD</u> did no more appear to Manoah and to his wife. Then Manoah knew that he *was* an <u>angel of the LORD</u>.

²² And Manoah said unto his wife, We shall surely die, because we have seen God.

²³ But his wife said unto him, If the LORD were pleased to kill us, he would not have received a burnt offering and a meat offering at our hands, neither would he have shewed us all these *things*, nor would as at this time have told us *such things* as these.

²⁴ And the woman bare a son, and called his name Samson: and the child grew, and the LORD blessed him.

²⁵ And the Spirit of the LORD began to move him at times in the camp of Dan between Zorah and Eshtaol.

1 Samuel 29:1-11 - Achish Calling David as an Angel of God

¹ Now the Philistines gathered together all their armies to Aphek: and the Israelites pitched by a fountain which *is* in Jezreel.

² And the lords of the Philistines passed on by hundreds, and by thousands: but David and his men passed on in the rereward with Achish.

³ Then said the princes of the Philistines, What *do* these Hebrews *here*? And Achish said unto the princes of the Philistines, *Is* not this David, the servant of Saul the king of Israel, which hath been with me these days, or these years, and I have found no fault in him since he fell *unto me* unto this day?

⁴ And the princes of the Philistines were wroth with him; and the princes of the Philistines said unto him, Make this fellow return, that he may go again to his place which thou hast appointed him, and let him not go down with us to battle, lest in the battle he be an adversary to us: for wherewith should he reconcile himself unto his master? *should it* not *be* with the heads of these men?

⁵ *Is* not this David, of whom they sang one to another in dances, saying, Saul slew his thousands, and David his ten thousands?

⁶ Then Achish called David, and said unto him, Surely, *as* the LORD liveth, thou hast been upright, and thy going out and thy coming in with me in the host *is* good in my sight: for I have not found evil in thee since the day of thy coming unto me unto this day: nevertheless the lords favour thee not.

⁷ Wherefore now return, and go in peace, that thou displease not the lords of the Philistines.

⁸ And David said unto Achish, But what have I done? and what hast thou found in thy servant so long as I have been with thee unto this day, that I may not go fight against the enemies of my lord the king?

⁹ And Achish answered and said to David, I know that thou *art* good in my sight, as an <u>angel of God</u>: notwithstanding the princes of the Philistines have said, He shall not go up with us to the battle.

¹⁰ Wherefore now rise up early in the morning with thy master's servants that are come with thee: and as soon as ye be up early in the morning, and have light, depart.

¹¹ So David and his men rose up early to depart in the morning, to return into the land of the Philistines. And the Philistines went up to Jezreel.

2 Samuel 14:1-23 - Joab Sending Wise Woman to King David – Wise as the Wisdom of an Angel of God

¹ Now Joab the son of Zeruiah perceived that the king's heart *was* toward Absalom.

² And Joab sent to Tekoah, and fetched thence a wise woman, and said unto her, I pray thee, feign thyself to be a mourner, and put on now mourning apparel, and anoint not thyself with oil, but be as a woman that had a long time mourned for the dead:

³ And come to the king, and speak on this manner unto him. So Joab put the words in her mouth.

⁴ And when the woman of Tekoah spake to the king, she fell on her face to the ground, and did obeisance, and said, Help, O king.

⁵ And the king said unto her, What aileth thee? And she answered, I *am* indeed a widow woman, and mine husband is dead.

⁶ And thy handmaid had two sons, and they two strove together in the field, and *there was* none to part them, but the one smote the other, and slew him.

⁷ And, behold, the whole family is risen against thine handmaid, and they said, Deliver him that smote his brother, that we may kill him, for the life of his brother whom he slew; and we will destroy the heir also: and so they shall quench my coal which is left, and shall not leave to my husband *neither* name nor remainder upon the earth.

⁸ And the king said unto the woman, Go to thine house, and I will give charge concerning thee.

⁹ And the woman of Tekoah said unto the king, My lord, O king, the iniquity *be* on me, and on my father's house: and the king and his throne *be* guiltless.

¹⁰ And the king said, Whosoever saith *ought* unto thee, bring him to me, and he shall not touch thee any more.

¹¹ Then said she, I pray thee, let the king remember the LORD thy God, that thou wouldest not suffer the revengers of blood to destroy any more, lest they destroy my son. And he said, *As* the LORD liveth, there shall not one hair of thy son fall to the earth.

¹² Then the woman said, Let thine handmaid, I pray thee, speak *one* word unto my lord the king. And he said, Say on.

¹³ And the woman said, Wherefore then hast thou thought such a thing against the people of God? for the king doth speak this thing as one which is faulty, in that the king doth not fetch home again his banished.

¹⁴ For we must needs die, and *are* as water spilt on the ground, which cannot be gathered up again; neither doth God respect *any* person: yet doth he devise means, that his banished be not expelled from him.

¹⁵ Now therefore that I am come to speak of this thing unto my lord the king, *it is* because the people have made me afraid: and thy handmaid said, I will now speak unto the king; it may be that the king will perform the request of his handmaid.

¹⁶ For the king will hear, to deliver his handmaid out of the hand of the man *that would* destroy me and my son together out of the inheritance of God.

¹⁷ Then thine handmaid said, The word of my lord the king shall now be comfortable: for as an <u>angel of God</u>, so *is* my lord the king to discern good and bad: therefore the LORD thy God will be with thee.

¹⁸ Then the king answered and said unto the woman, Hide not from me, I pray thee, the thing that I shall ask thee. And the woman said, Let my lord the king now speak.

¹⁹ And the king said, *Is not* the hand of Joab with thee in all this? And the woman answered and said, *As* thy soul liveth, my lord the king, none can turn to the right hand or to the left from ought that my lord the king hath spoken: for thy servant Joab, he bade me, and he put all these words in the mouth of thine handmaid:

²⁰ To fetch about this form of speech hath thy servant Joab done this thing: and my lord *is* wise, according to the wisdom of an <u>angel of God</u>, to know all *things* that *are* in the earth.

²¹ And the king said unto Joab, Behold now, I have done this thing: go therefore, bring the young man Absalom again.

²² And Joab fell to the ground on his face, and bowed himself, and thanked the king: and Joab said, To day thy servant knoweth that I have found grace in thy sight, my lord, O king, in that the king hath fulfilled the request of his servant.

²³ So Joab arose and went to Geshur, and brought Absalom to Jerusalem.

2 Samuel 19:24-27 - Mephibosheth Saying the King is Like the Angel of God

²⁴ And Mephibosheth the son of Saul came down to meet the king, and had neither dressed his feet, nor trimmed his beard, nor washed his clothes, from the day the king departed until the day he came *again* in peace.

²⁵ And it came to pass, when he was come to Jerusalem to meet the king, that the king said unto him, Wherefore wentest not thou with me, Mephibosheth?

²⁶ And he answered, My lord, O king, my servant deceived me: for thy servant said, I will saddle me an ass, that I may ride thereon, and go to the king; because thy servant *is* lame.

²⁷ And he hath slandered thy servant unto my lord the king; but my lord the king *is* as an <u>angel of God</u>: do therefore *what is* good in thine eyes.

2 Samuel 24:1-25 - Angel of the Lord Destroying Jerusalem

¹ And again the anger of the LORD was kindled against Israel, and he moved David against them to say, Go, number Israel and Judah.

² For the king said to Joab the captain of the host, which *was* with him, Go now through all the tribes of Israel, from Dan even to Beersheba, and number ye the people, that I may know the number of the people.

³ And Joab said unto the king, Now the LORD thy God add unto the people, how many soever they be, an hundredfold, and that the eyes of my lord the king may see *it*: but why doth my lord the king delight in this thing?

⁴ Notwithstanding the king's word prevailed against Joab, and against the captains of the host. And Joab and the captains of the host went out from the presence of the king, to number the people of Israel.

⁵ And they passed over Jordan, and pitched in Aroer, on the right side of the city that *lieth* in the midst of the river of Gad, and toward Jazer:

⁶ Then they came to Gilead, and to the land of Tahtimhodshi; and they came to Danjaan, and about to Zidon,

⁷ And came to the strong hold of Tyre, and to all the cities of the Hivites, and of the Canaanites: and they went out to the south of Judah, *even* to Beersheba.

⁸ So when they had gone through all the land, they came to Jerusalem at the end of nine months and twenty days.

⁹ And Joab gave up the sum of the number of the people unto the king: and there were in Israel eight hundred thousand valiant men that drew the sword; and the men of Judah *were* five hundred thousand men.

¹⁰ And David's heart smote him after that he had numbered the people. And David said unto the LORD, I have sinned greatly in that I have done: and now, I beseech thee, O LORD, take away the iniquity of thy servant; for I have done very foolishly.

¹¹ For when David was up in the morning, the word of the LORD came unto the prophet Gad, David's seer, saying,

¹² Go and say unto David, Thus saith the LORD, I offer thee three *things*; choose thee one of them, that I may *do it* unto thee.

¹³ So Gad came to David, and told him, and said unto him, Shall seven years of famine come unto thee in thy land? or wilt thou flee three months before thine enemies, while they pursue thee? or that there be three days' pestilence in thy land? now advise, and see what answer I shall return to him that sent me.

¹⁴ And David said unto Gad, I am in a great strait: let us fall now into the hand of the LORD; for his mercies *are* great: and let me not fall into the hand of man.

¹⁵ So the LORD sent a pestilence upon Israel from the morning even to the time appointed: and there died of the people from Dan even to Beersheba seventy thousand men.

¹⁶ And when the <u>angel</u> stretched out his hand upon Jerusalem to destroy it, the LORD repented him of the evil, and said to the <u>angel</u> that destroyed the people, It is enough: stay now thine hand. And the <u>angel of the LORD</u> was by the threshingplace of Araunah the Jebusite.

¹⁷ And David spake unto the LORD when he saw the <u>angel</u> that smote the people, and said, Lo, I have sinned, and I have done wickedly: but these sheep, what have they done? let thine hand, I pray thee, be against me, and against my father's house.

¹⁸ And Gad came that day to David, and said unto him, Go up, rear an altar unto the LORD in the threshingfloor of Araunah the Jebusite.

¹⁹ And David, according to the saying of Gad, went up as the LORD commanded.

²⁰ And Araunah looked, and saw the king and his servants coming on toward him: and Araunah went out, and bowed himself before the king on his face upon the ground.

²¹ And Araunah said, Wherefore is my lord the king come to his servant? And David said, To buy the threshingfloor of thee, to build an altar unto the LORD, that the plague may be stayed from the people.

²² And Araunah said unto David, Let my lord the king take and offer up what *seemeth* good unto him: behold, *here be* oxen for burnt sacrifice, and threshing instruments and *other* instruments of the oxen for wood.

²³ All these *things* did Araunah, *as* a king, give unto the king. And Araunah said unto the king, The LORD thy God accept thee.

²⁴ And the king said unto Araunah, Nay; but I will surely buy *it* of thee at a price: neither will I offer burnt offerings unto the LORD my God of that which doth cost me nothing. So David bought the threshingfloor and the oxen for fifty shekels of silver.

²⁵ And David built there an altar unto the LORD, and offered burnt offerings and peace offerings. So the LORD was intreated for the land, and the plague was stayed from Israel.

1 Kings 13:1-34 - Bethel Lying about what Angel told Him

¹ And, behold, there came a man of God out of Judah by the word of the LORD unto Bethel: and Jeroboam stood by the altar to burn incense.

² And he cried against the altar in the word of the LORD, and said, O altar, altar, thus saith the LORD; Behold, a child shall be born unto the house of David, Josiah by name; and upon thee shall he offer the priests of the high places that burn incense upon thee, and men's bones shall be burnt upon thee.

³ And he gave a sign the same day, saying, This *is* the sign which the LORD hath spoken; Behold, the altar shall be rent, and the ashes that *are* upon it shall be poured out.

⁴ And it came to pass, when king Jeroboam heard the saying of the man of God, which had cried against the altar in Bethel, that he put forth his hand from the altar, saying, Lay hold on him. And his hand, which he put forth against him, dried up, so that he could not pull it in again to him.

⁵ The altar also was rent, and the ashes poured out from the altar, according to the sign which the man of God had given by the word of the LORD.

⁶ And the king answered and said unto the man of God, Intreat now the face of the LORD thy God, and pray for me, that my hand may be restored me again. And the man of God besought the LORD, and the king's hand was restored him again, and became as *it was* before.

⁷ And the king said unto the man of God, Come home with me, and refresh thyself, and I will give thee a reward.

⁸ And the man of God said unto the king, If thou wilt give me half thine house, I will not go in with thee, neither will I eat bread nor drink water in this place:

⁹ For so was it charged me by the word of the LORD, saying, Eat no bread, nor drink water, nor turn again by the same way that thou camest.

¹⁰ So he went another way, and returned not by the way that he came to Bethel.

¹¹ Now there dwelt an old prophet in Bethel; and his sons came and told him all the works that the man of God had done that day in Bethel: the words which he had spoken unto the king, them they told also to their father.

¹² And their father said unto them, What way went he? For his sons had seen what way the man of God went, which came from Judah.

¹³ And he said unto his sons, Saddle me the ass. So they saddled him the ass: and he rode thereon,

¹⁴ And went after the man of God, and found him sitting under an oak: and he said unto him, *Art* thou the man of God that camest from Judah? And he said, I *am*.

¹⁵ Then he said unto him, Come home with me, and eat bread.

¹⁶ And he said, I may not return with thee, nor go in with thee: neither will I eat bread nor drink water with thee in this place:

¹⁷ For it was said to me by the word of the LORD, Thou shalt eat no bread nor drink water there, nor turn again to go by the way that thou camest.

¹⁸ He said unto him, I *am* a prophet also as thou *art*; and an <u>angel</u> spake unto me by the word of the LORD, saying, Bring him back with thee into thine house, that he may eat bread and drink water. *But* he lied unto him.

¹⁹ So he went back with him, and did eat bread in his house, and drank water.

²⁰ And it came to pass, as they sat at the table, that the word of the LORD came unto the prophet that brought him back:

²¹ And he cried unto the man of God that came from Judah, saying, Thus saith the LORD, Forasmuch as thou hast disobeyed the mouth of the LORD, and hast not kept the commandment which the LORD thy God commanded thee,

²² But camest back, and hast eaten bread and drunk water in the place, of the which *the LORD* did say to thee, Eat no bread, and drink no water; thy carcase shall not come unto the sepulchre of thy fathers.

²³ And it came to pass, after he had eaten bread, and after he had drunk, that he saddled for him the ass, *to wit*, for the prophet whom he had brought back.

²⁴ And when he was gone, a lion met him by the way, and slew him: and his carcase was cast in the way, and the ass stood by it, the lion also stood by the carcase.

²⁵ And, behold, men passed by, and saw the carcase cast in the way, and the lion standing by the carcase: and they came and told *it* in the city where the old prophet dwelt.

²⁶ And when the prophet that brought him back from the way heard *thereof*, he said, It *is* the man of God, who was disobedient unto the word of the LORD: therefore the LORD hath delivered him unto the lion, which hath torn him, and slain him, according to the word of the LORD, which he spake unto him.

²⁷ And he spake to his sons, saying, Saddle me the ass. And they saddled *him*.

²⁸ And he went and found his carcase cast in the way, and the ass and the lion standing by the carcase: the lion had not eaten the carcase, nor torn the ass.

²⁹ And the prophet took up the carcase of the man of God, and laid it upon the ass, and brought it back: and the old prophet came to the city, to mourn and to bury him.

³⁰ And he laid his carcase in his own grave; and they mourned over him, *saying*, Alas, my brother!

³¹ And it came to pass, after he had buried him, that he spake to his sons, saying, When I am dead, then bury me in the sepulchre wherein the man of God *is* buried; lay my bones beside his bones:

³² For the saying which he cried by the word of the LORD against the altar in Bethel, and against all the houses of the high places which *are* in the cities of Samaria, shall surely come to pass.

³³ After this thing Jeroboam returned not from his evil way, but made again of the lowest of the people priests of the high places: whosoever would, he consecrated him, and he became *one* of the priests of the high places.

³⁴ And this thing became sin unto the house of Jeroboam, even to cut *it* off, and to destroy *it* from off the face of the earth.

1 Kings 19:1-21- Angel of the Lord helps Elijah to Escape

¹ And Ahab told Jezebel all that Elijah had done, and withal how he had slain all the prophets with the sword.

² Then Jezebel sent a messenger unto Elijah, saying, So let the gods do *to me*, and more also, if I make not thy life as the life of one of them by to morrow about this time.

³ And when he saw *that*, he arose, and went for his life, and came to Beersheba, which *belongeth* to Judah, and left his servant there.

⁴ But he himself went a day's journey into the wilderness, and came and sat down under a juniper tree: and he requested for himself that he might die; and said, It is enough; now, O LORD, take away my life; for I *am* not better than my fathers.

⁵ And as he lay and slept under a juniper tree, behold, then an <u>angel</u> touched him, and said unto him, Arise *and* eat.

⁶ And he looked, and, behold, *there was* a cake baken on the coals, and a cruse of water at his head. And he did eat and drink, and laid him down again.

⁷ And the <u>angel of the LORD</u> came again the second time, and touched him, and said, Arise *and* eat; because the journey *is* too great for thee.

⁸ And he arose, and did eat and drink, and went in the strength of that meat forty days and forty nights unto Horeb the mount of God.

⁹ And he came thither unto a cave, and lodged there; and, behold, the word of the LORD *came* to him, and he said unto him, What doest thou here, Elijah?

¹⁰ And he said, I have been very jealous for the LORD God of hosts: for the children of Israel have forsaken thy covenant, thrown down thine altars, and slain thy prophets with the sword; and I, *even* I only, am left; and they seek my life, to take it away.

¹¹ And he said, Go forth, and stand upon the mount before the LORD. And, behold, the LORD passed by, and a great and strong wind rent the mountains, and brake in pieces the rocks before the LORD; *but* the LORD *was* not in the wind: and after the wind an earthquake; *but* the LORD *was* not in the earthquake:

¹² And after the earthquake a fire; *but* the LORD *was* not in the fire: and after the fire a still small voice.

¹³ And it was *so*, when Elijah heard *it*, that he wrapped his face in his mantle, and went out, and stood in the entering in of the cave. And, behold, *there came* a voice unto him, and said, What doest thou here, Elijah?

[14] And he said, I have been very jealous for the LORD God of hosts: because the children of Israel have forsaken thy covenant, thrown down thine altars, and slain thy prophets with the sword; and I, *even* I only, am left; and they seek my life, to take it away.

[15] And the LORD said unto him, Go, return on thy way to the wilderness of Damascus: and when thou comest, anoint Hazael *to be* king over Syria:

[16] And Jehu the son of Nimshi shalt thou anoint *to be* king over Israel: and Elisha the son of Shaphat of Abelmeholah shalt thou anoint *to be* prophet in thy room.

[17] And it shall come to pass, *that* him that escapeth the sword of Hazael shall Jehu slay: and him that escapeth from the sword of Jehu shall Elisha slay.

[18] Yet I have left *me* seven thousand in Israel, all the knees which have not bowed unto Baal, and every mouth which hath not kissed him.

[19] So he departed thence, and found Elisha the son of Shaphat, who *was* plowing *with* twelve yoke *of oxen* before him, and he with the twelfth: and Elijah passed by him, and cast his mantle upon him.

[20] And he left the oxen, and ran after Elijah, and said, Let me, I pray thee, kiss my father and my mother, and *then* I will follow thee. And he said unto him, Go back again: for what have I done to thee?

[21] And he returned back from him, and took a yoke of oxen, and slew them, and boiled their flesh with the instruments of the oxen, and gave unto the people, and they did eat. Then he arose, and went after Elijah, and ministered unto him.

2 Kings 1:1-18 - Angel of the Lord gives Elijah a Message

[1] Then Moab rebelled against Israel after the death of Ahab.

[2] And Ahaziah fell down through a lattice in his upper chamber that *was* in Samaria, and was sick: and he sent messengers, and said unto them, Go, enquire of Baalzebub the god of Ekron whether I shall recover of this disease.

³ But the <u>angel of the LORD</u> said to Elijah the Tishbite, Arise, go up to meet the messengers of the king of Samaria, and say unto them, *Is it* not because *there is* not a God in Israel, *that* ye go to enquire of Baalzebub the god of Ekron?

⁴ Now therefore thus saith the LORD, Thou shalt not come down from that bed on which thou art gone up, but shalt surely die. And Elijah departed.

⁵ And when the messengers turned back unto him, he said unto them, Why are ye now turned back?

⁶ And they said unto him, There came a man up to meet us, and said unto us, Go, turn again unto the king that sent you, and say unto him, Thus saith the LORD, *Is it* not because *there is* not a God in Israel, *that* thou sendest to enquire of Baalzebub the god of Ekron? therefore thou shalt not come down from that bed on which thou art gone up, but shalt surely die.

⁷ And he said unto them, What manner of man *was he* which came up to meet you, and told you these words?

⁸ And they answered him, *He was* an hairy man, and girt with a girdle of leather about his loins. And he said, It *is* Elijah the Tishbite.

⁹ Then the king sent unto him a captain of fifty with his fifty. And he went up to him: and, behold, he sat on the top of an hill. And he spake unto him, Thou man of God, the king hath said, Come down.

¹⁰ And Elijah answered and said to the captain of fifty, If I *be* a man of God, then let fire come down from heaven, and consume thee and thy fifty. And there came down fire from heaven, and consumed him and his fifty.

¹¹ Again also he sent unto him another captain of fifty with his fifty. And he answered and said unto him, O man of God, thus hath the king said, Come down quickly.

¹² And Elijah answered and said unto them, If I *be* a man of God, let fire come down from heaven, and consume thee and thy fifty. And the fire of God came down from heaven, and consumed him and his fifty.

[13] And he sent again a captain of the third fifty with his fifty. And the third captain of fifty went up, and came and fell on his knees before Elijah, and besought him, and said unto him, O man of God, I pray thee, let my life, and the life of these fifty thy servants, be precious in thy sight.

[14] Behold, there came fire down from heaven, and burnt up the two captains of the former fifties with their fifties: therefore let my life now be precious in thy sight.

[15] And the <u>angel of the LORD</u> said unto Elijah, Go down with him: be not afraid of him. And he arose, and went down with him unto the king.

[16] And he said unto him, Thus saith the LORD, Forasmuch as thou hast sent messengers to enquire of Baalzebub the god of Ekron, *is it* not because *there is* no God in Israel to enquire of his word? therefore thou shalt not come down off that bed on which thou art gone up, but shalt surely die.

[17] So he died according to the word of the LORD which Elijah had spoken. And Jehoram reigned in his stead in the second year of Jehoram the son of Jehoshaphat king of Judah; because he had no son.

[18] Now the rest of the acts of Ahaziah which he did, *are* they not written in the book of the chronicles of the kings of Israel?

2 Kings 19:1-37 - Angel of the Lord Kills 185,000 Assyrians

[1] And it came to pass, when king Hezekiah heard *it*, that he rent his clothes, and covered himself with sackcloth, and went into the house of the LORD.

[2] And he sent Eliakim, which *was* over the household, and Shebna the scribe, and the elders of the priests, covered with sackcloth, to Isaiah the prophet the son of Amoz.

[3] And they said unto him, Thus saith Hezekiah, This day *is* a day of trouble, and of rebuke, and blasphemy: for the children are come to the birth, and *there is* not strength to bring forth.

⁴ It may be the LORD thy God will hear all the words of Rabshakeh, whom the king of Assyria his master hath sent to reproach the living God; and will reprove the words which the LORD thy God hath heard: wherefore lift up *thy* prayer for the remnant that are left.

⁵ So the servants of king Hezekiah came to Isaiah.

⁶ And Isaiah said unto them, Thus shall ye say to your master, Thus saith the LORD, Be not afraid of the words which thou hast heard, with which the servants of the king of Assyria have blasphemed me.

⁷ Behold, I will send a blast upon him, and he shall hear a rumour, and shall return to his own land; and I will cause him to fall by the sword in his own land.

⁸ So Rabshakeh returned, and found the king of Assyria warring against Libnah: for he had heard that he was departed from Lachish.

⁹ And when he heard say of Tirhakah king of Ethiopia, Behold, he is come out to fight against thee: he sent messengers again unto Hezekiah, saying,

¹⁰ Thus shall ye speak to Hezekiah king of Judah, saying, Let not thy God in whom thou trustest deceive thee, saying, Jerusalem shall not be delivered into the hand of the king of Assyria.

¹¹ Behold, thou hast heard what the kings of Assyria have done to all lands, by destroying them utterly: and shalt thou be delivered?

¹² Have the gods of the nations delivered them which my fathers have destroyed; *as* Gozan, and Haran, and Rezeph, and the children of Eden which *were* in Thelasar?

¹³ Where *is* the king of Hamath, and the king of Arpad, and the king of the city of Sepharvaim, of Hena, and Ivah?

¹⁴ And Hezekiah received the letter of the hand of the messengers, and read it: and Hezekiah went up into the house of the LORD, and spread it before the LORD.

¹⁵ And Hezekiah prayed before the LORD, and said, O LORD God of Israel, which dwellest *between* the cherubims, thou art the God, *even* thou alone, of all the kingdoms of the earth; thou hast made heaven and earth.

¹⁶ LORD, bow down thine ear, and hear: open, LORD, thine eyes, and see: and hear the words of Sennacherib, which hath sent him to reproach the living God.

¹⁷ Of a truth, LORD, the kings of Assyria have destroyed the nations and their lands,

¹⁸ And have cast their gods into the fire: for they *were* no gods, but the work of men's hands, wood and stone: therefore they have destroyed them.

¹⁹ Now therefore, O LORD our God, I beseech thee, save thou us out of his hand, that all the kingdoms of the earth may know that thou *art* the LORD God, *even* thou only.

²⁰ Then Isaiah the son of Amoz sent to Hezekiah, saying, Thus saith the LORD God of Israel, *That* which thou hast prayed to me against Sennacherib king of Assyria I have heard.

²¹ This *is* the word that the LORD hath spoken concerning him; The virgin the daughter of Zion hath despised thee, *and* laughed thee to scorn; the daughter of Jerusalem hath shaken her head at thee.

²² Whom hast thou reproached and blasphemed? and against whom hast thou exalted *thy* voice, and lifted up thine eyes on high? *even* against the Holy *One* of Israel.

²³ By thy messengers thou hast reproached the Lord, and hast said, With the multitude of my chariots I am come up to the height of the mountains, to the sides of Lebanon, and will cut down the tall cedar trees thereof, *and* the choice fir trees thereof: and I will enter into the lodgings of his borders, *and into* the forest of his Carmel.

²⁴ I have digged and drunk strange waters, and with the sole of my feet have I dried up all the rivers of besieged places.

²⁵ Hast thou not heard long ago *how* I have done it, *and* of ancient times that I have formed it? now have I brought it to pass, that thou shouldest be to lay waste fenced cities *into* ruinous heaps.

²⁶ Therefore their inhabitants were of small power, they were dismayed and confounded; they were *as* the grass of the field, and *as* the green herb, *as* the grass on the housetops, and *as corn* blasted before it be grown up.

27 But I know thy abode, and thy going out, and thy coming in, and thy rage against me.

28 Because thy rage against me and thy tumult is come up into mine ears, therefore I will put my hook in thy nose, and my bridle in thy lips, and I will turn thee back by the way by which thou camest.

29 And this *shall be* a sign unto thee, Ye shall eat this year such things as grow of themselves, and in the second year that which springeth of the same; and in the third year sow ye, and reap, and plant vineyards, and eat the fruits thereof.

30 And the remnant that is escaped of the house of Judah shall yet again take root downward, and bear fruit upward.

31 For out of Jerusalem shall go forth a remnant, and they that escape out of mount Zion: the zeal of the LORD *of hosts* shall do this.

32 Therefore thus saith the LORD concerning the king of Assyria, He shall not come into this city, nor shoot an arrow there, nor come before it with shield, nor cast a bank against it.

33 By the way that he came, by the same shall he return, and shall not come into this city, saith the LORD.

34 For I will defend this city, to save it, for mine own sake, and for my servant David's sake.

35 And it came to pass that night, that the <u>angel of the LORD</u> went out, and smote in the camp of the Assyrians an hundred fourscore and five thousand: and when they arose early in the morning, behold, they *were* all dead corpses.

36 So Sennacherib king of Assyria departed, and went and returned, and dwelt at Nineveh.

37 And it came to pass, as he was worshipping in the house of Nisroch his god, that Adrammelech and Sharezer his sons smote him with the sword: and they escaped into the land of Armenia. And Esarhaddon his son reigned in his stead.

Kermie Wohlenhaus, Ph.D.

1 Chronicles 21:1-30 - King David and the Census of Israel - as Punishment, Angel of the Lord Destroys Jerusalem

¹ And Satan stood up against Israel, and provoked David to number Israel.

² And David said to Joab and to the rulers of the people, Go, number Israel from Beersheba even to Dan; and bring the number of them to me, that I may know *it*.

³ And Joab answered, The LORD make his people an hundred times so many more as they *be*: but, my lord the king, *are* they not all my lord's servants? why then doth my lord require this thing? why will he be a cause of trespass to Israel?

⁴ Nevertheless the king's word prevailed against Joab. Wherefore Joab departed, and went throughout all Israel, and came to Jerusalem.

⁵ And Joab gave the sum of the number of the people unto David. And all *they of* Israel were a thousand thousand and an hundred thousand men that drew sword: and Judah *was* four hundred threescore and ten thousand men that drew sword.

⁶ But Levi and Benjamin counted he not among them: for the king's word was abominable to Joab.

⁷ And God was displeased with this thing; therefore he smote Israel.

⁸ And David said unto God, I have sinned greatly, because I have done this thing: but now, I beseech thee, do away the iniquity of thy servant; for I have done very foolishly.

⁹ And the LORD spake unto Gad, David's seer, saying,

¹⁰ Go and tell David, saying, Thus saith the LORD, I offer thee three *things*: choose thee one of them, that I may do *it* unto thee.

¹¹ So Gad came to David, and said unto him, Thus saith the LORD, Choose thee

¹² Either three years' famine; or three months to be destroyed before thy foes, while that the sword of thine enemies overtaketh *thee*; or else three days the sword of the LORD, even the pestilence, in the land, and the <u>angel of the LORD</u> destroying throughout all the coasts of Israel. Now therefore advise thyself what word I shall bring again to him that sent me.

¹³ And David said unto Gad, I am in a great strait: let me fall now into the hand of the LORD; for very great *are* his mercies: but let me not fall into the hand of man.

¹⁴ So the LORD sent pestilence upon Israel: and there fell of Israel seventy thousand men.

¹⁵ And God sent an <u>angel</u> unto Jerusalem to destroy it: and as he was destroying, the LORD beheld, and he repented him of the evil, and said to the <u>angel</u> that destroyed, It is enough, stay now thine hand. And the <u>angel of the LORD</u> stood by the threshingfloor of Ornan the Jebusite.

¹⁶ And David lifted up his eyes, and saw the <u>angel of the LORD</u> stand between the earth and the heaven, having a drawn sword in his hand stretched out over Jerusalem. Then David and the elders *of Israel, who were* clothed in sackcloth, fell upon their faces.

¹⁷ And David said unto God, *Is it* not I *that* commanded the people to be numbered? even I it is that have sinned and done evil indeed; but *as for* these sheep, what have they done? let thine hand, I pray thee, O LORD my God, be on me, and on my father's house; but not on thy people, that they should be plagued.

¹⁸ Then the <u>angel of the LORD</u> commanded Gad to say to David, that David should go up, and set up an altar unto the LORD in the threshingfloor of Ornan the Jebusite.

¹⁹ And David went up at the saying of Gad, which he spake in the name of the LORD.

²⁰ And Ornan turned back, and saw the <u>angel</u>; and his four sons with him hid themselves. Now Ornan was threshing wheat.

²¹ And as David came to Ornan, Ornan looked and saw David, and went out of the threshingfloor, and bowed himself to David with *his* face to the ground.

²² Then David said to Ornan, Grant me the place of *this* threshingfloor, that I may build an altar therein unto the LORD: thou shalt grant it me for the full price: that the plague may be stayed from the people.

²³ And Ornan said unto David, Take *it* to thee, and let my lord the king do *that which is* good in his eyes: lo, I give *thee* the oxen *also* for burnt offerings, and the threshing instruments for wood, and the wheat for the meat offering; I give it all.

²⁴ And king David said to Ornan, Nay; but I will verily buy it for the full price: for I will not take *that* which *is* thine for the LORD, nor offer burnt offerings without cost.

²⁵ So David gave to Ornan for the place six hundred shekels of gold by weight.

²⁶ And David built there an altar unto the LORD, and offered burnt offerings and peace offerings, and called upon the LORD; and he answered him from heaven by fire upon the altar of burnt offering.

²⁷ And the LORD commanded the <u>angel</u>; and he put up his sword again into the sheath thereof.

²⁸ At that time when David saw that the LORD had answered him in the threshingfloor of Ornan the Jebusite, then he sacrificed there.

²⁹ For the tabernacle of the LORD, which Moses made in the wilderness, and the altar of the burnt offering, *were* at that season in the high place at Gibeon.

³⁰ But David could not go before it to enquire of God: for he was afraid because of the sword of the <u>angel of the LORD</u>.

2 Chronicles 32:1-33 - Isaiah Prays for Help and the Lord Sent an Angel

¹ After these things, and the establishment thereof, Sennacherib king of Assyria came, and entered into Judah, and encamped against the fenced cities, and thought to win them for himself.

² And when Hezekiah saw that Sennacherib was come, and that he was purposed to fight against Jerusalem,

³ He took counsel with his princes and his mighty men to stop the waters of the fountains which *were* without the city: and they did help him.

⁴ So there was gathered much people together, who stopped all the fountains, and the brook that ran through the midst of the land, saying, Why should the kings of Assyria come, and find much water?

⁵ Also he strengthened himself, and built up all the wall that was broken, and raised *it* up to the towers, and another wall without, and repaired Millo *in* the city of David, and made darts and shields in abundance.

⁶ And he set captains of war over the people, and gathered them together to him in the street of the gate of the city, and spake comfortably to them, saying,

⁷ Be strong and courageous, be not afraid nor dismayed for the king of Assyria, nor for all the multitude that *is* with him: for *there be* more with us than with him:

⁸ With him *is* an arm of flesh; but with us *is* the LORD our God to help us, and to fight our battles. And the people rested themselves upon the words of Hezekiah king of Judah.

⁹ After this did Sennacherib king of Assyria send his servants to Jerusalem, (but he *himself laid siege* against Lachish, and all his power with him,) unto Hezekiah king of Judah, and unto all Judah that *were* at Jerusalem, saying,

¹⁰ Thus saith Sennacherib king of Assyria, Whereon do ye trust, that ye abide in the siege in Jerusalem?

¹¹ Doth not Hezekiah persuade you to give over yourselves to die by famine and by thirst, saying, The LORD our God shall deliver us out of the hand of the king of Assyria?

¹² Hath not the same Hezekiah taken away his high places and his altars, and commanded Judah and Jerusalem, saying, Ye shall worship before one altar, and burn incense upon it?

¹³ Know ye not what I and my fathers have done unto all the people of *other* lands? were the gods of the nations of those lands any ways able to deliver their lands out of mine hand?

¹⁴ Who *was there* among all the gods of those nations that my fathers utterly destroyed, that could deliver his people out of mine hand, that your God should be able to deliver you out of mine hand?

¹⁵ Now therefore let not Hezekiah deceive you, nor persuade you on this manner, neither yet believe him: for no god of any nation or kingdom was able to deliver his people out of mine hand, and out of the hand of my fathers: how much less shall your God deliver you out of mine hand?

¹⁶ And his servants spake yet *more* against the LORD God, and against his servant Hezekiah.

¹⁷ He wrote also letters to rail on the LORD God of Israel, and to speak against him, saying, As the gods of the nations of *other* lands have not delivered their people out of mine hand, so shall not the God of Hezekiah deliver his people out of mine hand.

¹⁸ Then they cried with a loud voice in the Jews' speech unto the people of Jerusalem that *were* on the wall, to affright them, and to trouble them; that they might take the city.

¹⁹ And they spake against the God of Jerusalem, as against the gods of the people of the earth, *which were* the work of the hands of man.

²⁰ And for this *cause* Hezekiah the king, and the prophet Isaiah the son of Amoz, prayed and cried to heaven.

²¹ And the LORD sent an <u>angel</u>, which cut off all the mighty men of valour, and the leaders and captains in the camp of the king of Assyria. So he returned with shame of face to his own land. And when he was come into the house of his god, they that came forth of his own bowels slew him there with the sword.

²² Thus the LORD saved Hezekiah and the inhabitants of Jerusalem from the hand of Sennacherib the king of Assyria, and from the hand of all *other*, and guided them on every side.

²³ And many brought gifts unto the LORD to Jerusalem, and presents to Hezekiah king of Judah: so that he was magnified in the sight of all nations from thenceforth.

²⁴ In those days Hezekiah was sick to the death, and prayed unto the LORD: and he spake unto him, and he gave him a sign.

²⁵ But Hezekiah rendered not again according to the benefit *done* unto him; for his heart was lifted up: therefore there was wrath upon him, and upon Judah and Jerusalem.

²⁶ Notwithstanding Hezekiah humbled himself for the pride of his heart, *both* he and the inhabitants of Jerusalem, so that the wrath of the LORD came not upon them in the days of Hezekiah.

²⁷ And Hezekiah had exceeding much riches and honour: and he made himself treasuries for silver, and for gold, and for precious stones, and for spices, and for shields, and for all manner of pleasant jewels;

²⁸ Storehouses also for the increase of corn, and wine, and oil; and stalls for all manner of beasts, and cotes for flocks.

²⁹ Moreover he provided him cities, and possessions of flocks and herds in abundance: for God had given him substance very much.

³⁰ This same Hezekiah also stopped the upper watercourse of Gihon, and brought it straight down to the west side of the city of David. And Hezekiah prospered in all his works.

³¹ Howbeit in *the business of* the ambassadors of the princes of Babylon, who sent unto him to enquire of the wonder that was *done* in the land, God left him, to try him, that he might know all *that was* in his heart.

³² Now the rest of the acts of Hezekiah, and his goodness, behold, they *are* written in the vision of Isaiah the prophet, the son of Amoz, *and* in the book of the kings of Judah and Israel.

³³ And Hezekiah slept with his fathers, and they buried him in the chiefest of the sepulchres of the sons of David: and all Judah and the inhabitants of Jerusalem did him honour at his death. And Manasseh his son reigned in his stead.

Job 4:1-21 - Eliphaz tells Job, God Charges Angels with Folly

¹ Then Eliphaz the Temanite answered and said,

² *If* we assay to commune with thee, wilt thou be grieved? but who can withhold himself from speaking?

³ Behold, thou hast instructed many, and thou hast strengthened the weak hands.

⁴ Thy words have upholden him that was falling, and thou hast strengthened the feeble knees.

⁵ But now it is come upon thee, and thou faintest; it toucheth thee, and thou art troubled.

⁶ *Is* not *this* thy fear, thy confidence, thy hope, and the uprightness of thy ways?

⁷ Remember, I pray thee, who *ever* perished, being innocent? or where were the righteous cut off?

⁸ Even as I have seen, they that plow iniquity, and sow wickedness, reap the same.

⁹ By the blast of God they perish, and by the breath of his nostrils are they consumed.

¹⁰ The roaring of the lion, and the voice of the fierce lion, and the teeth of the young lions, are broken.

¹¹ The old lion perisheth for lack of prey, and the stout lion's whelps are scattered abroad.

¹² Now a thing was secretly brought to me, and mine ear received a little thereof.

¹³ In thoughts from the visions of the night, when deep sleep falleth on men,

¹⁴ Fear came upon me, and trembling, which made all my bones to shake.

¹⁵ Then a spirit passed before my face; the hair of my flesh stood up:

¹⁶ It stood still, but I could not discern the form thereof: an image *was* before mine eyes, *there was* silence, and I heard a voice, *saying*,

¹⁷ Shall mortal man be more just than God? shall a man be more pure than his maker?

¹⁸ Behold, he put no trust in his servants; and his <u>angels</u> he charged with folly:

¹⁹ How much less *in* them that dwell in houses of clay, whose foundation *is* in the dust, *which* are crushed before the moth?

²⁰ They are destroyed from morning to evening: they perish for ever without any regarding *it*.

²¹ Doth not their excellency *which is* in them go away? they die, even without wisdom.

Ecclesiastes 5:1-7 - What Not to Say before the Angel

¹ Keep thy foot when thou goest to the house of God, and be more ready to hear, than to give the sacrifice of fools: for they consider not that they do evil.

² Be not rash with thy mouth, and let not thine heart be hasty to utter *any* thing before God: for God *is* in heaven, and thou upon earth: therefore let thy words be few.

³ For a dream cometh through the multitude of business; and a fool's voice *is known* by multitude of words.

⁴ When thou vowest a vow unto God, defer not to pay it; for *he hath* no pleasure in fools: pay that which thou hast vowed.

⁵ Better *is it* that thou shouldest not vow, than that thou shouldest vow and not pay.

⁶ Suffer not thy mouth to cause thy flesh to sin; neither say thou before the angel, that it *was* an error: wherefore should God be angry at thy voice, and destroy the work of thine hands?

⁷ For in the multitude of dreams and many words *there are* also *divers* vanities: but fear thou God.

Isaiah 37:1-38 - Angel of the Lord Kills 185,000 Assyrians

¹ And it came to pass, when king Hezekiah heard *it*, that he rent his clothes, and covered himself with sackcloth, and went into the house of the LORD.

² And he sent Eliakim, who *was* over the household, and Shebna the scribe, and the elders of the priests covered with sackcloth, unto Isaiah the prophet the son of Amoz.

³ And they said unto him, Thus saith Hezekiah, This day *is* a day of trouble, and of rebuke, and of blasphemy: for the children are come to the birth, and *there is* not strength to bring forth.

⁴ It may be the LORD thy God will hear the words of Rabshakeh, whom the king of Assyria his master hath sent to reproach the living God, and will reprove the words which the LORD thy God hath heard: wherefore lift up *thy* prayer for the remnant that is left.

⁵ So the servants of king Hezekiah came to Isaiah.

⁶ And Isaiah said unto them, Thus shall ye say unto your master, Thus saith the LORD, Be not afraid of the words that thou hast heard, wherewith the servants of the king of Assyria have blasphemed me.

⁷ Behold, I will send a blast upon him, and he shall hear a rumour, and return to his own land; and I will cause him to fall by the sword in his own land.

⁸ So Rabshakeh returned, and found the king of Assyria warring against Libnah: for he had heard that he was departed from Lachish.

⁹ And he heard say concerning Tirhakah king of Ethiopia, He is come forth to make war with thee. And when he heard *it*, he sent messengers to Hezekiah, saying,

¹⁰ Thus shall ye speak to Hezekiah king of Judah, saying, Let not thy God, in whom thou trustest, deceive thee, saying, Jerusalem shall not be given into the hand of the king of Assyria.

¹¹ Behold, thou hast heard what the kings of Assyria have done to all lands by destroying them utterly; and shalt thou be delivered?

¹² Have the gods of the nations delivered them which my fathers have destroyed, *as* Gozan, and Haran, and Rezeph, and the children of Eden which *were* in Telassar?

¹³ Where *is* the king of Hamath, and the king of Arphad, and the king of the city of Sepharvaim, Hena, and Ivah?

14 And Hezekiah received the letter from the hand of the messengers, and read it: and Hezekiah went up unto the house of the LORD, and spread it before the LORD.

15 And Hezekiah prayed unto the LORD, saying,

16 O LORD of hosts, God of Israel, that dwellest *between* the cherubims, thou *art* the God, *even* thou alone, of all the kingdoms of the earth: thou hast made heaven and earth.

17 Incline thine ear, O LORD, and hear; open thine eyes, O LORD, and see: and hear all the words of Sennacherib, which hath sent to reproach the living God.

18 Of a truth, LORD, the kings of Assyria have laid waste all the nations, and their countries,

19 And have cast their gods into the fire: for they *were* no gods, but the work of men's hands, wood and stone: therefore they have destroyed them.

20 Now therefore, O LORD our God, save us from his hand, that all the kingdoms of the earth may know that thou *art* the LORD, *even* thou only.

21 Then Isaiah the son of Amoz sent unto Hezekiah, saying, Thus saith the LORD God of Israel, Whereas thou hast prayed to me against Sennacherib king of Assyria:

22 This *is* the word which the LORD hath spoken concerning him; The virgin, the daughter of Zion, hath despised thee, *and* laughed thee to scorn; the daughter of Jerusalem hath shaken her head at thee.

23 Whom hast thou reproached and blasphemed? and against whom hast thou exalted *thy* voice, and lifted up thine eyes on high? *even* against the Holy One of Israel.

24 By thy servants hast thou reproached the Lord, and hast said, By the multitude of my chariots am I come up to the height of the mountains, to the sides of Lebanon; and I will cut down the tall cedars thereof, *and* the choice fir trees thereof: and I will enter into the height of his border, *and* the forest of his Carmel.

²⁵ I have digged, and drunk water; and with the sole of my feet have I dried up all the rivers of the besieged places.

²⁶ Hast thou not heard long ago, *how* I have done it; *and* of ancient times, that I have formed it? now have I brought it to pass, that thou shouldest be to lay waste defenced cities *into* ruinous heaps.

²⁷ Therefore their inhabitants *were* of small power, they were dismayed and confounded: they were *as* the grass of the field, and *as* the green herb, *as* the grass on the housetops, and *as corn* blasted before it be grown up.

²⁸ But I know thy abode, and thy going out, and thy coming in, and thy rage against me.

²⁹ Because thy rage against me, and thy tumult, is come up into mine ears, therefore will I put my hook in thy nose, and my bridle in thy lips, and I will turn thee back by the way by which thou camest.

³⁰ And this *shall be* a sign unto thee, Ye shall eat *this* year such as groweth of itself; and the second year that which springeth of the same: and in the third year sow ye, and reap, and plant vineyards, and eat the fruit thereof.

³¹ And the remnant that is escaped of the house of Judah shall again take root downward, and bear fruit upward:

³² For out of Jerusalem shall go forth a remnant, and they that escape out of mount Zion: the zeal of the LORD of hosts shall do this.

³³ Therefore thus saith the LORD concerning the king of Assyria, He shall not come into this city, nor shoot an arrow there, nor come before it with shields, nor cast a bank against it.

³⁴ By the way that he came, by the same shall he return, and shall not come into this city, saith the LORD.

³⁵ For I will defend this city to save it for mine own sake, and for my servant David's sake.

³⁶ Then the <u>angel of the LORD</u> went forth, and smote in the camp of the Assyrians a hundred and fourscore and five thousand: and when they arose early in the morning, behold, they *were* all dead corpses.

⁳⁷ So Sennacherib king of Assyria departed, and went and returned, and dwelt at Nineveh.

³⁸ And it came to pass, as he was worshipping in the house of Nisroch his god, that Adrammelech and Sharezer his sons smote him with the sword; and they escaped into the land of Armenia: and Esarhaddon his son reigned in his stead.

Isaiah 63:1-19 - Angel of His Presence Saved the Afflicted

¹ Who *is* this that cometh from Edom, with dyed garments from Bozrah? this *that is* glorious in his apparel, travelling in the greatness of his strength? I that speak in righteousness, mighty to save.

² Wherefore *art thou* red in thine apparel, and thy garments like him that treadeth in the winefat?

³ I have trodden the winepress alone; and of the people *there was* none with me: for I will tread them in mine anger, and trample them in my fury; and their blood shall be sprinkled upon my garments, and I will stain all my raiment.

⁴ For the day of vengeance *is* in mine heart, and the year of my redeemed is come.

⁵ And I looked, and *there was* none to help; and I wondered that *there was* none to uphold: therefore mine own arm brought salvation unto me; and my fury, it upheld me.

⁶ And I will tread down the people in mine anger, and make them drunk in my fury, and I will bring down their strength to the earth.

⁷ I will mention the lovingkindnesses of the LORD, *and* the praises of the LORD, according to all that the LORD hath bestowed on us, and the great goodness toward the house of Israel, which he hath bestowed on them according to his mercies, and according to the multitude of his lovingkindnesses.

⁸ For he said, Surely they *are* my people, children *that* will not lie: so he was their Saviour.

⁹ In all their affliction he was afflicted, and the <u>angel</u> of his presence saved them: in his love and in his pity he redeemed them; and he bare them, and carried them all the days of old.

¹⁰ But they rebelled, and vexed his holy Spirit: therefore he was turned to be their enemy, *and* he fought against them.

¹¹ Then he remembered the days of old, Moses, *and* his people, *saying*, Where *is* he that brought them up out of the sea with the shepherd of his flock? where *is* he that put his holy Spirit within him?

¹² That led *them* by the right hand of Moses with his glorious arm, dividing the water before them, to make himself an everlasting name?

¹³ That led them through the deep, as an horse in the wilderness, *that* they should not stumble?

¹⁴ As a beast goeth down into the valley, the Spirit of the LORD caused him to rest: so didst thou lead thy people, to make thyself a glorious name.

¹⁵ Look down from heaven, and behold from the habitation of thy holiness and of thy glory: where *is* thy zeal and thy strength, the sounding of thy bowels and of thy mercies toward me? are they restrained?

¹⁶ Doubtless thou *art* our father, though Abraham be ignorant of us, and Israel acknowledge us not: thou, O LORD, *art* our father, our redeemer; thy name *is* from everlasting.

¹⁷ O LORD, why hast thou made us to err from thy ways, *and* hardened our heart from thy fear? Return for thy servants' sake, the tribes of thine inheritance.

¹⁸ The people of thy holiness have possessed *it* but a little while: our adversaries have trodden down thy sanctuary.

¹⁹ We are *thine*: thou never barest rule over them; they were not called by thy name.

Daniel 3:1-30 - Nebuchadnezzar Praises God and Angel for Delivering Shadrach, Meshach and Abed-Nego from Fiery Furnace

[1] Nebuchadnezzar the king made an image of gold, whose height *was* threescore cubits, *and* the breadth thereof six cubits: he set it up in the plain of Dura, in the province of Babylon.

[2] Then Nebuchadnezzar the king sent to gather together the princes, the governors, and the captains, the judges, the treasurers, the counsellors, the sheriffs, and all the rulers of the provinces, to come to the dedication of the image which Nebuchadnezzar the king had set up.

[3] Then the princes, the governors, and captains, the judges, the treasurers, the counsellors, the sheriffs, and all the rulers of the provinces, were gathered together unto the dedication of the image that Nebuchadnezzar the king had set up; and they stood before the image that Nebuchadnezzar had set up.

[4] Then an herald cried aloud, To you it is commanded, O people, nations, and languages,

[5] *That* at what time ye hear the sound of the cornet, flute, harp, sackbut, psaltery, dulcimer, and all kinds of musick, ye fall down and worship the golden image that Nebuchadnezzar the king hath set up:

[6] And whoso falleth not down and worshippeth shall the same hour be cast into the midst of a burning fiery furnace.

[7] Therefore at that time, when all the people heard the sound of the cornet, flute, harp, sackbut, psaltery, and all kinds of musick, all the people, the nations, and the languages, fell down *and* worshipped the golden image that Nebuchadnezzar the king had set up.

[8] Wherefore at that time certain Chaldeans came near, and accused the Jews.

[9] They spake and said to the king Nebuchadnezzar, O king, live for ever.

¹⁰ Thou, O king, hast made a decree, that every man that shall hear the sound of the cornet, flute, harp, sackbut, psaltery, and dulcimer, and all kinds of musick, shall fall down and worship the golden image:

¹¹ And whoso falleth not down and worshippeth, *that* he should be cast into the midst of a burning fiery furnace.

¹² There are certain Jews whom thou hast set over the affairs of the province of Babylon, Shadrach, Meshach, and Abednego; these men, O king, have not regarded thee: they serve not thy gods, nor worship the golden image which thou hast set up.

¹³ Then Nebuchadnezzar in *his* rage and fury commanded to bring Shadrach, Meshach, and Abednego. Then they brought these men before the king.

¹⁴ Nebuchadnezzar spake and said unto them, *Is it* true, O Shadrach, Meshach, and Abednego, do not ye serve my gods, nor worship the golden image which I have set up?

¹⁵ Now if ye be ready that at what time ye hear the sound of the cornet, flute, harp, sackbut, psaltery, and dulcimer, and all kinds of musick, ye fall down and worship the image which I have made; *well*: but if ye worship not, ye shall be cast the same hour into the midst of a burning fiery furnace; and who *is* that God that shall deliver you out of my hands?

¹⁶ Shadrach, Meshach, and Abednego, answered and said to the king, O Nebuchadnezzar, we *are* not careful to answer thee in this matter.

¹⁷ If it be *so*, our God whom we serve is able to deliver us from the burning fiery furnace, and he will deliver *us* out of thine hand, O king.

¹⁸ But if not, be it known unto thee, O king, that we will not serve thy gods, nor worship the golden image which thou hast set up.

¹⁹ Then was Nebuchadnezzar full of fury, and the form of his visage was changed against Shadrach, Meshach, and Abednego: *therefore* he spake, and commanded that they should heat the furnace one seven times more than it was wont to be heated.

²⁰ And he commanded the most mighty men that *were* in his army to bind Shadrach, Meshach, and Abednego, *and* to cast *them* into the burning fiery furnace.

²¹ Then these men were bound in their coats, their hosen, and their hats, and their *other* garments, and were cast into the midst of the burning fiery furnace.

²² Therefore because the king's commandment was urgent, and the furnace exceeding hot, the flame of the fire slew those men that took up Shadrach, Meshach, and Abednego.

²³ And these three men, Shadrach, Meshach, and Abednego, fell down bound into the midst of the burning fiery furnace.

²⁴ Then Nebuchadnezzar the king was astonied, and rose up in haste, *and* spake, and said unto his counsellors, Did not we cast three men bound into the midst of the fire? They answered and said unto the king, True, O king.

²⁵ He answered and said, Lo, I see four men loose, walking in the midst of the fire, and they have no hurt; and the form of the fourth is like the Son of God.

²⁶ Then Nebuchadnezzar came near to the mouth of the burning fiery furnace, *and* spake, and said, Shadrach, Meshach, and Abednego, ye servants of the most high God, come forth, and come *hither*. Then Shadrach, Meshach, and Abednego, came forth of the midst of the fire.

²⁷ And the princes, governors, and captains, and the king's counsellors, being gathered together, saw these men, upon whose bodies the fire had no power, nor was an hair of their head singed, neither were their coats changed, nor the smell of fire had passed on them.

²⁸ *Then* Nebuchadnezzar spake, and said, Blessed *be* the God of Shadrach, Meshach, and Abednego, who hath sent his <u>angel</u>, and delivered his servants that trusted in him, and have changed the king's word, and yielded their bodies, that they might not serve nor worship any god, except their own God.

²⁹ Therefore I make a decree, That every people, nation, and language, which speak any thing amiss against the God of Shadrach, Meshach, and Abednego, shall be cut in pieces, and their houses shall be made a dunghill: because there is no other God that can deliver after this sort.

³⁰ Then the king promoted Shadrach, Meshach, and Abednego, in the province of Babylon.

Daniel 6:1-28 - Angel Shut the Lions' Mouths for Daniel

¹ It pleased Darius to set over the kingdom an hundred and twenty princes, which should be over the whole kingdom;

² And over these three presidents; of whom Daniel *was* first: that the princes might give accounts unto them, and the king should have no damage.

³ Then this Daniel was preferred above the presidents and princes, because an excellent spirit *was* in him; and the king thought to set him over the whole realm.

⁴ Then the presidents and princes sought to find occasion against Daniel concerning the kingdom; but they could find none occasion nor fault; forasmuch as he *was* faithful, neither was there any error or fault found in him.

⁵ Then said these men, We shall not find any occasion against this Daniel, except we find *it* against him concerning the law of his God.

⁶ Then these presidents and princes assembled together to the king, and said thus unto him, King Darius, live for ever.

⁷ All the presidents of the kingdom, the governors, and the princes, the counsellors, and the captains, have consulted together to establish a royal statute, and to make a firm decree, that whosoever shall ask a petition of any God or man for thirty days, save of thee, O king, he shall be cast into the den of lions.

⁸ Now, O king, establish the decree, and sign the writing, that it be not changed, according to the law of the Medes and Persians, which altereth not.

⁹ Wherefore king Darius signed the writing and the decree.

¹⁰ Now when Daniel knew that the writing was signed, he went into his house; and his windows being open in his chamber toward Jerusalem, he kneeled upon his knees three times a day, and prayed, and gave thanks before his God, as he did aforetime.

¹¹ Then these men assembled, and found Daniel praying and making supplication before his God.

¹² Then they came near, and spake before the king concerning the king's decree; Hast thou not signed a decree, that every man that shall ask *a petition* of any God or man within thirty days, save of thee, O king, shall be cast into the den of lions? The king answered and said, The thing *is* true, according to the law of the Medes and Persians, which altereth not.

¹³ Then answered they and said before the king, That Daniel, which *is* of the children of the captivity of Judah, regardeth not thee, O king, nor the decree that thou hast signed, but maketh his petition three times a day.

¹⁴ Then the king, when he heard *these* words, was sore displeased with himself, and set *his* heart on Daniel to deliver him: and he laboured till the going down of the sun to deliver him.

¹⁵ Then these men assembled unto the king, and said unto the king, Know, O king, that the law of the Medes and Persians *is*, That no decree nor statute which the king establisheth may be changed.

¹⁶ Then the king commanded, and they brought Daniel, and cast *him* into the den of lions. *Now* the king spake and said unto Daniel, Thy God whom thou servest continually, he will deliver thee.

¹⁷ And a stone was brought, and laid upon the mouth of the den; and the king sealed it with his own signet, and with the signet of his lords; that the purpose might not be changed concerning Daniel.

¹⁸ Then the king went to his palace, and passed the night fasting: neither were instruments of musick brought before him: and his sleep went from him.

¹⁹ Then the king arose very early in the morning, and went in haste unto the den of lions.

²⁰ And when he came to the den, he cried with a lamentable voice unto Daniel: *and* the king spake and said to Daniel, O Daniel, servant of the living God, is thy God, whom thou servest continually, able to deliver thee from the lions?

²¹ Then said Daniel unto the king, O king, live for ever.

²² My God hath sent his <u>angel</u>, and hath shut the lions' mouths, that they have not hurt me: forasmuch as before him innocency was found in me; and also before thee, O king, have I done no hurt.

²³ Then was the king exceeding glad for him, and commanded that they should take Daniel up out of the den. So Daniel was taken up out of the den, and no manner of hurt was found upon him, because he believed in his God.

²⁴ And the king commanded, and they brought those men which had accused Daniel, and they cast *them* into the den of lions, them, their children, and their wives; and the lions had the mastery of them, and brake all their bones in pieces or ever they came at the bottom of the den.

²⁵ Then king Darius wrote unto all people, nations, and languages, that dwell in all the earth; Peace be multiplied unto you.

²⁶ I make a decree, That in every dominion of my kingdom men tremble and fear before the God of Daniel: for he *is* the living God, and stedfast for ever, and his kingdom *that* which shall not be destroyed, and his dominion *shall be even* unto the end.

²⁷ He delivereth and rescueth, and he worketh signs and wonders in heaven and in earth, who hath delivered Daniel from the power of the lions.

²⁸ So this Daniel prospered in the reign of Darius, and in the reign of Cyrus the Persian.

Hosea 12:1-14 - Hosea Saying that Jacob Struggled with the Angel

¹ Ephraim feedeth on wind, and followeth after the east wind: he daily increaseth lies and desolation; and they do make a covenant with the Assyrians, and oil is carried into Egypt.

² The LORD hath also a controversy with Judah, and will punish Jacob according to his ways; according to his doings will he recompense him.

³ He took his brother by the heel in the womb, and by his strength he had power with God:

⁴ Yea, he had power over the angel, and prevailed: he wept, and made supplication unto him: he found him *in* Bethel, and there he spake with us;

⁵ Even the LORD God of hosts; the LORD *is* his memorial.

⁶ Therefore turn thou to thy God: keep mercy and judgment, and wait on thy God continually.

⁷ *He is* a merchant, the balances of deceit *are* in his hand: he loveth to oppress.

⁸ And Ephraim said, Yet I am become rich, I have found me out substance: *in* all my labours they shall find none iniquity in me that *were* sin.

⁹ And I *that am* the LORD thy God from the land of Egypt will yet make thee to dwell in tabernacles, as in the days of the solemn feast.

¹⁰ I have also spoken by the prophets, and I have multiplied visions, and used similitudes, by the ministry of the prophets.

¹¹ *Is there* iniquity *in* Gilead? surely they are vanity: they sacrifice bullocks in Gilgal; yea, their altars *are* as heaps in the furrows of the fields.

¹² And Jacob fled into the country of Syria, and Israel served for a wife, and for a wife he kept *sheep*.

¹³ And by a prophet the LORD brought Israel out of Egypt, and by a prophet was he preserved.

¹⁴ Ephraim provoked *him* to anger most bitterly: therefore shall he leave his blood upon him, and his reproach shall his Lord return unto him.

Zechariah 1:1-21 - Zechariah's Visions of Angels

¹ In the eighth month, in the second year of Darius, came the word of the LORD unto Zechariah, the son of Berechiah, the son of Iddo the prophet, saying,

² The LORD hath been sore displeased with your fathers.

³ Therefore say thou unto them, Thus saith the LORD of hosts; Turn ye unto me, saith the LORD of hosts, and I will turn unto you, saith the LORD of hosts.

⁴ Be ye not as your fathers, unto whom the former prophets have cried, saying, Thus saith the LORD of hosts; Turn ye now from your evil ways, and *from* your evil doings: but they did not hear, nor hearken unto me, saith the LORD.

⁵ Your fathers, where *are* they? and the prophets, do they live for ever?

⁶ But my words and my statutes, which I commanded my servants the prophets, did they not take hold of your fathers? and they returned and said, Like as the LORD of hosts thought to do unto us, according to our ways, and according to our doings, so hath he dealt with us.

⁷ Upon the four and twentieth day of the eleventh month, which *is* the month Sebat, in the second year of Darius, came the word of the LORD unto Zechariah, the son of Berechiah, the son of Iddo the prophet, saying,

⁸ I saw by night, and behold a man riding upon a red horse, and he stood among the myrtle trees that *were* in the bottom; and behind him *were there* red horses, speckled, and white.

⁹ Then said I, O my lord, what *are* these? And the angel that talked with me said unto me, I will shew thee what these *be*.

¹⁰ And the man that stood among the myrtle trees answered and said, These *are they* whom the LORD hath sent to walk to and fro through the earth.

¹¹ And they answered the <u>angel of the LORD</u> that stood among the myrtle trees, and said, We have walked to and fro through the earth, and, behold, all the earth sitteth still, and is at rest.

¹² Then the <u>angel of the LORD</u> answered and said, O LORD of hosts, how long wilt thou not have mercy on Jerusalem and on the cities of Judah, against which thou hast had indignation these threescore and ten years?

¹³ And the LORD answered the <u>angel</u> that talked with me *with* good words *and* comfortable words.

¹⁴ So the <u>angel</u> that communed with me said unto me, Cry thou, saying, Thus saith the LORD of hosts; I am jealous for Jerusalem and for Zion with a great jealousy.

¹⁵ And I am very sore displeased with the heathen *that are* at ease: for I was but a little displeased, and they helped forward the affliction.

¹⁶ Therefore thus saith the LORD; I am returned to Jerusalem with mercies: my house shall be built in it, saith the LORD of hosts, and a line shall be stretched forth upon Jerusalem.

¹⁷ Cry yet, saying, Thus saith the LORD of hosts; My cities through prosperity shall yet be spread abroad; and the LORD shall yet comfort Zion, and shall yet choose Jerusalem.

¹⁸ Then lifted I up mine eyes, and saw, and behold four horns.

¹⁹ And I said unto the <u>angel</u> that talked with me, What *be* these? And he answered me, These *are* the horns which have scattered Judah, Israel, and Jerusalem.

²⁰ And the LORD shewed me four carpenters.

²¹ Then said I, What come these to do? And he spake, saying, These *are* the horns which have scattered Judah, so that no man did lift up his head: but these are come to fray them, to cast out the horns of the Gentiles, which lifted up *their* horn over the land of Judah to scatter it.

Zechariah 2:1-13 - Zechariah's Visions of Angels

¹ I lifted up mine eyes again, and looked, and behold a man with a measuring line in his hand.

² Then said I, Whither goest thou? And he said unto me, To measure Jerusalem, to see what *is* the breadth thereof, and what *is* the length thereof.

³ And, behold, the <u>angel</u> that talked with me went forth, and another <u>angel</u> went out to meet him,

⁴ And said unto him, Run, speak to this young man, saying, Jerusalem shall be inhabited *as* towns without walls for the multitude of men and cattle therein:

⁵ For I, saith the LORD, will be unto her a wall of fire round about, and will be the glory in the midst of her.

⁶ Ho, ho, *come forth*, and flee from the land of the north, saith the LORD: for I have spread you abroad as the four winds of the heaven, saith the LORD.

⁷ Deliver thyself, O Zion, that dwellest *with* the daughter of Babylon.

⁸ For thus saith the LORD of hosts; After the glory hath he sent me unto the nations which spoiled you: for he that toucheth you toucheth the apple of his eye.

⁹ For, behold, I will shake mine hand upon them, and they shall be a spoil to their servants: and ye shall know that the LORD of hosts hath sent me.

¹⁰ Sing and rejoice, O daughter of Zion: for, lo, I come, and I will dwell in the midst of thee, saith the LORD.

¹¹ And many nations shall be joined to the LORD in that day, and shall be my people: and I will dwell in the midst of thee, and thou shalt know that the LORD of hosts hath sent me unto thee.

¹² And the LORD shall inherit Judah his portion in the holy land, and shall choose Jerusalem again.

¹³ Be silent, O all flesh, before the LORD: for he is raised up out of his holy habitation.

Zechariah 3:1-10 - Zechariah's Visions of Angels

¹ And he shewed me Joshua the high priest standing before the <u>angel of the LORD</u>, and Satan standing at his right hand to resist him.

² And the LORD said unto Satan, The LORD rebuke thee, O Satan; even the LORD that hath chosen Jerusalem rebuke thee: *is* not this a brand plucked out of the fire?

³ Now Joshua was clothed with filthy garments, and stood before the <u>angel</u>.

⁴ And he answered and spake unto those that stood before him, saying, Take away the filthy garments from him. And unto him he said, Behold, I have caused thine iniquity to pass from thee, and I will clothe thee with change of raiment.

⁵ And I said, Let them set a fair mitre upon his head. So they set a fair mitre upon his head, and clothed him with garments. And the <u>angel of the LORD</u> stood by.

⁶ And the <u>angel of the LORD</u> protested unto Joshua, saying,

⁷ Thus saith the LORD of hosts; If thou wilt walk in my ways, and if thou wilt keep my charge, then thou shalt also judge my house, and shalt also keep my courts, and I will give thee places to walk among these that stand by.

⁸ Hear now, O Joshua the high priest, thou, and thy fellows that sit before thee: for they *are* men wondered at: for, behold, I will bring forth my servant the BRANCH.

⁹ For behold the stone that I have laid before Joshua; upon one stone *shall be* seven eyes: behold, I will engrave the graving thereof, saith the LORD of hosts, and I will remove the iniquity of that land in one day.

¹⁰ In that day, saith the LORD of hosts, shall ye call every man his neighbour under the vine and under the fig tree.

Kermie Wohlenhaus, Ph.D.

Zechariah 4:1-14 - Zechariah's Visions of Angels

¹ And the angel that talked with me came again, and waked me, as a man that is wakened out of his sleep,

² And said unto me, What seest thou? And I said, I have looked, and behold a candlestick all *of* gold, with a bowl upon the top of it, and his seven lamps thereon, and seven pipes to the seven lamps, which *are* upon the top thereof:

³ And two olive trees by it, one upon the right *side* of the bowl, and the other upon the left *side* thereof.

⁴ So I answered and spake to the angel that talked with me, saying, What *are* these, my lord?

⁵ Then the angel that talked with me answered and said unto me, Knowest thou not what these be? And I said, No, my lord.

⁶ Then he answered and spake unto me, saying, This *is* the word of the LORD unto Zerubbabel, saying, Not by might, nor by power, but by my spirit, saith the LORD of hosts.

⁷ Who *art* thou, O great mountain? before Zerubbabel *thou shalt become* a plain: and he shall bring forth the headstone *thereof with* shoutings, *crying,* Grace, grace unto it.

⁸ Moreover the word of the LORD came unto me, saying,

⁹ The hands of Zerubbabel have laid the foundation of this house; his hands shall also finish it; and thou shalt know that the LORD of hosts hath sent me unto you.

¹⁰ For who hath despised the day of small things? for they shall rejoice, and shall see the plummet in the hand of Zerubbabel *with* those seven; they *are* the eyes of the LORD, which run to and fro through the whole earth.

¹¹ Then answered I, and said unto him, What *are* these two olive trees upon the right *side* of the candlestick and upon the left *side* thereof?

¹² And I answered again, and said unto him, What *be these* two olive branches which through the two golden pipes empty the golden *oil* out of themselves?

¹³ And he answered me and said, Knowest thou not what these *be*? And I said, No, my lord.

¹⁴ Then said he, These *are* the two anointed ones, that stand by the Lord of the whole earth.

Zechariah 5:1-11 - Zechariah's Visions of Angels

¹ Then I turned, and lifted up mine eyes, and looked, and behold a flying roll.

² And he said unto me, What seest thou? And I answered, I see a flying roll; the length thereof *is* twenty cubits, and the breadth thereof ten cubits.

³ Then said he unto me, This *is* the curse that goeth forth over the face of the whole earth: for every one that stealeth shall be cut off *as* on this side according to it; and every one that sweareth shall be cut off *as* on that side according to it.

⁴ I will bring it forth, saith the LORD of hosts, and it shall enter into the house of the thief, and into the house of him that sweareth falsely by my name: and it shall remain in the midst of his house, and shall consume it with the timber thereof and the stones thereof.

⁵ Then the angel that talked with me went forth, and said unto me, Lift up now thine eyes, and see what *is* this that goeth forth.

⁶ And I said, What *is* it? And he said, This *is* an ephah that goeth forth. He said moreover, This *is* their resemblance through all the earth.

⁷ And, behold, there was lifted up a talent of lead: and this *is* a woman that sitteth in the midst of the ephah.

⁸ And he said, This *is* wickedness. And he cast it into the midst of the ephah; and he cast the weight of lead upon the mouth thereof.

⁹ Then lifted I up mine eyes, and looked, and, behold, there came out two women, and the wind *was* in their wings; for they had wings like the wings of a stork: and they lifted up the ephah between the earth and the heaven.

¹⁰ Then said I to the <u>angel</u> that talked with me, Whither do these bear the ephah?

¹¹ And he said unto me, To build it an house in the land of Shinar: and it shall be established, and set there upon her own base.

Zechariah 6:1-15 - Zechariah's Visions of Angels

¹ And I turned, and lifted up mine eyes, and looked, and, behold, there came four chariots out from between two mountains; and the mountains *were* mountains of brass.

² In the first chariot *were* red horses; and in the second chariot black horses;

³ And in the third chariot white horses; and in the fourth chariot grisled and bay horses.

⁴ Then I answered and said unto the <u>angel</u> that talked with me, What *are* these, my lord?

⁵ And the <u>angel</u> answered and said unto me, These *are* the four spirits of the heavens, which go forth from standing before the Lord of all the earth.

⁶ The black horses which *are* therein go forth into the north country; and the white go forth after them; and the grisled go forth toward the south country.

⁷ And the bay went forth, and sought to go that they might walk to and fro through the earth: and he said, Get you hence, walk to and fro through the earth. So they walked to and fro through the earth.

⁸ Then cried he upon me, and spake unto me, saying, Behold, these that go toward the north country have quieted my spirit in the north country.

⁹ And the word of the LORD came unto me, saying,

¹⁰ Take of *them of* the captivity, *even* of Heldai, of Tobijah, and of Jedaiah, which are come from Babylon, and come thou the same day, and go into the house of Josiah the son of Zephaniah;

¹¹ Then take silver and gold, and make crowns, and set *them* upon the head of Joshua the son of Josedech, the high priest;

¹² And speak unto him, saying, Thus speaketh the LORD of hosts, saying, Behold the man whose name *is* The BRANCH; and he shall grow up out of his place, and he shall build the temple of the LORD:

¹³ Even he shall build the temple of the LORD; and he shall bear the glory, and shall sit and rule upon his throne; and he shall be a priest upon his throne: and the counsel of peace shall be between them both.

¹⁴ And the crowns shall be to Helem, and to Tobijah, and to Jedaiah, and to Hen the son of Zephaniah, for a memorial in the temple of the LORD.

¹⁵ And they *that are* far off shall come and build in the temple of the LORD, and ye shall know that the LORD of hosts hath sent me unto you. And *this* shall come to pass, if ye will diligently obey the voice of the LORD your God.

Zechariah 12:1-14 - Zechariah's Visions of Angels

¹ The burden of the word of the LORD for Israel, saith the LORD, which stretcheth forth the heavens, and layeth the foundation of the earth, and formeth the spirit of man within him.

² Behold, I will make Jerusalem a cup of trembling unto all the people round about, when they shall be in the siege both against Judah *and* against Jerusalem.

³ And in that day will I make Jerusalem a burdensome stone for all people: all that burden themselves with it shall be cut in pieces, though all the people of the earth be gathered together against it.

⁴ In that day, saith the LORD, I will smite every horse with astonishment, and his rider with madness: and I will open mine eyes upon the house of Judah, and will smite every horse of the people with blindness.

⁵ And the governors of Judah shall say in their heart, The inhabitants of Jerusalem *shall be* my strength in the LORD of hosts their God.

⁶ In that day will I make the governors of Judah like an hearth of fire among the wood, and like a torch of fire in a sheaf; and they shall devour all the people round about, on the right hand and on the left: and Jerusalem shall be inhabited again in her own place, *even* in Jerusalem.

⁷ The LORD also shall save the tents of Judah first, that the glory of the house of David and the glory of the inhabitants of Jerusalem do not magnify *themselves* against Judah.

⁸ In that day shall the LORD defend the inhabitants of Jerusalem; and he that is feeble among them at that day shall be as David; and the house of David *shall be* as God, as the <u>angel of the LORD</u> before them.

⁹ And it shall come to pass in that day, *that* I will seek to destroy all the nations that come against Jerusalem.

¹⁰ And I will pour upon the house of David, and upon the inhabitants of Jerusalem, the spirit of grace and of supplications: and they shall look upon me whom they have pierced, and they shall mourn for him, as one mourneth for *his* only *son*, and shall be in bitterness for him, as one that is in bitterness for *his* firstborn.

¹¹ In that day shall there be a great mourning in Jerusalem, as the mourning of Hadadrimmon in the valley of Megiddon.

¹² And the land shall mourn, every family apart; the family of the house of David apart, and their wives apart; the family of the house of Nathan apart, and their wives apart;

¹³ The family of the house of Levi apart, and their wives apart; the family of Shimei apart, and their wives apart;

¹⁴ All the families that remain, every family apart, and their wives apart.

Angels in the Psalms

Psalm 8 - Humans a Little Lower than Angels

¹ (To the chief Musician upon Gittith, A Psalm of David.) O LORD our Lord, how excellent *is* thy name in all the earth! who hast set thy glory above the heavens.

² Out of the mouth of babes and sucklings hast thou ordained strength because of thine enemies, that thou mightest still the enemy and the avenger.

³ When I consider thy heavens, the work of thy fingers, the moon and the stars, which thou hast ordained;

⁴ What is man, that thou art mindful of him? and the son of man, that thou visitest him?

⁵ For thou hast made him a little lower than the <u>angels</u>, and hast crowned him with glory and honour.

⁶ Thou madest him to have dominion over the works of thy hands; thou hast put all *things* under his feet:

⁷ All sheep and oxen, yea, and the beasts of the field;

⁸ The fowl of the air, and the fish of the sea, *and whatsoever* passeth through the paths of the seas.

⁹ O LORD our Lord, how excellent *is* thy name in all the earth!

Psalm 34 - Angel of the Lord Encamps and Delivers Those Who Revere God

¹ (*A Psalm* of David, when he changed his behaviour before Abimelech; who drove him away, and he departed.) I will bless the LORD at all times: his praise *shall* continually *be* in my mouth.

² My soul shall make her boast in the LORD: the humble shall hear *thereof*, and be glad.

³ O magnify the LORD with me, and let us exalt his name together.

⁴ I sought the LORD, and he heard me, and delivered me from all my fears.

⁵ They looked unto him, and were lightened: and their faces were not ashamed.

⁶ This poor man cried, and the LORD heard *him*, and saved him out of all his troubles.

⁷ The <u>angel of the LORD</u> encampeth round about them that fear him, and delivereth them.

⁸ O taste and see that the LORD *is* good: blessed *is* the man *that* trusteth in him.

⁹ O fear the LORD, ye his saints: for *there is* no want to them that fear him.

¹⁰ The young lions do lack, and suffer hunger: but they that seek the LORD shall not want any good *thing*.

¹¹ Come, ye children, hearken unto me: I will teach you the fear of the LORD.

¹² What man *is he that* desireth life, *and* loveth *many* days, that he may see good?

¹³ Keep thy tongue from evil, and thy lips from speaking guile.

¹⁴ Depart from evil, and do good; seek peace, and pursue it.

¹⁵ The eyes of the LORD *are* upon the righteous, and his ears *are open* unto their cry.

¹⁶ The face of the LORD *is* against them that do evil, to cut off the remembrance of them from the earth.

¹⁷ *The righteous* cry, and the LORD heareth, and delivereth them out of all their troubles.

¹⁸ The LORD *is* nigh unto them that are of a broken heart; and saveth such as be of a contrite spirit.

¹⁹ Many *are* the afflictions of the righteous: but the LORD delivereth him out of them all.

²⁰ He keepeth all his bones: not one of them is broken.

²¹ Evil shall slay the wicked: and they that hate the righteous shall be desolate.

²² The LORD redeemeth the soul of his servants: and none of them that trust in him shall be desolate.

Psalm 35 – Let the Angel of the Lord Chase and Persecute Those Who Fight Against Me

¹ (*A Psalm* of David.) Plead *my cause*, O LORD, with them that strive with me: fight against them that fight against me.

² Take hold of shield and buckler, and stand up for mine help.

³ Draw out also the spear, and stop *the way* against them that persecute me: say unto my soul, I *am* thy salvation.

⁴ Let them be confounded and put to shame that seek after my soul: let them be turned back and brought to confusion that devise my hurt.

⁵ Let them be as chaff before the wind: and let the <u>angel of the LORD</u> chase *them*.

⁶ Let their way be dark and slippery: and let the <u>angel of the LORD</u> persecute them.

⁷ For without cause have they hid for me their net *in* a pit, *which* without cause they have digged for my soul.

⁸ Let destruction come upon him at unawares; and let his net that he hath hid catch himself: into that very destruction let him fall.

⁹ And my soul shall be joyful in the LORD: it shall rejoice in his salvation.

¹⁰ All my bones shall say, LORD, who *is* like unto thee, which deliverest the poor from him that is too strong for him, yea, the poor and the needy from him that spoileth him?

¹¹ False witnesses did rise up; they laid to my charge *things* that I knew not.

¹² They rewarded me evil for good *to* the spoiling of my soul.

¹³ But as for me, when they were sick, my clothing *was* sackcloth: I humbled my soul with fasting; and my prayer returned into mine own bosom.

¹⁴ I behaved myself as though *he had been* my friend *or* brother: I bowed down heavily, as one that mourneth *for his* mother.

¹⁵ But in mine adversity they rejoiced, and gathered themselves together: *yea*, the abjects gathered themselves together against me, and I knew *it* not; they did tear *me*, and ceased not:

¹⁶ With hypocritical mockers in feasts, they gnashed upon me with their teeth.

¹⁷ Lord, how long wilt thou look on? rescue my soul from their destructions, my darling from the lions.

¹⁸ I will give thee thanks in the great congregation: I will praise thee among much people.

¹⁹ Let not them that are mine enemies wrongfully rejoice over me: *neither* let them wink with the eye that hate me without a cause.

²⁰ For they speak not peace: but they devise deceitful matters against *them that are* quiet in the land.

²¹ Yea, they opened their mouth wide against me, *and* said, Aha, aha, our eye hath seen *it*.

²² *This* thou hast seen, O LORD: keep not silence: O Lord, be not far from me.

²³ Stir up thyself, and awake to my judgment, *even* unto my cause, my God and my Lord.

²⁴ Judge me, O LORD my God, according to thy righteousness; and let them not rejoice over me.

²⁵ Let them not say in their hearts, Ah, so would we have it: let them not say, We have swallowed him up.

²⁶ Let them be ashamed and brought to confusion together that rejoice at mine hurt: let them be clothed with shame and dishonour that magnify *themselves* against me.

²⁷ Let them shout for joy, and be glad, that favour my righteous cause: yea, let them say continually, Let the LORD be magnified, which hath pleasure in the prosperity of his servant.

²⁸ And my tongue shall speak of thy righteousness *and* of thy praise all the day long.

Psalm 68 - Thousands of Angels

¹ (To the chief Musician, A Psalm *or* Song of David.) Let God arise, let his enemies be scattered: let them also that hate him flee before him.

² As smoke is driven away, *so* drive *them* away: as wax melteth before the fire, *so* let the wicked perish at the presence of God.

³ But let the righteous be glad; let them rejoice before God: yea, let them exceedingly rejoice.

⁴ Sing unto God, sing praises to his name: extol him that rideth upon the heavens by his name JAH, and rejoice before him.

⁵ A father of the fatherless, and a judge of the widows, *is* God in his holy habitation.

⁶ God setteth the solitary in families: he bringeth out those which are bound with chains: but the rebellious dwell in a dry *land*.

⁷ O God, when thou wentest forth before thy people, when thou didst march through the wilderness; Selah:

⁸ The earth shook, the heavens also dropped at the presence of God: *even* Sinai itself *was moved* at the presence of God, the God of Israel.

⁹ Thou, O God, didst send a plentiful rain, whereby thou didst confirm thine inheritance, when it was weary.

¹⁰ Thy congregation hath dwelt therein: thou, O God, hast prepared of thy goodness for the poor.

¹¹ The Lord gave the word: great *was* the company of those that published *it*.

¹² Kings of armies did flee apace: and she that tarried at home divided the spoil.

¹³ Though ye have lien among the pots, *yet shall ye be as* the wings of a dove covered with silver, and her feathers with yellow gold.

¹⁴ When the Almighty scattered kings in it, it was *white* as snow in Salmon.

¹⁵ The hill of God *is as* the hill of Bashan; an high hill *as* the hill of Bashan.

¹⁶ Why leap ye, ye high hills? *this is* the hill *which* God desireth to dwell in; yea, the LORD will dwell *in it* for ever.

¹⁷ The chariots of God *are* twenty thousand, *even* thousands of <u>angels</u>: the Lord *is* among them, *as in* Sinai, in the holy *place*.

¹⁸ Thou hast ascended on high, thou hast led captivity captive: thou hast received gifts for men; yea, *for* the rebellious also, that the LORD God might dwell *among them*.

¹⁹ Blessed *be* the Lord, *who* daily loadeth us *with benefits, even* the God of our salvation. Selah.

²⁰ *He that is* our God *is* the God of salvation; and unto GOD the Lord *belong* the issues from death.

²¹ But God shall wound the head of his enemies, *and* the hairy scalp of such an one as goeth on still in his trespasses.

²² The Lord said, I will bring again from Bashan, I will bring *my people* again from the depths of the sea:

²³ That thy foot may be dipped in the blood of *thine* enemies, *and* the tongue of thy dogs in the same.

²⁴ They have seen thy goings, O God; *even* the goings of my God, my King, in the sanctuary.

²⁵ The singers went before, the players on instruments *followed* after; among *them were* the damsels playing with timbrels.

²⁶ Bless ye God in the congregations, *even* the Lord, from the fountain of Israel.

²⁷ There *is* little Benjamin *with* their ruler, the princes of Judah *and* their council, the princes of Zebulun, *and* the princes of Naphtali.

²⁸ Thy God hath commanded thy strength: strengthen, O God, that which thou hast wrought for us.

²⁹ Because of thy temple at Jerusalem shall kings bring presents unto thee.

³⁰ Rebuke the company of spearmen, the multitude of the bulls, with the calves of the people, *till every one* submit himself with pieces of silver: scatter thou the people *that* delight in war.

³¹ Princes shall come out of Egypt; Ethiopia shall soon stretch out her hands unto God.

³² Sing unto God, ye kingdoms of the earth; O sing praises unto the Lord; Selah:

³³ To him that rideth upon the heavens of heavens, *which were* of old; lo, he doth send out his voice, *and that* a mighty voice.

³⁴ Ascribe ye strength unto God: his excellency *is* over Israel, and his strength *is* in the clouds.

³⁵ O God, *thou art* terrible out of thy holy places: the God of Israel *is* he that giveth strength and power unto *his* people. Blessed *be* God.

Psalm 78 - Manna, the Bread of Angels

¹ (Maschil of Asaph.) Give ear, O my people, *to* my law: incline your ears to the words of my mouth.

² I will open my mouth in a parable: I will utter dark sayings of old:

³ Which we have heard and known, and our fathers have told us.

⁴ We will not hide *them* from their children, shewing to the generation to come the praises of the LORD, and his strength, and his wonderful works that he hath done.

⁵ For he established a testimony in Jacob, and appointed a law in Israel, which he commanded our fathers, that they should make them known to their children:

⁶ That the generation to come might know *them, even* the children *which* should be born; *who* should arise and declare *them* to their children:

⁷ That they might set their hope in God, and not forget the works of God, but keep his commandments:

⁸ And might not be as their fathers, a stubborn and rebellious generation; a generation *that* set not their heart aright, and whose spirit was not stedfast with God.

⁹ The children of Ephraim, *being* armed, *and* carrying bows, turned back in the day of battle.

¹⁰ They kept not the covenant of God, and refused to walk in his law;

¹¹ And forgat his works, and his wonders that he had shewed them.

¹² Marvellous things did he in the sight of their fathers, in the land of Egypt, *in* the field of Zoan.

¹³ He divided the sea, and caused them to pass through; and he made the waters to stand as an heap.

¹⁴ In the daytime also he led them with a cloud, and all the night with a light of fire.

¹⁵ He clave the rocks in the wilderness, and gave *them* drink as *out of* the great depths.

¹⁶ He brought streams also out of the rock, and caused waters to run down like rivers.

¹⁷ And they sinned yet more against him by provoking the most High in the wilderness.

¹⁸ And they tempted God in their heart by asking meat for their lust.

¹⁹ Yea, they spake against God; they said, Can God furnish a table in the wilderness?

[20] Behold, he smote the rock, that the waters gushed out, and the streams overflowed; can he give bread also? can he provide flesh for his people?

[21] Therefore the LORD heard *this*, and was wroth: so a fire was kindled against Jacob, and anger also came up against Israel;

[22] Because they believed not in God, and trusted not in his salvation:

[23] Though he had commanded the clouds from above, and opened the doors of heaven,

[24] And had rained down manna upon them to eat, and had given them of the corn of heaven.

[25] Man did eat <u>angels</u>' food: he sent them meat to the full.

[26] He caused an east wind to blow in the heaven: and by his power he brought in the south wind.

[27] He rained flesh also upon them as dust, and feathered fowls like as the sand of the sea:

[28] And he let *it* fall in the midst of their camp, round about their habitations.

[29] So they did eat, and were well filled: for he gave them their own desire;

[30] They were not estranged from their lust. But while their meat *was* yet in their mouths,

[31] The wrath of God came upon them, and slew the fattest of them, and smote down the chosen *men* of Israel.

[32] For all this they sinned still, and believed not for his wondrous works.

[33] Therefore their days did he consume in vanity, and their years in trouble.

[34] When he slew them, then they sought him: and they returned and enquired early after God.

[35] And they remembered that God *was* their rock, and the high God their redeemer.

³⁶ Nevertheless they did flatter him with their mouth, and they lied unto him with their tongues.

³⁷ For their heart was not right with him, neither were they stedfast in his covenant.

³⁸ But he, *being* full of compassion, forgave *their* iniquity, and destroyed *them* not: yea, many a time turned he his anger away, and did not stir up all his wrath.

³⁹ For he remembered that they *were but* flesh; a wind that passeth away, and cometh not again.

⁴⁰ How oft did they provoke him in the wilderness, *and* grieve him in the desert!

⁴¹ Yea, they turned back and tempted God, and limited the Holy One of Israel.

⁴² They remembered not his hand, *nor* the day when he delivered them from the enemy.

⁴³ How he had wrought his signs in Egypt, and his wonders in the field of Zoan:

⁴⁴ And had turned their rivers into blood; and their floods, that they could not drink.

⁴⁵ He sent divers sorts of flies among them, which devoured them; and frogs, which destroyed them.

⁴⁶ He gave also their increase unto the caterpiller, and their labour unto the locust.

⁴⁷ He destroyed their vines with hail, and their sycomore trees with frost.

⁴⁸ He gave up their cattle also to the hail, and their flocks to hot thunderbolts.

⁴⁹ He cast upon them the fierceness of his anger, wrath, and indignation, and trouble, by sending evil <u>angels</u> *among them*.

⁵⁰ He made a way to his anger; he spared not their soul from death, but gave their life over to the pestilence;

⁵¹ And smote all the firstborn in Egypt; the chief of *their* strength in the tabernacles of Ham:

⁵² But made his own people to go forth like sheep, and guided them in the wilderness like a flock.

⁵³ And he led them on safely, so that they feared not: but the sea overwhelmed their enemies.

⁵⁴ And he brought them to the border of his sanctuary, *even to* this mountain, *which* his right hand had purchased.

⁵⁵ He cast out the heathen also before them, and divided them an inheritance by line, and made the tribes of Israel to dwell in their tents.

⁵⁶ Yet they tempted and provoked the most high God, and kept not his testimonies:

⁵⁷ But turned back, and dealt unfaithfully like their fathers: they were turned aside like a deceitful bow.

⁵⁸ For they provoked him to anger with their high places, and moved him to jealousy with their graven images.

⁵⁹ When God heard *this*, he was wroth, and greatly abhorred Israel:

⁶⁰ So that he forsook the tabernacle of Shiloh, the tent *which* he placed among men;

⁶¹ And delivered his strength into captivity, and his glory into the enemy's hand.

⁶² He gave his people over also unto the sword; and was wroth with his inheritance.

⁶³ The fire consumed their young men; and their maidens were not given to marriage.

⁶⁴ Their priests fell by the sword; and their widows made no lamentation.

⁶⁵ Then the Lord awaked as one out of sleep, *and* like a mighty man that shouteth by reason of wine.

⁶⁶ And he smote his enemies in the hinder parts: he put them to a perpetual reproach.

⁶⁷ Moreover he refused the tabernacle of Joseph, and chose not the tribe of Ephraim:

⁶⁸ But chose the tribe of Judah, the mount Zion which he loved.

⁶⁹ And he built his sanctuary like high *palaces*, like the earth which he hath established for ever.

⁷⁰ He chose David also his servant, and took him from the sheepfolds:

⁷¹ From following the ewes great with young he brought him to feed Jacob his people, and Israel his inheritance.

⁷² So he fed them according to the integrity of his heart; and guided them by the skilfulness of his hands.

Psalm 91 - God Gives Angels Charge Over You to Keep You in All Your Ways

¹ He that dwelleth in the secret place of the most High shall abide under the shadow of the Almighty.

² I will say of the LORD, *He is* my refuge and my fortress: my God; in him will I trust.

³ Surely he shall deliver thee from the snare of the fowler, *and* from the noisome pestilence.

⁴ He shall cover thee with his feathers, and under his wings shalt thou trust: his truth *shall be thy* shield and buckler.

⁵ Thou shalt not be afraid for the terror by night; *nor* for the arrow *that* flieth by day;

⁶ *Nor* for the pestilence *that* walketh in darkness; *nor* for the destruction *that* wasteth at noonday.

⁷ A thousand shall fall at thy side, and ten thousand at thy right hand; *but* it shall not come nigh thee.

⁸ Only with thine eyes shalt thou behold and see the reward of the wicked.

⁹ Because thou hast made the LORD, *which is* my refuge, *even* the most High, thy habitation;

¹⁰ There shall no evil befall thee, neither shall any plague come nigh thy dwelling.

¹¹ For he shall give his <u>angels</u> charge over thee, to keep thee in all thy ways.

¹² They shall bear thee up in *their* hands, lest thou dash thy foot against a stone.

¹³ Thou shalt tread upon the lion and adder: the young lion and the dragon shalt thou trample under feet.

¹⁴ Because he hath set his love upon me, therefore will I deliver him: I will set him on high, because he hath known my name.

¹⁵ He shall call upon me, and I will answer him: I *will be* with him in trouble; I will deliver him, and honour him.

¹⁶ With long life will I satisfy him, and shew him my salvation.

Psalm 103 - Bless the Lord, Ye Angels

¹ (*A Psalm* of David.) Bless the LORD, O my soul: and all that is within me, *bless* his holy name.

² Bless the LORD, O my soul, and forget not all his benefits:

³ Who forgiveth all thine iniquities; who healeth all thy diseases;

⁴ Who redeemeth thy life from destruction; who crowneth thee with lovingkindness and tender mercies;

⁵ Who satisfieth thy mouth with good *things; so that* thy youth is renewed like the eagle's.

⁶ The LORD executeth righteousness and judgment for all that are oppressed.

⁷ He made known his ways unto Moses, his acts unto the children of Israel.

⁸ The LORD *is* merciful and gracious, slow to anger, and plenteous in mercy.

⁹ He will not always chide: neither will he keep *his anger* for ever.

¹⁰ He hath not dealt with us after our sins; nor rewarded us according to our iniquities.

¹¹ For as the heaven is high above the earth, *so* great is his mercy toward them that fear him.

¹² As far as the east is from the west, *so* far hath he removed our transgressions from us.

¹³ Like as a father pitieth *his* children, *so* the LORD pitieth them that fear him.

¹⁴ For he knoweth our frame; he remembereth that we *are* dust.

¹⁵ *As for* man, his days *are* as grass: as a flower of the field, so he flourisheth.

¹⁶ For the wind passeth over it, and it is gone; and the place thereof shall know it no more.

¹⁷ But the mercy of the LORD *is* from everlasting to everlasting upon them that fear him, and his righteousness unto children's children;

¹⁸ To such as keep his covenant, and to those that remember his commandments to do them.

¹⁹ The LORD hath prepared his throne in the heavens; and his kingdom ruleth over all.

²⁰ Bless the LORD, ye his <u>angels,</u> that excel in strength, that do his commandments, hearkening unto the voice of his word.

²¹ Bless ye the LORD, all *ye* his hosts; *ye* ministers of his, that do his pleasure.

²² Bless the LORD, all his works in all places of his dominion: bless the LORD, O my soul.

Psalm 104 - Who Makes God's Angels Spirits; Ministers of Flaming Fire

¹ Bless the LORD, O my soul. O LORD my God, thou art very great; thou art clothed with honour and majesty.

² Who coverest *thyself* with light as *with* a garment: who stretchest out the heavens like a curtain:

³ Who layeth the beams of his chambers in the waters: who maketh the clouds his chariot: who walketh upon the wings of the wind:

⁴ Who maketh his <u>angels</u> spirits; his ministers a flaming fire:

⁵ *Who* laid the foundations of the earth, *that* it should not be removed for ever.

⁶ Thou coveredst it with the deep as *with* a garment: the waters stood above the mountains.

⁷ At thy rebuke they fled; at the voice of thy thunder they hasted away.

⁸ They go up by the mountains; they go down by the valleys unto the place which thou hast founded for them.

⁹ Thou hast set a bound that they may not pass over; that they turn not again to cover the earth.

¹⁰ He sendeth the springs into the valleys, *which* run among the hills.

¹¹ They give drink to every beast of the field: the wild asses quench their thirst.

¹² By them shall the fowls of the heaven have their habitation, *which* sing among the branches.

¹³ He watereth the hills from his chambers: the earth is satisfied with the fruit of thy works.

¹⁴ He causeth the grass to grow for the cattle, and herb for the service of man: that he may bring forth food out of the earth;

¹⁵ And wine *that* maketh glad the heart of man, *and* oil to make *his* face to shine, and bread *which* strengtheneth man's heart.

¹⁶ The trees of the LORD are full *of sap*; the cedars of Lebanon, which he hath planted;

¹⁷ Where the birds make their nests: *as for* the stork, the fir trees *are* her house.

¹⁸ The high hills *are* a refuge for the wild goats; *and* the rocks for the conies.

¹⁹ He appointed the moon for seasons: the sun knoweth his going down.

²⁰ Thou makest darkness, and it is night: wherein all the beasts of the forest do creep *forth*.

²¹ The young lions roar after their prey, and seek their meat from God.

²² The sun ariseth, they gather themselves together, and lay them down in their dens.

²³ Man goeth forth unto his work and to his labour until the evening.

²⁴ O LORD, how manifold are thy works! in wisdom hast thou made them all: the earth is full of thy riches.

²⁵ *So is* this great and wide sea, wherein *are* things creeping innumerable, both small and great beasts.

²⁶ There go the ships: *there is* that leviathan, *whom* thou hast made to play therein.

²⁷ These wait all upon thee; that thou mayest give *them* their meat in due season.

²⁸ *That* thou givest them they gather: thou openest thine hand, they are filled with good.

²⁹ Thou hidest thy face, they are troubled: thou takest away their breath, they die, and return to their dust.

³⁰ Thou sendest forth thy spirit, they are created: and thou renewest the face of the earth.

³¹ The glory of the LORD shall endure for ever: the LORD shall rejoice in his works.

³² He looketh on the earth, and it trembleth: he toucheth the hills, and they smoke.

³³ I will sing unto the LORD as long as I live: I will sing praise to my God while I have my being.

³⁴ My meditation of him shall be sweet: I will be glad in the LORD.

³⁵ Let the sinners be consumed out of the earth, and let the wicked be no more. Bless thou the LORD, O my soul. Praise ye the LORD.

Psalm 148 - Praise God, All God's Angels

¹ Praise ye the LORD. Praise ye the LORD from the heavens: praise him in the heights.

² Praise ye him, all his <u>angels</u>: praise ye him, all his hosts.

³ Praise ye him, sun and moon: praise him, all ye stars of light.

⁴ Praise him, ye heavens of heavens, and ye waters that *be* above the heavens.

⁵ Let them praise the name of the LORD: for he commanded, and they were created.

⁶ He hath also stablished them for ever and ever: he hath made a decree which shall not pass.

⁷ Praise the LORD from the earth, ye dragons, and all deeps:

⁸ Fire, and hail; snow, and vapour; stormy wind fulfilling his word:

⁹ Mountains, and all hills; fruitful trees, and all cedars:

¹⁰ Beasts, and all cattle; creeping things, and flying fowl:

¹¹ Kings of the earth, and all people; princes, and all judges of the earth:

¹² Both young men, and maidens; old men, and children:

¹³ Let them praise the name of the LORD: for his name alone is excellent; his glory *is* above the earth and heaven.

[14] He also exalteth the horn of his people, the praise of all his saints; *even* of the children of Israel, a people near unto him. Praise ye the LORD.

Angels in the New Testament

Angels in the Life of Jesus in Chronological Order

Luke 1:1-45 - Angel of the Lord Proclaims Birth of Son to Zacharias and Gabriel Foretells to Mary the Gender, Name, Destiny and that the Conception of her Child, Jesus, was from the Holy Ghost

¹ Forasmuch as many have taken in hand to set forth in order a declaration of those things which are most surely believed among us,

² Even as they delivered them unto us, which from the beginning were eyewitnesses, and ministers of the word;

³ It seemed good to me also, having had perfect understanding of all things from the very first, to write unto thee in order, most excellent Theophilus,

⁴ That thou mightest know the certainty of those things, wherein thou hast been instructed.

⁵ There was in the days of Herod, the king of Judaea, a certain priest named Zacharias, of the course of Abia: and his wife *was* of the daughters of Aaron, and her name *was* Elisabeth.

⁶ And they were both righteous before God, walking in all the commandments and ordinances of the Lord blameless.

⁷ And they had no child, because that Elisabeth was barren, and they both were *now* well stricken in years.

⁸ And it came to pass, that while he executed the priest's office before God in the order of his course,

⁹ According to the custom of the priest's office, his lot was to burn incense when he went into the temple of the Lord.

¹⁰ And the whole multitude of the people were praying without at the time of incense.

¹¹ And there appeared unto him an <u>angel of the Lord</u> standing on the right side of the altar of incense.

¹² And when Zacharias saw *him*, he was troubled, and fear fell upon him.

¹³ But the <u>angel</u> said unto him, Fear not, Zacharias: for thy prayer is heard; and thy wife Elisabeth shall bear thee a son, and thou shalt call his name John.

¹⁴ And thou shalt have joy and gladness; and many shall rejoice at his birth.

¹⁵ For he shall be great in the sight of the Lord, and shall drink neither wine nor strong drink; and he shall be filled with the Holy Ghost, even from his mother's womb.

¹⁶ And many of the children of Israel shall he turn to the Lord their God.

¹⁷ And he shall go before him in the spirit and power of Elias, to turn the hearts of the fathers to the children, and the disobedient to the wisdom of the just; to make ready a people prepared for the Lord.

¹⁸ And Zacharias said unto the <u>angel</u>, Whereby shall I know this? for I am an old man, and my wife well stricken in years.

¹⁹ And the <u>angel</u> answering said unto him, I am Gabriel, that stand in the presence of God; and am sent to speak unto thee, and to shew thee these glad tidings.

²⁰ And, behold, thou shalt be dumb, and not able to speak, until the day that these things shall be performed, because thou believest not my words, which shall be fulfilled in their season.

²¹ And the people waited for Zacharias, and marvelled that he tarried so long in the temple.

²² And when he came out, he could not speak unto them: and they perceived that he had seen a vision in the temple: for he beckoned unto them, and remained speechless.

²³ And it came to pass, that, as soon as the days of his ministration were accomplished, he departed to his own house.

²⁴ And after those days his wife Elisabeth conceived, and hid herself five months, saying,

²⁵ Thus hath the Lord dealt with me in the days wherein he looked on *me*, to take away my reproach among men.

²⁶ And in the sixth month the angel Gabriel was sent from God unto a city of Galilee, named Nazareth,

²⁷ To a virgin espoused to a man whose name was Joseph, of the house of David; and the virgin's name *was* Mary.

²⁸ And the angel came in unto her, and said, Hail, *thou that art* highly favoured, the Lord *is* with thee: blessed *art* thou among women.

²⁹ And when she saw *him*, she was troubled at his saying, and cast in her mind what manner of salutation this should be.

³⁰ And the angel said unto her, Fear not, Mary: for thou hast found favour with God.

³¹ And, behold, thou shalt conceive in thy womb, and bring forth a son, and shalt call his name JESUS.

³² He shall be great, and shall be called the Son of the Highest: and the Lord God shall give unto him the throne of his father David:

³³ And he shall reign over the house of Jacob for ever; and of his kingdom there shall be no end.

³⁴ Then said Mary unto the angel, How shall this be, seeing I know not a man?

³⁵ And the angel answered and said unto her, The Holy Ghost shall come upon thee, and the power of the Highest shall overshadow thee: therefore also that holy thing which shall be born of thee shall be called the Son of God.

³⁶ And, behold, thy cousin Elisabeth, she hath also conceived a son in her old age: and this is the sixth month with her, who was called barren.

³⁷ For with God nothing shall be impossible.

³⁸ And Mary said, Behold the handmaid of the Lord; be it unto me according to thy word. And the <u>angel</u> departed from her.

³⁹ And Mary arose in those days, and went into the hill country with haste, into a city of Juda;

⁴⁰ And entered into the house of Zacharias, and saluted Elisabeth.

⁴¹ And it came to pass, that, when Elisabeth heard the salutation of Mary, the babe leaped in her womb; and Elisabeth was filled with the Holy Ghost:

⁴² And she spake out with a loud voice, and said, Blessed *art* thou among women, and blessed *is* the fruit of thy womb.

⁴³ And whence *is* this to me, that the mother of my Lord should come to me?

⁴⁴ For, lo, as soon as the voice of thy salutation sounded in mine ears, the babe leaped in my womb for joy.

⁴⁵ And blessed *is* she that believed: for there shall be a performance of those things which were told her from the Lord.

Matthew 1:17-25 - Angel of the Lord in a Dream told Joseph about Taking Mary as His Wife and that the Baby was Conceived by the Holy Ghost and told Him the Child's Gender, Name and Destiny

¹⁷ So all the generations from Abraham to David *are* fourteen generations; and from David until the carrying away into Babylon *are* fourteen generations; and from the carrying away into Babylon unto Christ *are* fourteen generations.

¹⁸ Now the birth of Jesus Christ was on this wise: When as his mother Mary was espoused to Joseph, before they came together, she was found with child of the Holy Ghost.

¹⁹ Then Joseph her husband, being a just *man*, and not willing to make her a publick example, was minded to put her away privily.

²⁰ But while he thought on these things, behold, the <u>angel of the Lord</u> appeared unto him in a dream, saying, Joseph, thou son of David, fear not to take unto thee Mary thy wife: for that which is conceived in her is of the Holy Ghost.

²¹ And she shall bring forth a son, and thou shalt call his name JESUS: for he shall save his people from their sins.

²² Now all this was done, that it might be fulfilled which was spoken of the Lord by the prophet, saying,

²³ Behold, a virgin shall be with child, and shall bring forth a son, and they shall call his name Emmanuel, which being interpreted is, God with us.

²⁴ Then Joseph being raised from sleep did as the <u>angel of the Lord</u> had bidden him, and took unto him his wife:

²⁵ And knew her not till she had brought forth her firstborn son: and he called his name JESUS.

Luke 2:1-20 - Angel of the Lord Announces the Birth of Jesus to the Shepherds, followed by a Multitude of Angels Praising God

¹ And it came to pass in those days, that there went out a decree from Caesar Augustus, that all the world should be taxed.

² (*And* this taxing was first made when Cyrenius was governor of Syria.)

³ And all went to be taxed, every one into his own city.

⁴ And Joseph also went up from Galilee, out of the city of Nazareth, into Judaea, unto the city of David, which is called Bethlehem; (because he was of the house and lineage of David:)

⁵ To be taxed with Mary his espoused wife, being great with child.

⁶ And so it was, that, while they were there, the days were accomplished that she should be delivered.

⁷ And she brought forth her firstborn son, and wrapped him in swaddling clothes, and laid him in a manger; because there was no room for them in the inn.

⁸ And there were in the same country shepherds abiding in the field, keeping watch over their flock by night.

⁹ And, lo, the <u>angel of the Lord</u> came upon them, and the glory of the Lord shone round about them: and they were sore afraid.

¹⁰ And the <u>angel</u> said unto them, Fear not: for, behold, I bring you good tidings of great joy, which shall be to all people.

¹¹ For unto you is born this day in the city of David a Saviour, which is Christ the Lord.

¹² And this *shall be* a sign unto you; Ye shall find the babe wrapped in swaddling clothes, lying in a manger.

¹³ And suddenly there was with the <u>angel</u> a multitude of the heavenly host praising God, and saying,

¹⁴ Glory to God in the highest, and on earth peace, good will toward men.

¹⁵ And it came to pass, as the <u>angels</u> were gone away from them into heaven, the shepherds said one to another, Let us now go even unto Bethlehem, and see this thing which is come to pass, which the Lord hath made known unto us.

¹⁶ And they came with haste, and found Mary, and Joseph, and the babe lying in a manger.

¹⁷ And when they had seen *it*, they made known abroad the saying which was told them concerning this child.

[18] And all they that heard *it* wondered at those things which were told them by the shepherds.

[19] But Mary kept all these things, and pondered *them* in her heart.

[20] And the shepherds returned, glorifying and praising God for all the things that they had heard and seen, as it was told unto them.

Matthew 2:1-23 - Joseph Instructed in a Dream by the Angel of the Lord to Flee to Egypt and when to Return Safely to Israel

[1] Now when Jesus was born in Bethlehem of Judaea in the days of Herod the king, behold, there came wise men from the east to Jerusalem,

[2] Saying, Where is he that is born King of the Jews? for we have seen his star in the east, and are come to worship him.

[3] When Herod the king had heard *these things*, he was troubled, and all Jerusalem with him.

[4] And when he had gathered all the chief priests and scribes of the people together, he demanded of them where Christ should be born.

[5] And they said unto him, In Bethlehem of Judaea: for thus it is written by the prophet,

[6] And thou Bethlehem, *in* the land of Juda, art not the least among the princes of Juda: for out of thee shall come a Governor, that shall rule my people Israel.

[7] Then Herod, when he had privily called the wise men, enquired of them diligently what time the star appeared.

[8] And he sent them to Bethlehem, and said, Go and search diligently for the young child; and when ye have found *him*, bring me word again, that I may come and worship him also.

[9] When they had heard the king, they departed; and, lo, the star, which they saw in the east, went before them, till it came and stood over where the young child was.

¹⁰ When they saw the star, they rejoiced with exceeding great joy.

¹¹ And when they were come into the house, they saw the young child with Mary his mother, and fell down, and worshipped him: and when they had opened their treasures, they presented unto him gifts; gold, and frankincense, and myrrh.

¹² And being warned of God in a dream that they should not return to Herod, they departed into their own country another way.

¹³ And when they were departed, behold, the <u>angel of the Lord</u> appeareth to Joseph in a dream, saying, Arise, and take the young child and his mother, and flee into Egypt, and be thou there until I bring thee word: for Herod will seek the young child to destroy him.

¹⁴ When he arose, he took the young child and his mother by night, and departed into Egypt:

¹⁵ And was there until the death of Herod: that it might be fulfilled which was spoken of the Lord by the prophet, saying, Out of Egypt have I called my son.

¹⁶ Then Herod, when he saw that he was mocked of the wise men, was exceeding wroth, and sent forth, and slew all the children that were in Bethlehem, and in all the coasts thereof, from two years old and under, according to the time which he had diligently enquired of the wise men.

¹⁷ Then was fulfilled that which was spoken by Jeremy the prophet, saying,

¹⁸ In Rama was there a voice heard, lamentation, and weeping, and great mourning, Rachel weeping *for* her children, and would not be comforted, because they are not.

¹⁹ But when Herod was dead, behold, an <u>angel of the Lord</u> appeareth in a dream to Joseph in Egypt,

²⁰ Saying, Arise, and take the young child and his mother, and go into the land of Israel: for they are dead which sought the young child's life.

²¹ And he arose, and took the young child and his mother, and came into the land of Israel.

²² But when he heard that Archelaus did reign in Judaea in the room of his father Herod, he was afraid to go thither: notwithstanding, being warned of God in a dream, he turned aside into the parts of Galilee:

²³ And he came and dwelt in a city called Nazareth: that it might be fulfilled which was spoken by the prophets, He shall be called a Nazarene.

Mark 1:9-13 - Angels Ministered to Jesus after the 40-day Temptation

⁹ And it came to pass in those days, that Jesus came from Nazareth of Galilee, and was baptized of John in Jordan.

¹⁰ And straightway coming up out of the water, he saw the heavens opened, and the Spirit like a dove descending upon him:

¹¹ And there came a voice from heaven, *saying*, Thou art my beloved Son, in whom I am well pleased.

¹² And immediately the Spirit driveth him into the wilderness.

¹³ And he was there in the wilderness forty days, tempted of Satan; and was with the wild beasts; and the <u>angels</u> ministered unto him.

Matthew 4:1-11- Angels Ministered to Jesus after the 40-day Temptation

¹ Then was Jesus led up of the Spirit into the wilderness to be tempted of the devil.

² And when he had fasted forty days and forty nights, he was afterward an hungred.

³ And when the tempter came to him, he said, If thou be the Son of God, command that these stones be made bread.

⁴ But he answered and said, It is written, Man shall not live by bread alone, but by every word that proceedeth out of the mouth of God.

⁵ Then the devil taketh him up into the holy city, and setteth him on a pinnacle of the temple,

⁶ And saith unto him, If thou be the Son of God, cast thyself down: for it is written, He shall give his <u>angels</u> charge concerning thee: and in *their* hands they shall bear thee up, lest at any time thou dash thy foot against a stone.

⁷ Jesus said unto him, It is written again, Thou shalt not tempt the Lord thy God.

⁸ Again, the devil taketh him up into an exceeding high mountain, and sheweth him all the kingdoms of the world, and the glory of them;

⁹ And saith unto him, All these things will I give thee, if thou wilt fall down and worship me.

¹⁰ Then saith Jesus unto him, Get thee hence, Satan: for it is written, Thou shalt worship the Lord thy God, and him only shalt thou serve.

¹¹ Then the devil leaveth him, and, behold, <u>angels</u> came and ministered unto him.

John 5:1-9 - Angel Troubled the Water at the Healing Pool in Bethesda

¹ After this there was a feast of the Jews; and Jesus went up to Jerusalem.

² Now there is at Jerusalem by the sheep *market* a pool, which is called in the Hebrew tongue Bethesda, having five porches.

³ In these lay a great multitude of impotent folk, of blind, halt, withered, waiting for the moving of the water.

⁴ For an <u>angel</u> went down at a certain season into the pool, and troubled the water: whosoever then first after the troubling of the water stepped in was made whole of whatsoever disease he had.

⁵ And a certain man was there, which had an infirmity thirty and eight years.

⁶ When Jesus saw him lie, and knew that he had been now a long time *in that case*, he saith unto him, Wilt thou be made whole?

⁷ The impotent man answered him, Sir, I have no man, when the water is troubled, to put me into the pool: but while I am coming, another steppeth down before me.

⁸ Jesus saith unto him, "Rise, take up thy bed, and walk".

⁹ And immediately the man was made whole, and took up his bed, and walked: and on the same day was the sabbath.

Luke 22:39-47 - Jesus Comforted by an Angel in His Agony at Mount of Olives

³⁹ And he came out, and went, as he was wont, to the mount of Olives; and his disciples also followed him.

⁴⁰ And when he was at the place, he said unto them, Pray that ye enter not into temptation.

⁴¹ And he was withdrawn from them about a stone's cast, and kneeled down, and prayed,

⁴² Saying, Father, if thou be willing, remove this cup from me: nevertheless not my will, but thine, be done.

⁴³ And there appeared an <u>angel</u> unto him from heaven, strengthening him.

⁴⁴ And being in an agony he prayed more earnestly: and his sweat was as it were great drops of blood falling down to the ground.

⁴⁵ And when he rose up from prayer, and was come to his disciples, he found them sleeping for sorrow,

⁴⁶ And said unto them, Why sleep ye? rise and pray, lest ye enter into temptation.

⁴⁷ And while he yet spake, behold a multitude, and he that was called Judas, one of the twelve, went before them, and drew near unto Jesus to kiss him.

Matthew 28:1-8 - Angel of the Lord Rolled Back the Stone from Jesus' Tomb and Announced Jesus' Resurrection to the Women at the Tomb

¹ In the end of the sabbath, as it began to dawn toward the first *day* of the week, came Mary Magdalene and the other Mary to see the sepulchre.

² And, behold, there was a great earthquake: for the <u>angel of the Lord</u> descended from heaven, and came and rolled back the stone from the door, and sat upon it.

³ His countenance was like lightning, and his raiment white as snow:

⁴ And for fear of him the keepers did shake, and became as dead *men*.

⁵ And the <u>angel</u> answered and said unto the women, Fear not ye: for I know that ye seek Jesus, which was crucified.

⁶ He is not here: for he is risen, as he said. Come, see the place where the Lord lay.

⁷ And go quickly, and tell his disciples that he is risen from the dead; and, behold, he goeth before you into Galilee; there shall ye see him: lo, I have told you.

⁸ And they departed quickly from the sepulchre with fear and great joy; and did run to bring his disciples word.

John 20:1-18 - Angels Question Mary Magdalene's Grief at the Tomb

¹ The first *day* of the week cometh Mary Magdalene early, when it was yet dark, unto the sepulchre, and seeth the stone taken away from the sepulchre.

² Then she runneth, and cometh to Simon Peter, and to the other disciple, whom Jesus loved, and saith unto them, They have taken away the Lord out of the sepulchre, and we know not where they have laid him.

³ Peter therefore went forth, and that other disciple, and came to the sepulchre.

⁴ So they ran both together: and the other disciple did outrun Peter, and came first to the sepulchre.

⁵ And he stooping down, *and looking in*, saw the linen clothes lying; yet went he not in.

⁶ Then cometh Simon Peter following him, and went into the sepulchre, and seeth the linen clothes lie,

⁷ And the napkin, that was about his head, not lying with the linen clothes, but wrapped together in a place by itself.

⁸ Then went in also that other disciple, which came first to the sepulchre, and he saw, and believed.

⁹ For as yet they knew not the scripture, that he must rise again from the dead.

¹⁰ Then the disciples went away again unto their own home.

¹¹ But Mary stood without at the sepulchre weeping: and as she wept, she stooped down, *and looked* into the sepulchre,

¹² And seeth two angels in white sitting, the one at the head, and the other at the feet, where the body of Jesus had lain.

¹³ And they say unto her, Woman, why weepest thou? She saith unto them, Because they have taken away my Lord, and I know not where they have laid him.

¹⁴ And when she had thus said, she turned herself back, and saw Jesus standing, and knew not that it was Jesus.

¹⁵ Jesus saith unto her, Woman, why weepest thou? whom seekest thou? She, supposing him to be the gardener, saith unto him, Sir, if thou have borne him hence, tell me where thou hast laid him, and I will take him away.

¹⁶ Jesus saith unto her, Mary. She turned herself, and saith unto him, Rabboni; which is to say, Master.

¹⁷ Jesus saith unto her, Touch me not; for I am not yet ascended to my Father: but go to my brethren, and say unto them, I ascend unto my Father, and your Father; and *to* my God, and your God.

¹⁸ Mary Magdalene came and told the disciples that she had seen the Lord, and *that* he had spoken these things unto her.

Matthew 13:1-58 - Parable of the Seeds and Angels to Harvest Righteous and Unrighteous for Jesus at the End of the Age

¹ The same day went Jesus out of the house, and sat by the sea side.

² And great multitudes were gathered together unto him, so that he went into a ship, and sat; and the whole multitude stood on the shore.

³ And he spake many things unto them in parables, saying, Behold, a sower went forth to sow;

⁴ And when he sowed, some *seeds* fell by the way side, and the fowls came and devoured them up:

⁵ Some fell upon stony places, where they had not much earth: and forthwith they sprung up, because they had no deepness of earth:

⁶ And when the sun was up, they were scorched; and because they had no root, they withered away.

⁷ And some fell among thorns; and the thorns sprung up, and choked them:

⁸ But other fell into good ground, and brought forth fruit, some an hundredfold, some sixtyfold, some thirtyfold.

⁹ Who hath ears to hear, let him hear.

¹⁰ And the disciples came, and said unto him, Why speakest thou unto them in parables?

¹¹ He answered and said unto them, Because it is given unto you to know the mysteries of the kingdom of heaven, but to them it is not given.

¹² For whosoever hath, to him shall be given, and he shall have more abundance: but whosoever hath not, from him shall be taken away even that he hath.

¹³ Therefore speak I to them in parables: because they seeing see not; and hearing they hear not, neither do they understand.

¹⁴ And in them is fulfilled the prophecy of Esaias, which saith, By hearing ye shall hear, and shall not understand; and seeing ye shall see, and shall not perceive:

¹⁵ For this people's heart is waxed gross, and *their* ears are dull of hearing, and their eyes they have closed; lest at any time they should see with *their* eyes, and hear with *their* ears, and should understand with *their* heart, and should be converted, and I should heal them.

¹⁶ But blessed *are* your eyes, for they see: and your ears, for they hear.

¹⁷ For verily I say unto you, That many prophets and righteous *men* have desired to see *those things* which ye see, and have not seen *them*; and to hear *those things* which ye hear, and have not heard *them*.

¹⁸ Hear ye therefore the parable of the sower.

¹⁹ When any one heareth the word of the kingdom, and understandeth *it* not, then cometh the wicked *one*, and catcheth away that which was sown in his heart. This is he which received seed by the way side.

²⁰ But he that received the seed into stony places, the same is he that heareth the word, and anon with joy receiveth it;

²¹ Yet hath he not root in himself, but dureth for a while: for when tribulation or persecution ariseth because of the word, by and by he is offended.

²² He also that received seed among the thorns is he that heareth the word; and the care of this world, and the deceitfulness of riches, choke the word, and he becometh unfruitful.

²³ But he that received seed into the good ground is he that heareth the word, and understandeth *it*; which also beareth fruit, and bringeth forth, some an hundredfold, some sixty, some thirty.

24 Another parable put he forth unto them, saying, The kingdom of heaven is likened unto a man which sowed good seed in his field:

25 But while men slept, his enemy came and sowed tares among the wheat, and went his way.

26 But when the blade was sprung up, and brought forth fruit, then appeared the tares also.

27 So the servants of the householder came and said unto him, Sir, didst not thou sow good seed in thy field? from whence then hath it tares?

28 He said unto them, An enemy hath done this. The servants said unto him, Wilt thou then that we go and gather them up?

29 But he said, Nay; lest while ye gather up the tares, ye root up also the wheat with them.

30 Let both grow together until the harvest: and in the time of harvest I will say to the reapers, Gather ye together first the tares, and bind them in bundles to burn them: but gather the wheat into my barn.

31 Another parable put he forth unto them, saying, The kingdom of heaven is like to a grain of mustard seed, which a man took, and sowed in his field:

32 Which indeed is the least of all seeds: but when it is grown, it is the greatest among herbs, and becometh a tree, so that the birds of the air come and lodge in the branches thereof.

33 Another parable spake he unto them; The kingdom of heaven is like unto leaven, which a woman took, and hid in three measures of meal, till the whole was leavened.

34 All these things spake Jesus unto the multitude in parables; and without a parable spake he not unto them:

35 That it might be fulfilled which was spoken by the prophet, saying, I will open my mouth in parables; I will utter things which have been kept secret from the foundation of the world.

36 Then Jesus sent the multitude away, and went into the house: and his disciples came unto him, saying, Declare unto us the parable of the tares of the field.

³⁷ He answered and said unto them, He that soweth the good seed is the Son of man;

³⁸ The field is the world; the good seed are the children of the kingdom; but the tares are the children of the wicked *one*;

³⁹ The enemy that sowed them is the devil; the harvest is the end of the world; and the reapers are the <u>angels</u>.

⁴⁰ As therefore the tares are gathered and burned in the fire; so shall it be in the end of this world.

⁴¹ The Son of man shall send forth his <u>angels,</u> and they shall gather out of his kingdom all things that offend, and them which do iniquity;

⁴² And shall cast them into a furnace of fire: there shall be wailing and gnashing of teeth.

⁴³ Then shall the righteous shine forth as the sun in the kingdom of their Father. Who hath ears to hear, let him hear.

⁴⁴ Again, the kingdom of heaven is like unto treasure hid in a field; the which when a man hath found, he hideth, and for joy thereof goeth and selleth all that he hath, and buyeth that field.

⁴⁵ Again, the kingdom of heaven is like unto a merchant man, seeking goodly pearls:

⁴⁶ Who, when he had found one pearl of great price, went and sold all that he had, and bought it.

⁴⁷ Again, the kingdom of heaven is like unto a net, that was cast into the sea, and gathered of every kind:

⁴⁸ Which, when it was full, they drew to shore, and sat down, and gathered the good into vessels, but cast the bad away.

⁴⁹ So shall it be at the end of the world: the <u>angels</u> shall come forth, and sever the wicked from among the just,

⁵⁰ And shall cast them into the furnace of fire: there shall be wailing and gnashing of teeth.

⁵¹ Jesus saith unto them, Have ye understood all these things? They say unto him, Yea, Lord.

⁵² Then said he unto them, Therefore every scribe *which is* instructed unto the kingdom of heaven is like unto a man *that is* an householder, which bringeth forth out of his treasure *things* new and old.

⁵³ And it came to pass, *that* when Jesus had finished these parables, he departed thence.

⁵⁴ And when he was come into his own country, he taught them in their synagogue, insomuch that they were astonished, and said, Whence hath this *man* this wisdom, and *these* mighty works?

⁵⁵ Is not this the carpenter's son? is not his mother called Mary? and his brethren, James, and Joses, and Simon, and Judas?

⁵⁶ And his sisters, are they not all with us? Whence then hath this *man* all these things?

⁵⁷ And they were offended in him. But Jesus said unto them, A prophet is not without honour, save in his own country, and in his own house.

⁵⁸ And he did not many mighty works there because of their unbelief.

Matthew 24:25-31 - Jesus will send his Angels with a Great Sound of a Trumpet to Gather His Elect

²⁵ Behold, I have told you before.

²⁶ Wherefore if they shall say unto you, Behold, he is in the desert; go not forth: behold, *he is* in the secret chambers; believe *it* not.

²⁷ For as the lightning cometh out of the east, and shineth even unto the west; so shall also the coming of the Son of man be.

²⁸ For wheresoever the carcase is, there will the eagles be gathered together.

²⁹ Immediately after the tribulation of those days shall the sun be darkened, and the moon shall not give her light, and the stars shall fall from heaven, and the powers of the heavens shall be shaken:

³⁰ And then shall appear the sign of the Son of man in heaven: and then shall all the tribes of the earth mourn, and they shall see the Son of man coming in the clouds of heaven with power and great glory.

³¹ And he shall send his angels with a great sound of a trumpet, and they shall gather together his elect from the four winds, from one end of heaven to the other.

Mark 13:21-27 - He Shall Send His Angels to Gather Together His Elect

²¹ And then if any man shall say to you, Lo, here *is* Christ; or, lo, *he is* there; believe *him* not:

²² For false Christs and false prophets shall rise, and shall shew signs and wonders, to seduce, if *it were* possible, even the elect.

²³ But take ye heed: behold, I have foretold you all things.

²⁴ But in those days, after that tribulation, the sun shall be darkened, and the moon shall not give her light,

²⁵ And the stars of heaven shall fall, and the powers that are in heaven shall be shaken.

²⁶ And then shall they see the Son of man coming in the clouds with great power and glory.

²⁷ And then shall he send his angels, and shall gather together his elect from the four winds, from the uttermost part of the earth to the uttermost part of heaven.

Mark 8:34-38 - Jesus Comes with the Holy Angels

³⁴ And when he had called the people *unto him* with his disciples also, he said unto them, Whosoever will come after me, let him deny himself, and take up his cross, and follow me.

³⁵ For whosoever will save his life shall lose it; but whosoever shall lose his life for my sake and the gospel's, the same shall save it.

³⁶ For what shall it profit a man, if he shall gain the whole world, and lose his own soul?

³⁷ Or what shall a man give in exchange for his soul?

³⁸ Whosoever therefore shall be ashamed of me and of my words in this adulterous and sinful generation; of him also shall the Son of man be ashamed, when he cometh in the glory of his Father with the holy <u>angels</u>.

Matthew 16:24-28 - The Son of Man Shall Come in the Glory of His Father with His Angels

²⁴ Then said Jesus unto his disciples, If any *man* will come after me, let him deny himself, and take up his cross, and follow me.

²⁵ For whosoever will save his life shall lose it: and whosoever will lose his life for my sake shall find it.

²⁶ For what is a man profited, if he shall gain the whole world, and lose his own soul? or what shall a man give in exchange for his soul?

²⁷ For the Son of man shall come in the glory of his Father with his <u>angels</u>; and then he shall reward every man according to his works.

²⁸ Verily I say unto you, There be some standing here, which shall not taste of death, till they see the Son of man coming in his kingdom.

Matthew 25:31-46 - Son of Man Shall Come in His Glory and all the Holy Angels; He Shall Separate Them One from Another, the Devil and his angels

³¹ When the Son of man shall come in his glory, and all the holy <u>angels</u> with him, then shall he sit upon the throne of his glory:

³² And before him shall be gathered all nations: and he shall separate them one from another, as a shepherd divideth *his* sheep from the goats:

[33] And he shall set the sheep on his right hand, but the goats on the left.

[34] Then shall the King say unto them on his right hand, Come, ye blessed of my Father, inherit the kingdom prepared for you from the foundation of the world:

[35] For I was an hungred, and ye gave me meat: I was thirsty, and ye gave me drink: I was a stranger, and ye took me in:

[36] Naked, and ye clothed me: I was sick, and ye visited me: I was in prison, and ye came unto me.

[37] Then shall the righteous answer him, saying, Lord, when saw we thee an hungred, and fed *thee*? or thirsty, and gave *thee* drink?

[38] When saw we thee a stranger, and took *thee* in? or naked, and clothed *thee*?

[39] Or when saw we thee sick, or in prison, and came unto thee?

[40] And the King shall answer and say unto them, Verily I say unto you, Inasmuch as ye have done *it* unto one of the least of these my brethren, ye have done *it* unto me.

[41] Then shall he say also unto them on the left hand, Depart from me, ye cursed, into everlasting fire, prepared for the devil and his <u>angels</u>:

[42] For I was an hungred, and ye gave me no meat: I was thirsty, and ye gave me no drink:

[43] I was a stranger, and ye took me not in: naked, and ye clothed me not: sick, and in prison, and ye visited me not.

[44] Then shall they also answer him, saying, Lord, when saw we thee an hungred, or a thirst, or a stranger, or naked, or sick, or in prison, and did not minister unto thee?

[45] Then shall he answer them, saying, Verily I say unto you, Inasmuch as ye did *it* not to one of the least of these, ye did *it* not to me.

[46] And these shall go away into everlasting punishment: but the righteous into life eternal.

Luke 9:18-26 - He Shall Come in His Own Glory and of the Holy Angels

¹⁸ And it came to pass, as he was alone praying, his disciples were with him: and he asked them, saying, Whom say the people that I am?

¹⁹ They answering said, John the Baptist; but some *say*, Elias; and others *say*, that one of the old prophets is risen again.

²⁰ He said unto them, But whom say ye that I am? Peter answering said, The Christ of God.

²¹ And he straitly charged them, and commanded *them* to tell no man that thing;

²² Saying, The Son of man must suffer many things, and be rejected of the elders and chief priests and scribes, and be slain, and be raised the third day.

²³ And he said to *them* all, If any *man* will come after me, let him deny himself, and take up his cross daily, and follow me.

²⁴ For whosoever will save his life shall lose it: but whosoever will lose his life for my sake, the same shall save it.

²⁵ For what is a man advantaged, if he gain the whole world, and lose himself, or be cast away?

²⁶ For whosoever shall be ashamed of me and of my words, of him shall the Son of man be ashamed, when he shall come in his own glory, and *in his* Father's, and of the holy angels.

Revelation 5:1-14 - Many Angels Praise the Lamb

¹ And I saw in the right hand of him that sat on the throne a book written within and on the backside, sealed with seven seals.

² And I saw a strong angel proclaiming with a loud voice, Who is worthy to open the book, and to loose the seals thereof?

³ And no man in heaven, nor in earth, neither under the earth, was able to open the book, neither to look thereon.

⁴ And I wept much, because no man was found worthy to open and to read the book, neither to look thereon.

⁵ And one of the elders saith unto me, Weep not: behold, the Lion of the tribe of Juda, the Root of David, hath prevailed to open the book, and to loose the seven seals thereof.

⁶ And I beheld, and, lo, in the midst of the throne and of the four beasts, and in the midst of the elders, stood a Lamb as it had been slain, having seven horns and seven eyes, which are the seven Spirits of God sent forth into all the earth.

⁷ And he came and took the book out of the right hand of him that sat upon the throne.

⁸ And when he had taken the book, the four beasts and four *and* twenty elders fell down before the Lamb, having every one of them harps, and golden vials full of odours, which are the prayers of saints.

⁹ And they sung a new song, saying, Thou art worthy to take the book, and to open the seals thereof: for thou wast slain, and hast redeemed us to God by thy blood out of every kindred, and tongue, and people, and nation;

¹⁰ And hast made us unto our God kings and priests: and we shall reign on the earth.

¹¹ And I beheld, and I heard the voice of many <u>angels</u> round about the throne and the beasts and the elders: and the number of them was ten thousand times ten thousand, and thousands of thousands;

¹² Saying with a loud voice, Worthy is the Lamb that was slain to receive power, and riches, and wisdom, and strength, and honour, and glory, and blessing.

¹³ And every creature which is in heaven, and on the earth, and under the earth, and such as are in the sea, and all that are in them, heard I saying, Blessing, and honour, and glory, and power, *be* unto him that sitteth upon the throne, and unto the Lamb for ever and ever.

¹⁴ And the four beasts said, Amen. And the four *and* twenty elders fell down and worshipped him that liveth for ever and ever.

Revelation 12:1-17 - Michael and His Angels Cast Out Dragon

¹ And there appeared a great wonder in heaven; a woman clothed with the sun, and the moon under her feet, and upon her head a crown of twelve stars:

² And she being with child cried, travailing in birth, and pained to be delivered.

³ And there appeared another wonder in heaven; and behold a great red dragon, having seven heads and ten horns, and seven crowns upon his heads.

⁴ And his tail drew the third part of the stars of heaven, and did cast them to the earth: and the dragon stood before the woman which was ready to be delivered, for to devour her child as soon as it was born.

⁵ And she brought forth a man child, who was to rule all nations with a rod of iron: and her child was caught up unto God, and *to* his throne.

⁶ And the woman fled into the wilderness, where she hath a place prepared of God, that they should feed her there a thousand two hundred *and* threescore days.

⁷ And there was war in heaven: Michael and his <u>angels</u> fought against the dragon; and the dragon fought and his <u>angels,</u>

⁸ And prevailed not; neither was their place found any more in heaven.

⁹ And the great dragon was cast out, that old serpent, called the Devil, and Satan, which deceiveth the whole world: he was cast out into the earth, and his <u>angels</u> were cast out with him.

¹⁰ And I heard a loud voice saying in heaven, Now is come salvation, and strength, and the kingdom of our God, and the power of his Christ: for the accuser of our brethren is cast down, which accused them before our God day and night.

¹¹ And they overcame him by the blood of the Lamb, and by the word of their testimony; and they loved not their lives unto the death.

¹² Therefore rejoice, *ye* heavens, and ye that dwell in them. Woe to the inhabiters of the earth and of the seal for the devil is come down unto you, having great wrath, because he knoweth that he hath but a short time.

¹³ And when the dragon saw that he was cast unto the earth, he persecuted the woman which brought forth the man *child*.

¹⁴ And to the woman were given two wings of a great eagle, that she might fly into the wilderness, into her place, where she is nourished for a time, and times, and half a time, from the face of the serpent.

¹⁵ And the serpent cast out of his mouth water as a flood after the woman, that he might cause her to be carried away of the flood.

¹⁶ And the earth helped the woman, and the earth opened her mouth, and swallowed up the flood which the dragon cast out of his mouth.

¹⁷ And the dragon was wroth with the woman, and went to make war with the remnant of her seed, which keep the commandments of God, and have the testimony of Jesus Christ.

Jesus' Teachings Regarding the Angels

Matthew 18:1-10 - In Heaven, Children's Angels Do Always Behold the Face of God

¹ At the same time came the disciples unto Jesus, saying, Who is the greatest in the kingdom of heaven?

² And Jesus called a little child unto him, and set him in the midst of them,

³ And said, Verily I say unto you, Except ye be converted, and become as little children, ye shall not enter into the kingdom of heaven.

⁴ Whosoever therefore shall humble himself as this little child, the same is greatest in the kingdom of heaven.

⁵ And whoso shall receive one such little child in my name receiveth me.

⁶ But whoso shall offend one of these little ones which believe in me, it were better for him that a millstone were hanged about his neck, and *that* he were drowned in the depth of the sea.

⁷ Woe unto the world because of offences! for it must needs be that offences come; but woe to that man by whom the offence cometh!

⁸ Wherefore if thy hand or thy foot offend thee, cut them off, and cast *them* from thee: it is better for thee to enter into life halt or maimed, rather than having two hands or two feet to be cast into everlasting fire.

⁹ And if thine eye offend thee, pluck it out, and cast *it* from thee: it is better for thee to enter into life with one eye, rather than having two eyes to be cast into hell fire.

¹⁰ Take heed that ye despise not one of these little ones; for I say unto you, That in heaven their <u>angels</u> do always behold the face of my Father which is in heaven.

Matthew 22:23-30 - Angels of God Do Not Marry

²³ The same day came to him the Sadducees, which say that there is no resurrection, and asked him,

²⁴ Saying, Master, Moses said, If a man die, having no children, his brother shall marry his wife, and raise up seed unto his brother.

²⁵ Now there were with us seven brethren: and the first, when he had married a wife, deceased, and, having no issue, left his wife unto his brother:

²⁶ Likewise the second also, and the third, unto the seventh.

²⁷ And last of all the woman died also.

²⁸ Therefore in the resurrection whose wife shall she be of the seven? for they all had her.

²⁹ Jesus answered and said unto them, Ye do err, not knowing the scriptures, nor the power of God.

³⁰ For in the resurrection they neither marry, nor are given in marriage, but are as the angels of God in heaven.

Matthew 24:34-37 - Angels of Heaven Do Not Know all that God Knows - Time of Jesus' Coming

³⁴ Verily I say unto you, This generation shall not pass, till all these things be fulfilled.

³⁵ Heaven and earth shall pass away, but my words shall not pass away.

³⁶ But of that day and hour knoweth no *man*, no, not the angels of heaven, but my Father only.

³⁷ But as the days of Noe *were*, so shall also the coming of the Son of man be.

Matthew 26:46-56 - Jesus Could Pray to God and God Would Send 12 Legions of Angels (72,000) to Save Him

⁴⁶ Rise, let us be going: behold, he is at hand that doth betray me.

⁴⁷ And while he yet spake, lo, Judas, one of the twelve, came, and with him a great multitude with swords and staves, from the chief priests and elders of the people.

⁴⁸ Now he that betrayed him gave them a sign, saying, Whomsoever I shall kiss, that same is he: hold him fast.

⁴⁹ And forthwith he came to Jesus, and said, Hail, master; and kissed him.

⁵⁰ And Jesus said unto him, Friend, wherefore art thou come? Then came they, and laid hands on Jesus, and took him.

⁵¹ And, behold, one of them which were with Jesus stretched out *his* hand, and drew his sword, and struck a servant of the high priest's, and smote off his ear.

⁵² Then said Jesus unto him, Put up again thy sword into his place: for all they that take the sword shall perish with the sword.

⁵³ Thinkest thou that I cannot now pray to my Father, and he shall presently give me more than twelve legions of <u>angels</u>?

⁵⁴ But how then shall the scriptures be fulfilled, that thus it must be?

⁵⁵ In that same hour said Jesus to the multitudes, Are ye come out as against a thief with swords and staves for to take me? I sat daily with you teaching in the temple, and ye laid no hold on me.

⁵⁶ But all this was done, that the scriptures of the prophets might be fulfilled. Then all the disciples forsook him, and fled.

Mark 12:18-25 - Angels Do Not Marry

¹⁸ Then come unto him the Sadducees, which say there is no resurrection; and they asked him, saying,

¹⁹ Master, Moses wrote unto us, If a man's brother die, and leave *his* wife *behind him*, and leave no children, that his brother should take his wife, and raise up seed unto his brother.

²⁰ Now there were seven brethren: and the first took a wife, and dying left no seed.

²¹ And the second took her, and died, neither left he any seed: and the third likewise.

²² And the seven had her, and left no seed: last of all the woman died also.

²³ In the resurrection therefore, when they shall rise, whose wife shall she be of them? for the seven had her to wife.

²⁴ And Jesus answering said unto them, Do ye not therefore err, because ye know not the scriptures, neither the power of God?

²⁵ For when they shall rise from the dead, they neither marry, nor are given in marriage; but are as the <u>angels</u> which are in heaven.

Mark 13:31-33 - Angels Do Not Know but God Knows the Time of Jesus' Coming

³¹ Heaven and earth shall pass away: but my words shall not pass away.

³² But of that day and *that* hour knoweth no man, no, not the <u>angels</u> which are in heaven, neither the Son, but the Father.

³³ Take ye heed, watch and pray: for ye know not when the time is.

Luke 9: 23-27 - Whosoever Shall be Ashamed of Me . . . of Him Shall the Son of Man be Ashamed When He Shall Come in His Own Glory and of the Holy Angels

²³ And he said to *them* all, If any *man* will come after me, let him deny himself, and take up his cross daily, and follow me.

²⁴ For whosoever will save his life shall lose it: but whosoever will lose his life for my sake, the same shall save it.

²⁵ For what is a man advantaged, if he gain the whole world, and lose himself, or be cast away?

²⁶ For whosoever shall be ashamed of me and of my words, of him shall the Son of man be ashamed, when he shall come in his own glory, and *in his* Father's, and of the holy <u>angels</u>.

²⁷ But I tell you of a truth, there be some standing here, which shall not taste of death, till they see the kingdom of God.

Luke 12:8-12 - Whosoever Confesses Me before Men, Him Shall the Son of Man Also Confess Before the Angels of God

⁸ Also I say unto you, Whosoever shall confess me before men, him shall the Son of man also confess before the <u>angels of God</u>:

⁹ But he that denieth me before men shall be denied before the <u>angels of God</u>.

¹⁰ And whosoever shall speak a word against the Son of man, it shall be forgiven him: but unto him that blasphemeth against the Holy Ghost it shall not be forgiven.

¹¹ And when they bring you unto the synagogues, and *unto* magistrates, and powers, take ye no thought how or what thing ye shall answer, or what ye shall say:

¹² For the Holy Ghost shall teach you in the same hour what ye ought to say.

Luke 15:1-10 - There is Joy in the Presence of the Angels of God Over One Sinner that Repents

¹ Then drew near unto him all the publicans and sinners for to hear him.

² And the Pharisees and scribes murmured, saying, This man receiveth sinners, and eateth with them.

³ And he spake this parable unto them, saying,

⁴ What man of you, having an hundred sheep, if he lose one of them, doth not leave the ninety and nine in the wilderness, and go after that which is lost, until he find it?

⁵ And when he hath found *it*, he layeth *it* on his shoulders, rejoicing.

⁶ And when he cometh home, he calleth together *his* friends and neighbours, saying unto them, Rejoice with me; for I have found my sheep which was lost.

⁷ I say unto you, that likewise joy shall be in heaven over one sinner that repenteth, more than over ninety and nine just persons, which need no repentance.

⁸ Either what woman having ten pieces of silver, if she lose one piece, doth not light a candle, and sweep the house, and seek diligently till she find *it*?

⁹ And when she hath found *it*, she calleth *her* friends and *her* neighbours together, saying, Rejoice with me; for I have found the piece which I had lost.

¹⁰ Likewise, I say unto you, there is joy in the presence of the <u>angels of God</u> over one sinner that repenteth.

Luke 16:14-31 - The Humble Beggar Lazarus Carried by the Angels into Abraham's Bosom

¹⁴ And the Pharisees also, who were covetous, heard all these things: and they derided him.

¹⁵ And he said unto them, Ye are they which justify yourselves before men; but God knoweth your hearts: for that which is highly esteemed among men is abomination in the sight of God.

¹⁶ The law and the prophets *were* until John: since that time the kingdom of God is preached, and every man presseth into it.

¹⁷ And it is easier for heaven and earth to pass, than one tittle of the law to fail.

¹⁸ Whosoever putteth away his wife, and marrieth another, committeth adultery: and whosoever marrieth her that is put away from *her* husband committeth adultery.

¹⁹ There was a certain rich man, which was clothed in purple and fine linen, and fared sumptuously every day:

²⁰ And there was a certain beggar named Lazarus, which was laid at his gate, full of sores,

²¹ And desiring to be fed with the crumbs which fell from the rich man's table: moreover the dogs came and licked his sores.

²² And it came to pass, that the beggar died, and was carried by the <u>angels</u> into Abraham's bosom: the rich man also died, and was buried;

²³ And in hell he lift up his eyes, being in torments, and seeth Abraham afar off, and Lazarus in his bosom.

²⁴ And he cried and said, Father Abraham, have mercy on me, and send Lazarus, that he may dip the tip of his finger in water, and cool my tongue; for I am tormented in this flame.

²⁵ But Abraham said, Son, remember that thou in thy lifetime receivedst thy good things, and likewise Lazarus evil things: but now he is comforted, and thou art tormented.

²⁶ And beside all this, between us and you there is a great gulf fixed: so that they which would pass from hence to you cannot; neither can they pass to us, that *would come* from thence.

²⁷ Then he said, I pray thee therefore, father, that thou wouldest send him to my father's house:

²⁸ For I have five brethren; that he may testify unto them, lest they also come into this place of torment.

²⁹ Abraham saith unto him, They have Moses and the prophets; let them hear them.

³⁰ And he said, Nay, father Abraham: but if one went unto them from the dead, they will repent.

³¹ And he said unto him, If they hear not Moses and the prophets, neither will they be persuaded, though one rose from the dead.

Luke 20:27-36 - Angels Do Not Marry

²⁷ Then came to *him* certain of the Sadducees, which deny that there is any resurrection; and they asked him,

[28] Saying, Master, Moses wrote unto us, If any man's brother die, having a wife, and he die without children, that his brother should take his wife, and raise up seed unto his brother.

[29] There were therefore seven brethren: and the first took a wife, and died without children.

[30] And the second took her to wife, and he died childless.

[31] And the third took her; and in like manner the seven also: and they left no children, and died.

[32] Last of all the woman died also.

[33] Therefore in the resurrection whose wife of them is she? for seven had her to wife.

[34] And Jesus answering said unto them, The children of this world marry, and are given in marriage:

[35] But they which shall be accounted worthy to obtain that world, and the resurrection from the dead, neither marry, nor are given in marriage:

[36] Neither can they die any more: for they are equal unto the angels; and are the children of God, being the children of the resurrection.

John 1:44-51 - Ye Shall See Heaven Open and the Angels of God Ascending and Descending upon the Son of Man

[44] Now Philip was of Bethsaida, the city of Andrew and Peter.

[45] Philip findeth Nathanael, and saith unto him, We have found him, of whom Moses in the law, and the prophets, did write, Jesus of Nazareth, the son of Joseph.

[46] And Nathanael said unto him, Can there any good thing come out of Nazareth? Philip saith unto him, Come and see.

[47] Jesus saw Nathanael coming to him, and saith of him, Behold an Israelite indeed, in whom is no guile!

⁴⁸ Nathanael saith unto him, Whence knowest thou me? Jesus answered and said unto him, Before that Philip called thee, when thou wast under the fig tree, I saw thee.

⁴⁹ Nathanael answered and saith unto him, Rabbi, thou art the Son of God; thou art the King of Israel.

⁵⁰ Jesus answered and said unto him, Because I said unto thee, I saw thee under the fig tree, believest thou? thou shalt see greater things than these.

⁵¹ And he saith unto him, Verily, verily, I say unto you, Hereafter ye shall see heaven open, and the <u>angels of God</u> ascending and descending upon the Son of man.

Acts of the Apostles, Paul's letters, the General Letters

Acts 5:12-29 - Angel of the Lord Frees the Apostles from Prison

¹² And by the hands of the apostles were many signs and wonders wrought among the people; (and they were all with one accord in Solomon's porch.

¹³ And of the rest durst no man join himself to them: but the people magnified them.

¹⁴ And believers were the more added to the Lord, multitudes both of men and women.)

¹⁵ Insomuch that they brought forth the sick into the streets, and laid *them* on beds and couches, that at the least the shadow of Peter passing by might overshadow some of them.

¹⁶ There came also a multitude *out* of the cities round about unto Jerusalem, bringing sick folks, and them which were vexed with unclean spirits: and they were healed every one.

¹⁷ Then the high priest rose up, and all they that were with him, (which is the sect of the Sadducees,) and were filled with indignation,

¹⁸ And laid their hands on the apostles, and put them in the common prison.

¹⁹ But the <u>angel of the Lord</u> by night opened the prison doors, and brought them forth, and said,

²⁰ Go, stand and speak in the temple to the people all the words of this life.

²¹ And when they heard *that*, they entered into the temple early in the morning, and taught. But the high priest came, and they that were with him, and called the council together, and all the senate of the children of Israel, and sent to the prison to have them brought.

²² But when the officers came, and found them not in the prison, they returned, and told,

²³ Saying, The prison truly found we shut with all safety, and the keepers standing without before the doors: but when we had opened, we found no man within.

²⁴ Now when the high priest and the captain of the temple and the chief priests heard these things, they doubted of them whereunto this would grow.

²⁵ Then came one and told them, saying, Behold, the men whom ye put in prison are standing in the temple, and teaching the people.

²⁶ Then went the captain with the officers, and brought them without violence: for they feared the people, lest they should have been stoned.

²⁷ And when they had brought them, they set *them* before the council: and the high priest asked them,

²⁸ Saying, Did not we straitly command you that ye should not teach in this name? and, behold, ye have filled Jerusalem with your doctrine, and intend to bring this man's blood upon us.

²⁹ Then Peter and the *other* apostles answered and said, We ought to obey God rather than men.

Acts 6:1-15 - Saw Stephen's Face as it Had Been the Face of an Angel

¹ And in those days, when the number of the disciples was multiplied, there arose a murmuring of the Grecians against the Hebrews, because their widows were neglected in the daily ministration.

² Then the twelve called the multitude of the disciples *unto them*, and said, It is not reason that we should leave the word of God, and serve tables.

³ Wherefore, brethren, look ye out among you seven men of honest report, full of the Holy Ghost and wisdom, whom we may appoint over this business.

⁴ But we will give ourselves continually to prayer, and to the ministry of the word.

⁵ And the saying pleased the whole multitude: and they chose Stephen, a man full of faith and of the Holy Ghost, and Philip, and Prochorus, and Nicanor, and Timon, and Parmenas, and Nicolas a proselyte of Antioch:

⁶ Whom they set before the apostles: and when they had prayed, they laid *their* hands on them.

⁷ And the word of God increased; and the number of the disciples multiplied in Jerusalem greatly; and a great company of the priests were obedient to the faith.

⁸ And Stephen, full of faith and power, did great wonders and miracles among the people.

⁹ Then there arose certain of the synagogue, which is called *the synagogue* of the Libertines, and Cyrenians, and Alexandrians, and of them of Cilicia and of Asia, disputing with Stephen.

¹⁰ And they were not able to resist the wisdom and the spirit by which he spake.

¹¹ Then they suborned men, which said, We have heard him speak blasphemous words against Moses, and *against* God.

¹² And they stirred up the people, and the elders, and the scribes, and came upon *him*, and caught him, and brought *him* to the council,

¹³ And set up false witnesses, which said, This man ceaseth not to speak blasphemous words against this holy place, and the law:

¹⁴ For we have heard him say, that this Jesus of Nazareth shall destroy this place, and shall change the customs which Moses delivered us.

¹⁵ And all that sat in the council, looking stedfastly on him, saw his face as it had been the face of an <u>angel</u>.

Acts 7:22-40 - Stephen's Defense Against Charges Recounting the Angel of the Lord in the Burning Bush Appearing to Moses and Spoke to Him on the Mount of Sinai

²² And Moses was learned in all the wisdom of the Egyptians, and was mighty in words and in deeds.

²³ And when he was full forty years old, it came into his heart to visit his brethren the children of Israel.

²⁴ And seeing one *of them* suffer wrong, he defended *him*, and avenged him that was oppressed, and smote the Egyptian:

²⁵ For he supposed his brethren would have understood how that God by his hand would deliver them: but they understood not.

²⁶ And the next day he shewed himself unto them as they strove, and would have set them at one again, saying, Sirs, ye are brethren; why do ye wrong one to another?

²⁷ But he that did his neighbour wrong thrust him away, saying, Who made thee a ruler and a judge over us?

²⁸ Wilt thou kill me, as thou diddest the Egyptian yesterday?

²⁹ Then fled Moses at this saying, and was a stranger in the land of Madian, where he begat two sons.

30 And when forty years were expired, there appeared to him in the wilderness of mount Sinai an <u>angel of the Lord</u> in a flame of fire in a bush.

31 When Moses saw *it*, he wondered at the sight: and as he drew near to behold *it*, the voice of the Lord came unto him,

32 *Saying*, I *am* the God of thy fathers, the God of Abraham, and the God of Isaac, and the God of Jacob. Then Moses trembled, and durst not behold.

33 Then said the Lord to him, Put off thy shoes from thy feet: for the place where thou standest is holy ground.

34 I have seen, I have seen the affliction of my people which is in Egypt, and I have heard their groaning, and am come down to deliver them. And now come, I will send thee into Egypt.

35 This Moses whom they refused, saying, Who made thee a ruler and a judge? the same did God send *to be* a ruler and a deliverer by the hand of the <u>angel</u> which appeared to him in the bush.

36 He brought them out, after that he had shewed wonders and signs in the land of Egypt, and in the Red sea, and in the wilderness forty years.

37 This is that Moses, which said unto the children of Israel, A prophet shall the Lord your God raise up unto you of your brethren, like unto me; him shall ye hear.

38 This is he, that was in the church in the wilderness with the <u>angel</u> which spake to him in the mount Sina, and *with* our fathers: who received the lively oracles to give unto us:

39 To whom our fathers would not obey, but thrust *him* from them, and in their hearts turned back again into Egypt,

40 Saying unto Aaron, Make us gods to go before us: for *as for* this Moses, which brought us out of the land of Egypt, we wot not what is become of him.

Acts 7:46-53 - Stephen Refers to Law Given by the Dispostion of Angels

[46] Who found favour before God, and desired to find a tabernacle for the God of Jacob.

[47] But Solomon built him an house.

[48] Howbeit the most High dwelleth not in temples made with hands; as saith the prophet,

[49] Heaven *is* my throne, and earth *is* my footstool: what house will ye build me? saith the Lord: or what *is* the place of my rest?

[50] Hath not my hand made all these things?

[51] Ye stiffnecked and uncircumcised in heart and ears, ye do always resist the Holy Ghost: as your fathers *did*, so *do* ye.

[52] Which of the prophets have not your fathers persecuted? and they have slain them which shewed before of the coming of the Just One; of whom ye have been now the betrayers and murderers:

[53] Who have received the law by the disposition of <u>angels</u>, and have not kept *it*.

Acts 8:25-39 - Angel of the Lord Instructs Philip to Meet Ethiopian Eunuch

[25] And they, when they had testified and preached the word of the Lord, returned to Jerusalem, and preached the gospel in many villages of the Samaritans.

[26] And the <u>angel of the Lord</u> spake unto Philip, saying, Arise, and go toward the south unto the way that goeth down from Jerusalem unto Gaza, which is desert.

[27] And he arose and went: and, behold, a man of Ethiopia, an eunuch of great authority under Candace queen of the Ethiopians, who had the charge of all her treasure, and had come to Jerusalem for to worship,

²⁸ Was returning, and sitting in his chariot read Esaias the prophet.

²⁹ Then the Spirit said unto Philip, Go near, and join thyself to this chariot.

³⁰ And Philip ran thither to *him*, and heard him read the prophet Esaias, and said, Understandest thou what thou readest?

³¹ And he said, How can I, except some man should guide me? And he desired Philip that he would come up and sit with him.

³² The place of the scripture which he read was this, He was led as a sheep to the slaughter; and like a lamb dumb before his shearer, so opened he not his mouth:

³³ In his humiliation his judgment was taken away: and who shall declare his generation? for his life is taken from the earth.

³⁴ And the eunuch answered Philip, and said, I pray thee, of whom speaketh the prophet this? of himself, or of some other man?

³⁵ Then Philip opened his mouth, and began at the same scripture, and preached unto him Jesus.

³⁶ And as they went on *their* way, they came unto a certain water: and the eunuch said, See, *here is* water; what doth hinder me to be baptized?

³⁷ And Philip said, If thou believest with all thine heart, thou mayest. And he answered and said, I believe that Jesus Christ is the Son of God.

³⁸ And he commanded the chariot to stand still: and they went down both into the water, both Philip and the eunuch; and he baptized him.

³⁹ And when they were come up out of the water, the Spirit of the Lord caught away Philip, that the eunuch saw him no more: and he went on his way rejoicing.

Acts 10:1-35 - Angel of God Came to Cornelius the Centurion to Send for Peter

[1] There was a certain man in Caesarea called Cornelius, a centurion of the band called the Italian *band*,

[2] *A* devout *man*, and one that feared God with all his house, which gave much alms to the people, and prayed to God alway.

[3] He saw in a vision evidently about the ninth hour of the day an <u>angel of God</u> coming in to him, and saying unto him, Cornelius.

[4] And when he looked on him, he was afraid, and said, What is it, Lord? And he said unto him, Thy prayers and thine alms are come up for a memorial before God.

[5] And now send men to Joppa, and call for *one* Simon, whose surname is Peter:

[6] He lodgeth with one Simon a tanner, whose house is by the sea side: he shall tell thee what thou oughtest to do.

[7] And when the <u>angel</u> which spake unto Cornelius was departed, he called two of his household servants, and a devout soldier of them that waited on him continually;

[8] And when he had declared all *these* things unto them, he sent them to Joppa.

[9] On the morrow, as they went on their journey, and drew nigh unto the city, Peter went up upon the housetop to pray about the sixth hour:

[10] And he became very hungry, and would have eaten: but while they made ready, he fell into a trance,

[11] And saw heaven opened, and a certain vessel descending unto him, as it had been a great sheet knit at the four corners, and let down to the earth:

[12] Wherein were all manner of fourfooted beasts of the earth, and wild beasts, and creeping things, and fowls of the air.

[13] And there came a voice to him, Rise, Peter; kill, and eat.

¹⁴ But Peter said, Not so, Lord; for I have never eaten any thing that is common or unclean.

¹⁵ And the voice *spake* unto him again the second time, What God hath cleansed, *that* call not thou common.

¹⁶ This was done thrice: and the vessel was received up again into heaven.

¹⁷ Now while Peter doubted in himself what this vision which he had seen should mean, behold, the men which were sent from Cornelius had made enquiry for Simon's house, and stood before the gate,

¹⁸ And called, and asked whether Simon, which was surnamed Peter, were lodged there.

¹⁹ While Peter thought on the vision, the Spirit said unto him, Behold, three men seek thee.

²⁰ Arise therefore, and get thee down, and go with them, doubting nothing: for I have sent them.

²¹ Then Peter went down to the men which were sent unto him from Cornelius; and said, Behold, I am he whom ye seek: what *is* the cause wherefore ye are come?

²² And they said, Cornelius the centurion, a just man, and one that feareth God, and of good report among all the nation of the Jews, was warned from God by an holy <u>angel</u> to send for thee into his house, and to hear words of thee.

²³ Then called he them in, and lodged *them*. And on the morrow Peter went away with them, and certain brethren from Joppa accompanied him.

²⁴ And the morrow after they entered into Caesarea. And Cornelius waited for them, and had called together his kinsmen and near friends.

²⁵ And as Peter was coming in, Cornelius met him, and fell down at his feet, and worshipped *him*.

²⁶ But Peter took him up, saying, Stand up; I myself also am a man.

²⁷ And as he talked with him, he went in, and found many that were come together.

²⁸ And he said unto them, Ye know how that it is an unlawful thing for a man that is a Jew to keep company, or come unto one of another nation; but God hath shewed me that I should not call any man common or unclean.

²⁹ Therefore came I *unto you* without gainsaying, as soon as I was sent for: I ask therefore for what intent ye have sent for me?

³⁰ And Cornelius said, Four days ago I was fasting until this hour; and at the ninth hour I prayed in my house, and, behold, a man stood before me in bright clothing,

³¹ And said, Cornelius, thy prayer is heard, and thine alms are had in remembrance in the sight of God.

³² Send therefore to Joppa, and call hither Simon, whose surname is Peter; he is lodged in the house of *one* Simon a tanner by the sea side: who, when he cometh, shall speak unto thee.

³³ Immediately therefore I sent to thee; and thou hast well done that thou art come. Now therefore are we all here present before God, to hear all things that are commanded thee of God.

³⁴ Then Peter opened *his* mouth, and said, Of a truth I perceive that God is no respecter of persons:

³⁵ But in every nation he that feareth him, and worketh righteousness, is accepted with him.

Acts 11:1-18 - Peter Repeats to the Apostles and Brethren his Story about Cornelius and Gentiles Granted Repentance unto Life

¹ And the apostles and brethren that were in Judaea heard that the Gentiles had also received the word of God.

² And when Peter was come up to Jerusalem, they that were of the circumcision contended with him,

³ Saying, Thou wentest in to men uncircumcised, and didst eat with them.

⁴ But Peter rehearsed *the matter* from the beginning, and expounded *it* by order unto them, saying,

⁵ I was in the city of Joppa praying: and in a trance I saw a vision, A certain vessel descend, as it had been a great sheet, let down from heaven by four corners; and it came even to me:

⁶ Upon the which when I had fastened mine eyes, I considered, and saw fourfooted beasts of the earth, and wild beasts, and creeping things, and fowls of the air.

⁷ And I heard a voice saying unto me, Arise, Peter; slay and eat.

⁸ But I said, Not so, Lord: for nothing common or unclean hath at any time entered into my mouth.

⁹ But the voice answered me again from heaven, What God hath cleansed, *that* call not thou common.

¹⁰ And this was done three times: and all were drawn up again into heaven.

¹¹ And, behold, immediately there were three men already come unto the house where I was, sent from Caesarea unto me.

¹² And the Spirit bade me go with them, nothing doubting. Moreover these six brethren accompanied me, and we entered into the man's house:

¹³ And he shewed us how he had seen an <u>angel</u> in his house, which stood and said unto him, Send men to Joppa, and call for Simon, whose surname is Peter;

¹⁴ Who shall tell thee words, whereby thou and all thy house shall be saved.

¹⁵ And as I began to speak, the Holy Ghost fell on them, as on us at the beginning.

¹⁶ Then remembered I the word of the Lord, how that he said, John indeed baptized with water; but ye shall be baptized with the Holy Ghost.

¹⁷ Forasmuch then as God gave them the like gift as *he did* unto us, who believed on the Lord Jesus Christ; what was I, that I could withstand God?

¹⁸ When they heard these things, they held their peace, and glorified God, saying, Then hath God also to the Gentiles granted repentance unto life.

Acts 12:1-25 - Peter being Rescued from Prison by the Angel of the Lord

¹ Now about that time Herod the king stretched forth *his* hands to vex certain of the church.

² And he killed James the brother of John with the sword.

³ And because he saw it pleased the Jews, he proceeded further to take Peter also. (Then were the days of unleavened bread.)

⁴ And when he had apprehended him, he put *him* in prison, and delivered *him* to four quaternions of soldiers to keep him; intending after Easter to bring him forth to the people.

⁵ Peter therefore was kept in prison: but prayer was made without ceasing of the church unto God for him.

⁶ And when Herod would have brought him forth, the same night Peter was sleeping between two soldiers, bound with two chains: and the keepers before the door kept the prison.

⁷ And, behold, the angel of the Lord came upon *him*, and a light shined in the prison: and he smote Peter on the side, and raised him up, saying, Arise up quickly. And his chains fell off from *his* hands.

⁸ And the angel said unto him, Gird thyself, and bind on thy sandals. And so he did. And he saith unto him, Cast thy garment about thee, and follow me.

⁹ And he went out, and followed him; and wist not that it was true which was done by the angel; but thought he saw a vision.

¹⁰ When they were past the first and the second ward, they came unto the iron gate that leadeth unto the city; which opened to them of his own accord: and they went out, and passed on through one street; and forthwith the <u>angel</u> departed from him.

¹¹ And when Peter was come to himself, he said, Now I know of a surety, that the Lord hath sent his <u>angel</u>, and hath delivered me out of the hand of Herod, and *from* all the expectation of the people of the Jews.

¹² And when he had considered *the thing*, he came to the house of Mary the mother of John, whose surname was Mark; where many were gathered together praying.

¹³ And as Peter knocked at the door of the gate, a damsel came to hearken, named Rhoda.

¹⁴ And when she knew Peter's voice, she opened not the gate for gladness, but ran in, and told how Peter stood before the gate.

¹⁵ And they said unto her, Thou art mad. But she constantly affirmed that it was even so. Then said they, It is his <u>angel</u>.

¹⁶ But Peter continued knocking: and when they had opened *the door*, and saw him, they were astonished.

¹⁷ But he, beckoning unto them with the hand to hold their peace, declared unto them how the Lord had brought him out of the prison. And he said, Go shew these things unto James, and to the brethren. And he departed, and went into another place.

¹⁸ Now as soon as it was day, there was no small stir among the soldiers, what was become of Peter.

¹⁹ And when Herod had sought for him, and found him not, he examined the keepers, and commanded that *they* should be put to death. And he went down from Judaea to Caesarea, and *there* abode.

²⁰ And Herod was highly displeased with them of Tyre and Sidon: but they came with one accord to him, and, having made Blastus the king's chamberlain their friend, desired peace; because their country was nourished by the king's *country*.

[21] And upon a set day Herod, arrayed in royal apparel, sat upon his throne, and made an oration unto them.

[22] And the people gave a shout, *saying, It is* the voice of a god, and not of a man.

[23] And immediately the <u>angel of the Lord</u> smote him, because he gave not God the glory: and he was eaten of worms, and gave up the ghost.

[24] But the word of God grew and multiplied.

[25] And Barnabas and Saul returned from Jerusalem, when they had fulfilled *their* ministry, and took with them John, whose surname was Mark.

Acts 23:1-11 - Paul being Questioned by Pharisees and Sadducees; Sadducees say that there are No Angels and Pharisees Defend Paul and say there are Angels

[1] And Paul, earnestly beholding the council, said, Men *and* brethren, I have lived in all good conscience before God until this day.

[2] And the high priest Ananias commanded them that stood by him to smite him on the mouth.

[3] Then said Paul unto him, God shall smite thee, *thou* whited wall: for sittest thou to judge me after the law, and commandest me to be smitten contrary to the law?

[4] And they that stood by said, Revilest thou God's high priest?

[5] Then said Paul, I wist not, brethren, that he was the high priest: for it is written, Thou shalt not speak evil of the ruler of thy people.

[6] But when Paul perceived that the one part were Sadducees, and the other Pharisees, he cried out in the council, Men *and* brethren, I am a Pharisee, the son of a Pharisee: of the hope and resurrection of the dead I am called in question.

[7] And when he had so said, there arose a dissension between the Pharisees and the Sadducees: and the multitude was divided.

⁸ For the Sadducees say that there is no resurrection, neither <u>angel</u>, nor spirit: but the Pharisees confess both.

⁹ And there arose a great cry: and the scribes *that were* of the Pharisees' part arose, and strove, saying, We find no evil in this man: but if a spirit or an <u>angel</u> hath spoken to him, let us not fight against God.

¹⁰ And when there arose a great dissension, the chief captain, fearing lest Paul should have been pulled in pieces of them, commanded the soldiers to go down, and to take him by force from among them, and to bring *him* into the castle.

¹¹ And the night following the Lord stood by him, and said, Be of good cheer, Paul: for as thou hast testified of me in Jerusalem, so must thou bear witness also at Rome.

Acts 27:1-44 - Paul Being Told by Angel of God that Ship would be Lost but No Loss of Life

¹ And when it was determined that we should sail into Italy, they delivered Paul and certain other prisoners unto *one* named Julius, a centurion of Augustus' band.

² And entering into a ship of Adramyttium, we launched, meaning to sail by the coasts of Asia; *one* Aristarchus, a Macedonian of Thessalonica, being with us.

³ And the next *day* we touched at Sidon. And Julius courteously entreated Paul, and gave *him* liberty to go unto his friends to refresh himself.

⁴ And when we had launched from thence, we sailed under Cyprus, because the winds were contrary.

⁵ And when we had sailed over the sea of Cilicia and Pamphylia, we came to Myra, *a city* of Lycia.

⁶ And there the centurion found a ship of Alexandria sailing into Italy; and he put us therein.

⁷ And when we had sailed slowly many days, and scarce were come over against Cnidus, the wind not suffering us, we sailed under Crete, over against Salmone;

⁸ And, hardly passing it, came unto a place which is called The fair havens; nigh whereunto was the city *of* Lasea.

⁹ Now when much time was spent, and when sailing was now dangerous, because the fast was now already past, Paul admonished *them*,

¹⁰ And said unto them, Sirs, I perceive that this voyage will be with hurt and much damage, not only of the lading and ship, but also of our lives.

¹¹ Nevertheless the centurion believed the master and the owner of the ship, more than those things which were spoken by Paul.

¹² And because the haven was not commodious to winter in, the more part advised to depart thence also, if by any means they might attain to Phenice, *and there* to winter; *which is* an haven of Crete, and lieth toward the south west and north west.

¹³ And when the south wind blew softly, supposing that they had obtained *their* purpose, loosing *thence*, they sailed close by Crete.

¹⁴ But not long after there arose against it a tempestuous wind, called Euroclydon.

¹⁵ And when the ship was caught, and could not bear up into the wind, we let *her* drive.

¹⁶ And running under a certain island which is called Clauda, we had much work to come by the boat:

¹⁷ Which when they had taken up, they used helps, undergirding the ship; and, fearing lest they should fall into the quicksands, strake sail, and so were driven.

¹⁸ And we being exceedingly tossed with a tempest, the next *day* they lightened the ship;

¹⁹ And the third *day* we cast out with our own hands the tackling of the ship.

²⁰ And when neither sun nor stars in many days appeared, and no small tempest lay on *us*, all hope that we should be saved was then taken away.

²¹ But after long abstinence Paul stood forth in the midst of them, and said, Sirs, ye should have hearkened unto me, and not have loosed from Crete, and to have gained this harm and loss.

²² And now I exhort you to be of good cheer: for there shall be no loss of *any man's* life among you, but of the ship.

²³ For there stood by me this night the angel of God, whose I am, and whom I serve,

²⁴ Saying, Fear not, Paul; thou must be brought before Caesar: and, lo, God hath given thee all them that sail with thee.

²⁵ Wherefore, sirs, be of good cheer: for I believe God, that it shall be even as it was told me.

²⁶ Howbeit we must be cast upon a certain island.

²⁷ But when the fourteenth night was come, as we were driven up and down in Adria, about midnight the shipmen deemed that they drew near to some country;

²⁸ And sounded, and found *it* twenty fathoms: and when they had gone a little further, they sounded again, and found *it* fifteen fathoms.

²⁹ Then fearing lest we should have fallen upon rocks, they cast four anchors out of the stern, and wished for the day.

³⁰ And as the shipmen were about to flee out of the ship, when they had let down the boat into the sea, under colour as though they would have cast anchors out of the foreship,

³¹ Paul said to the centurion and to the soldiers, Except these abide in the ship, ye cannot be saved.

³² Then the soldiers cut off the ropes of the boat, and let her fall off.

³³ And while the day was coming on, Paul besought *them* all to take meat, saying, This day is the fourteenth day that ye have tarried and continued fasting, having taken nothing.

³⁴ Wherefore I pray you to take *some* meat: for this is for your health: for there shall not an hair fall from the head of any of you.

³⁵ And when he had thus spoken, he took bread, and gave thanks to God in presence of them all: and when he had broken *it*, he began to eat.

³⁶ Then were they all of good cheer, and they also took *some* meat.

³⁷ And we were in all in the ship two hundred threescore and sixteen souls.

³⁸ And when they had eaten enough, they lightened the ship, and cast out the wheat into the sea.

³⁹ And when it was day, they knew not the land: but they discovered a certain creek with a shore, into the which they were minded, if it were possible, to thrust in the ship.

⁴⁰ And when they had taken up the anchors, they committed *themselves* unto the sea, and loosed the rudder bands, and hoised up the mainsail to the wind, and made toward shore.

⁴¹ And falling into a place where two seas met, they ran the ship aground; and the forepart stuck fast, and remained unmoveable, but the hinder part was broken with the violence of the waves.

⁴² And the soldiers' counsel was to kill the prisoners, lest any of them should swim out, and escape.

⁴³ But the centurion, willing to save Paul, kept them from *their* purpose; and commanded that they which could swim should cast *themselves* first *into the sea*, and get to land:

⁴⁴ And the rest, some on boards, and some on *broken pieces* of the ship. And so it came to pass, that they escaped all safe to land.

Romans 8:35-39 - Paul Asking who shall Separate them from the Love of Christ? Not Angels

³⁵ Who shall separate us from the love of Christ? *shall* tribulation, or distress, or persecution, or famine, or nakedness, or peril, or sword?

³⁶ As it is written, For thy sake we are killed all the day long; we are accounted as sheep for the slaughter.

³⁷ Nay, in all these things we are more than conquerors through him that loved us.

³⁸ For I am persuaded, that neither death, nor life, nor <u>angels</u>, nor principalities, nor powers, nor things present, nor things to come,

³⁹ Nor height, nor depth, nor any other creature, shall be able to separate us from the love of God, which is in Christ Jesus our Lord.

1 Corinthians 4:4-10 - Paul Saying how Apostles are made Spectacles unto the World and to the Angels

⁴ For I know nothing by myself; yet am I not hereby justified: but he that judgeth me is the Lord.

⁵ Therefore judge nothing before the time, until the Lord come, who both will bring to light the hidden things of darkness, and will make manifest the counsels of the hearts: and then shall every man have praise of God.

⁶ And these things, brethren, I have in a figure transferred to myself and *to* Apollos for your sakes; that ye might learn in us not to think *of men* above that which is written, that no one of you be puffed up for one against another.

⁷ For who maketh thee to differ *from another*? and what hast thou that thou didst not receive? now if thou didst receive *it*, why dost thou glory, as if thou hadst not received *it*?

⁸ Now ye are full, now ye are rich, ye have reigned as kings without us: and I would to God ye did reign, that we also might reign with you.

⁹ For I think that God hath set forth us the apostles last, as it were appointed to death: for we are made a spectacle unto the world, and to <u>angels</u>, and to men.

¹⁰ We *are* fools for Christ's sake, but ye *are* wise in Christ; we *are* weak, but ye *are* strong; ye *are* honourable, but we *are* despised.

1 Corinthians 6:1-8 - Paul Warns to not Judge and Telling Apostles that They shall not Judge Angels

[1] Dare any of you, having a matter against another, go to law before the unjust, and not before the saints?

[2] Do ye not know that the saints shall judge the world? and if the world shall be judged by you, are ye unworthy to judge the smallest matters?

[3] Know ye not that we shall judge <u>angels</u>? how much more things that pertain to this life?

[4] If then ye have judgments of things pertaining to this life, set them to judge who are least esteemed in the church.

[5] I speak to your shame. Is it so, that there is not a wise man among you? no, not one that shall be able to judge between his brethren?

[6] But brother goeth to law with brother, and that before the unbelievers.

[7] Now therefore there is utterly a fault among you, because ye go to law one with another. Why do ye not rather take wrong? why do ye not rather *suffer yourselves to* be defrauded?

[8] Nay, ye do wrong, and defraud, and that *your* brethren.

1 Corinthians 11:1-16 - Paul Instructs Women Covering their Heads while Praying and Prophesying because of the Angels

[1] Be ye followers of me, even as I also *am* of Christ.

[2] Now I praise you, brethren, that ye remember me in all things, and keep the ordinances, as I delivered *them* to you.

[3] But I would have you know, that the head of every man is Christ; and the head of the woman *is* the man; and the head of Christ *is* God.

[4] Every man praying or prophesying, having *his* head covered, dishonoureth his head.

⁵ But every woman that prayeth or prophesieth with *her* head uncovered dishonoureth her head: for that is even all one as if she were shaven.

⁶ For if the woman be not covered, let her also be shorn: but if it be a shame for a woman to be shorn or shaven, let her be covered.

⁷ For a man indeed ought not to cover *his* head, forasmuch as he is the image and glory of God: but the woman is the glory of the man.

⁸ For the man is not of the woman; but the woman of the man.

⁹ Neither was the man created for the woman; but the woman for the man.

¹⁰ For this cause ought the woman to have power on *her* head because of the angels.

¹¹ Nevertheless neither is the man without the woman, neither the woman without the man, in the Lord.

¹² For as the woman *is* of the man, even so *is* the man also by the woman; but all things of God.

¹³ Judge in yourselves: is it comely that a woman pray unto God uncovered?

¹⁴ Doth not even nature itself teach you, that, if a man have long hair, it is a shame unto him?

¹⁵ But if a woman have long hair, it is a glory to her: for *her* hair is given her for a covering.

¹⁶ But if any man seem to be contentious, we have no such custom, neither the churches of God.

1 Corinthians 13:1-3 - Speaking with the Tongues of Angels

¹ Though I speak with the tongues of men and of angels, and have not charity, I am become *as* sounding brass, or a tinkling cymbal.

² And though I have *the gift of* prophecy, and understand all mysteries, and all knowledge; and though I have all faith, so that I could remove mountains, and have not charity, I am nothing.

³ And though I bestow all my goods to feed *the poor*, and though I give my body to be burned, and have not charity, it profiteth me nothing.

2 Corinthians 11:1-15 - Satan being Transformed into an Angel of Light

¹ Would to God ye could bear with me a little in *my* folly: and indeed bear with me.

² For I am jealous over you with godly jealousy: for I have espoused you to one husband, that I may present *you as* a chaste virgin to Christ.

³ But I fear, lest by any means, as the serpent beguiled Eve through his subtilty, so your minds should be corrupted from the simplicity that is in Christ.

⁴ For if he that cometh preacheth another Jesus, whom we have not preached, or *if* ye receive another spirit, which ye have not received, or another gospel, which ye have not accepted, ye might well bear with *him*.

⁵ For I suppose I was not a whit behind the very chiefest apostles.

⁶ But though *I be* rude in speech, yet not in knowledge; but we have been throughly made manifest among you in all things.

⁷ Have I committed an offence in abasing myself that ye might be exalted, because I have preached to you the gospel of God freely?

⁸ I robbed other churches, taking wages *of them*, to do you service.

⁹ And when I was present with you, and wanted, I was chargeable to no man: for that which was lacking to me the brethren which came from Macedonia supplied: and in all *things* I have kept myself from being burdensome unto you, and *so* will I keep *myself*.

[10] As the truth of Christ is in me, no man shall stop me of this boasting in the regions of Achaia.

[11] Wherefore? because I love you not? God knoweth.

[12] But what I do, that I will do, that I may cut off occasion from them which desire occasion; that wherein they glory, they may be found even as we.

[13] For such *are* false apostles, deceitful workers, transforming themselves into the apostles of Christ.

[14] And no marvel; for Satan himself is transformed into an <u>angel</u> of light.

[15] Therefore *it is* no great thing if his ministers also be transformed as the ministers of righteousness; whose end shall be according to their works.

Galatians 1:1-8 - Paul Instructing the Church that we or an Angel Preach any Other Gospel, let Him be Accursed

[1] Paul, an apostle, (not of men, neither by man, but by Jesus Christ, and God the Father, who raised him from the dead;)

[2] And all the brethren which are with me, unto the churches of Galatia:

[3] Grace *be* to you and peace from God the Father, and *from* our Lord Jesus Christ,

[4] Who gave himself for our sins, that he might deliver us from this present evil world, according to the will of God and our Father:

[5] To whom *be* glory for ever and ever. Amen.

[6] I marvel that ye are so soon removed from him that called you into the grace of Christ unto another gospel:

[7] Which is not another; but there be some that trouble you, and would pervert the gospel of Christ.

⁸ But though we, or an <u>angel</u> from heaven, preach any other gospel unto you than that which we have preached unto you, let him be accursed.

Galatians 3:18-20 - Paul Speaking of the Law Being Ordained by Angels in the Hand of a Mediator

¹⁸ For if the inheritance *be* of the law, *it is* no more of promise: but God gave *it* to Abraham by promise.

¹⁹ Wherefore then *serveth* the law? It was added because of transgressions, till the seed should come to whom the promise was made; *and it was* ordained by <u>angels</u> in the hand of a mediator.

²⁰ Now a mediator is not *a mediator* of one, but God is one.

Galatians 4:6-14 - Paul is Received as an Angel of God

⁶ And because ye are sons, God hath sent forth the Spirit of his Son into your hearts, crying, Abba, Father.

⁷ Wherefore thou art no more a servant, but a son; and if a son, then an heir of God through Christ.

⁸ Howbeit then, when ye knew not God, ye did service unto them which by nature are no gods.

⁹ But now, after that ye have known God, or rather are known of God, how turn ye again to the weak and beggarly elements, whereunto ye desire again to be in bondage?

¹⁰ Ye observe days, and months, and times, and years.

¹¹ I am afraid of you, lest I have bestowed upon you labour in vain.

¹² Brethren, I beseech you, be as I *am*; for I *am* as ye *are*: ye have not injured me at all.

¹³ Ye know how through infirmity of the flesh I preached the gospel unto you at the first.

[14] And my temptation which was in my flesh ye despised not, nor rejected; but received me as an <u>angel of God</u>, *even* as Christ Jesus.

Colossians 2:16-19 - Paul Warning to Let no Man Begile You of Your Reward in the Worshipping of Angels

[16] Let no man therefore judge you in meat, or in drink, or in respect of an holyday, or of the new moon, or of the sabbath *days*:

[17] Which are a shadow of things to come; but the body *is* of Christ.

[18] Let no man beguile you of your reward in a voluntary humility and worshipping of <u>angels</u>, intruding into those things which he hath not seen, vainly puffed up by his fleshly mind,

[19] And not holding the Head, from which all the body by joints and bands having nourishment ministered, and knit together, increaseth with the increase of God.

2 Thessalonians 1:3-10 - When Jesus Shall be Revealed from Heaven with His Mighty Angels

[3] We are bound to thank God always for you, brethren, as it is meet, because that your faith grows exceedingly, and the charity of every one of you all toward each other abounds;

[4] So that we ourselves glory in you in the churches of God for your patience and faith in all your persecutions and tribulations that ye endure:

[5] *Which is* a manifest token of the righteous judgment of God, that ye may be counted worthy of the kingdom of God, for which ye also suffer:

[6] Seeing *it is* a righteous thing with God to recompense tribulation to them the Lord that trouble you;

[7] And to you who are troubled rest with us, when the Lord Jesus shall be revealed from heaven with his mighty <u>angels</u>,

⁸ In flaming fire taking vengeance on them that know not God, and that obey not the gospel of our Lord Jesus Christ:

⁹ Who shall be punished with everlasting destruction from the presence of the Lord, and from the glory of his power;

¹⁰ When he shall come to be glorified in his saints, and to be admired in all them that believe (because our testimony among you was believed) in that day.

1 Timothy 5:17-25 - Paul Charging Timothy to Carry out his Instructions by Jesus Christ and the Elect Angels

¹⁷ Let the elders that rule well be counted worthy of double honour, especially they who labour in the word and doctrine.

¹⁸ For the scripture saith, Thou shalt not muzzle the ox that treadeth out the corn. And, the labourer *is* worthy of his reward.

¹⁹ Against an elder receive not an accusation, but before two or three witnesses.

²⁰ Them that sin rebuke before all, that others also may fear.

²¹ I charge *thee* before God, and the Lord Jesus Christ, and the elect angels, that thou observe these things without preferring one before another, doing nothing by partiality.

²² Lay hands suddenly on no man, neither be partaker of other men's sins: keep thyself pure.

²³ Drink no longer water, but use a little wine for thy stomach's sake and thine often infirmities.

²⁴ Some men's sins are open beforehand, going before to judgment; and some *men* they follow after.

²⁵ Likewise also the good works *of some* are manifest beforehand; and they that are otherwise cannot be hid.

Hebrews 1:1-14 - Jesus Made Better than Angels, Let All the Angels of God Worship Him and Sit on Right Hand of God and Ministering Spirits of the Heirs of Salvation

¹ God, who at sundry times and in divers manners spake in time past unto the fathers by the prophets,

² Hath in these last days spoken unto us by *his* Son, whom he hath appointed heir of all things, by whom also he made the worlds;

³ Who being the brightness of *his* glory, and the express image of his person, and upholding all things by the word of his power, when he had by himself purged our sins, sat down on the right hand of the Majesty on high;

⁴ Being made so much better than the <u>angels</u>, as he hath by inheritance obtained a more excellent name than they.

⁵ For unto which of the <u>angels</u> said he at any time, Thou art my Son, this day have I begotten thee? And again, I will be to him a Father, and he shall be to me a Son?

⁶ And again, when he bringeth in the firstbegotten into the world, he saith, And let all the <u>angels of God</u> worship him.

⁷ And of the <u>angels</u> he saith, Who maketh his <u>angels</u> spirits, and his ministers a flame of fire.

⁸ But unto the Son *he saith*, Thy throne, O God, *is* for ever and ever: a sceptre of righteousness *is* the sceptre of thy kingdom.

⁹ Thou hast loved righteousness, and hated iniquity; therefore God, *even* thy God, hath anointed thee with the oil of gladness above thy fellows.

¹⁰ And, Thou, Lord, in the beginning hast laid the foundation of the earth; and the heavens are the works of thine hands:

¹¹ They shall perish; but thou remainest; and they all shall wax old as doth a garment;

¹² And as a vesture shalt thou fold them up, and they shall be changed: but thou art the same, and thy years shall not fail.

¹³ But to which of the angels said he at any time, Sit on my right hand, until I make thine enemies thy footstool?

¹⁴ Are they not all ministering spirits, sent forth to minister for them who shall be heirs of salvation?

Hebrews 2:1-18 - Word Spoken by Angels and Made Him a Little Lower than the Angels

¹ Therefore we ought to give the more earnest heed to the things which we have heard, lest at any time we should let *them* slip.

² For if the word spoken by angels was stedfast, and every transgression and disobedience received a just recompence of reward;

³ How shall we escape, if we neglect so great salvation; which at the first began to be spoken by the Lord, and was confirmed unto us by them that heard *him*;

⁴ God also bearing *them* witness, both with signs and wonders, and with divers miracles, and gifts of the Holy Ghost, according to his own will?

⁵ For unto the angels hath he not put in subjection the world to come, whereof we speak.

⁶ But one in a certain place testified, saying, What is man, that thou art mindful of him? or the son of man, that thou visitest him?

⁷ Thou madest him a little lower than the angels; thou crownedst him with glory and honour, and didst set him over the works of thy hands:

⁸ Thou hast put all things in subjection under his feet. For in that he put all in subjection under him, he left nothing *that is* not put under him. But now we see not yet all things put under him.

⁹ But we see Jesus, who was made a little lower than the angels for the suffering of death, crowned with glory and honour; that he by the grace of God should taste death for every man.

¹⁰ For it became him, for whom *are* all things, and by whom *are* all things, in bringing many sons unto glory, to make the captain of their salvation perfect through sufferings.

¹¹ For both he that sanctifieth and they who are sanctified *are* all of one: for which cause he is not ashamed to call them brethren,

¹² Saying, I will declare thy name unto my brethren, in the midst of the church will I sing praise unto thee.

¹³ And again, I will put my trust in him. And again, Behold I and the children which God hath given me.

¹⁴ Forasmuch then as the children are partakers of flesh and blood, he also himself likewise took part of the same; that through death he might destroy him that had the power of death, that is, the devil;

¹⁵ And deliver them who through fear of death were all their lifetime subject to bondage.

¹⁶ For verily he took not on *him the nature of* <u>angels</u>; but he took on *him* the seed of Abraham.

¹⁷ Wherefore in all things it behoved him to be made like unto *his* brethren, that he might be a merciful and faithful high priest in things *pertaining* to God, to make reconciliation for the sins of the people.

¹⁸ For in that he himself hath suffered being tempted, he is able to succour them that are tempted.

Hebrews 12:18-24 - Innumerable Company of Angels in Heaven

¹⁸ For ye are not come unto the mount that might be touched, and that burned with fire, nor unto blackness, and darkness, and tempest,

¹⁹ And the sound of a trumpet, and the voice of words; which *voice* they that heard intreated that the word should not be spoken to them any more:

²⁰ (For they could not endure that which was commanded, And if so much as a beast touch the mountain, it shall be stoned, or thrust through with a dart:

²¹ And so terrible was the sight, *that* Moses said, I exceedingly fear and quake:)

²² But ye are come unto mount Sion, and unto the city of the living God, the heavenly Jerusalem, and to an innumerable company of angels,

²³ To the general assembly and church of the firstborn, which are written in heaven, and to God the Judge of all, and to the spirits of just men made perfect,

²⁴ And to Jesus the mediator of the new covenant, and to the blood of sprinkling, that speaketh better things than *that of* Abel.

Hebrews 13:1-2 - Entertain Strangers, Unwittingly Entertain Angels

¹ Let brotherly love continue.

² Be not forgetful to entertain strangers: for thereby some have entertained angels unawares.

1 Peter 1:1-12 - Angels Desire to Look into those Things Preached

¹ Peter, an apostle of Jesus Christ, to the strangers scattered throughout Pontus, Galatia, Cappadocia, Asia, and Bithynia,

² Elect according to the foreknowledge of God the Father, through sanctification of the Spirit, unto obedience and sprinkling of the blood of Jesus Christ: Grace unto you, and peace, be multiplied.

³ Blessed *be* the God and Father of our Lord Jesus Christ, which according to his abundant mercy hath begotten us again unto a lively hope by the resurrection of Jesus Christ from the dead,

⁴ To an inheritance incorruptible, and undefiled, and that fadeth not away, reserved in heaven for you,

⁵ Who are kept by the power of God through faith unto salvation ready to be revealed in the last time.

⁶ Wherein ye greatly rejoice, though now for a season, if need be, ye are in heaviness through manifold temptations:

⁷ That the trial of your faith, being much more precious than of gold that perisheth, though it be tried with fire, might be found unto praise and honour and glory at the appearing of Jesus Christ:

⁸ Whom having not seen, ye love; in whom, though now ye see *him* not, yet believing, ye rejoice with joy unspeakable and full of glory:

⁹ Receiving the end of your faith, *even* the salvation of *your* souls.

¹⁰ Of which salvation the prophets have enquired and searched diligently, who prophesied of the grace *that should come* unto you:

¹¹ Searching what, or what manner of time the Spirit of Christ which was in them did signify, when it testified beforehand the sufferings of Christ, and the glory that should follow.

¹² Unto whom it was revealed, that not unto themselves, but unto us they did minister the things, which are now reported unto you by them that have preached the gospel unto you with the Holy Ghost sent down from heaven; which things the <u>angels</u> desire to look into.

1 Peter 3:18-22 - Angels Subject to Jesus Christ

¹⁸ For Christ also hath once suffered for sins, the just for the unjust, that he might bring us to God, being put to death in the flesh, but quickened by the Spirit:

¹⁹ By which also he went and preached unto the spirits in prison;

²⁰ Which sometime were disobedient, when once the longsuffering of God waited in the days of Noah, while the ark was a preparing, wherein few, that is, eight souls were saved by water.

²¹ The like figure whereunto *even* baptism doth also now save us (not the putting away of the filth of the flesh, but the answer of a good conscience toward God,) by the resurrection of Jesus Christ:

²² Who is gone into heaven, and is on the right hand of God; <u>angels</u> and authorities and powers being made subject unto him.

2 Peter 2:1-10 - God not Sparing Punishment on the Angels who Sinned

¹ But there were false prophets also among the people, even as there shall be false teachers among you, who privily shall bring in damnable heresies, even denying the Lord that bought them, and bring upon themselves swift destruction.

² And many shall follow their pernicious ways; by reason of whom the way of truth shall be evil spoken of.

³ And through covetousness shall they with feigned words make merchandise of you: whose judgment now of a long time lingereth not, and their damnation slumbereth not.

⁴ For if God spared not the <u>angels</u> that sinned, but cast *them* down to hell, and delivered *them* into chains of darkness, to be reserved unto judgment;

⁵ And spared not the old world, but saved Noah the eighth *person*, a preacher of righteousness, bringing in the flood upon the world of the ungodly;

⁶ And turning the cities of Sodom and Gomorrha into ashes condemned *them* with an overthrow, making *them* an ensample unto those that after should live ungodly;

⁷ And delivered just Lot, vexed with the filthy conversation of the wicked:

⁸ (For that righteous man dwelling among them, in seeing and hearing, vexed *his* righteous soul from day to day with *their* unlawful deeds;)

⁹ The Lord knoweth how to deliver the godly out of temptations, and to reserve the unjust unto the day of judgment to be punished:

¹⁰ But chiefly them that walk after the flesh in the lust of uncleanness, and despise government. Presumptuous *are they*, selfwilled, they are not afraid to speak evil of dignities.

Jude 1:1-6 - Angels who did not Keep their Proper Domain

¹ Jude, the servant of Jesus Christ, and brother of James, to them that are sanctified by God the Father, and preserved in Jesus Christ, *and* called:

² Mercy unto you, and peace, and love, be multiplied.

³ Beloved, when I gave all diligence to write unto you of the common salvation, it was needful for me to write unto you, and exhort *you* that ye should earnestly contend for the faith which was once delivered unto the saints.

⁴ For there are certain men crept in unawares, who were before of old ordained to this condemnation, ungodly men, turning the grace of our God into lasciviousness, and denying the only Lord God, and our Lord Jesus Christ.

⁵ I will therefore put you in remembrance, though ye once knew this, how that the Lord, having saved the people out of the land of Egypt, afterward destroyed them that believed not.

⁶ And the <u>angels</u> which kept not their first estate, but left their own habitation, he hath reserved in everlasting chains under darkness unto the judgment of the great day.

The Book of Revelation and the Angels

Revelation 1:1-20 - Jesus Christ Sent and Signified Angel with this Revelation - Seven Stars are Seven Angels of the Seven Churches and Seven Candlesticks are the Seven Churches

[1] The Revelation of Jesus Christ, which God gave unto him, to shew unto his servants things which must shortly come to pass; and he sent and signified *it* by his <u>angel</u> unto his servant John:

[2] Who bare record of the word of God, and of the testimony of Jesus Christ, and of all things that he saw.

[3] Blessed *is* he that readeth, and they that hear the words of this prophecy, and keep those things which are written therein: for the time *is* at hand.

[4] John to the seven churches which are in Asia: Grace *be* unto you, and peace, from him which is, and which was, and which is to come; and from the seven Spirits which are before his throne;

[5] And from Jesus Christ, *who is* the faithful witness, *and* the first begotten of the dead, and the prince of the kings of the earth. Unto him that loved us, and washed us from our sins in his own blood,

[6] And hath made us kings and priests unto God and his Father; to him *be* glory and dominion for ever and ever. Amen.

[7] Behold, he cometh with clouds; and every eye shall see him, and they *also* which pierced him: and all kindreds of the earth shall wail because of him. Even so, Amen.

[8] I am Alpha and Omega, the beginning and the ending, saith the Lord, which is, and which was, and which is to come, the Almighty.

[9] I John, who also am your brother, and companion in tribulation, and in the kingdom and patience of Jesus Christ, was in the isle that is called Patmos, for the word of God, and for the testimony of Jesus Christ.

¹⁰ I was in the Spirit on the Lord's day, and heard behind me a great voice, as of a trumpet,

¹¹ Saying, I am Alpha and Omega, the first and the last: and, What thou seest, write in a book, and send *it* unto the seven churches which are in Asia; unto Ephesus, and unto Smyrna, and unto Pergamos, and unto Thyatira, and unto Sardis, and unto Philadelphia, and unto Laodicea.

¹² And I turned to see the voice that spake with me. And being turned, I saw seven golden candlesticks;

¹³ And in the midst of the seven candlesticks *one* like unto the Son of man, clothed with a garment down to the foot, and girt about the paps with a golden girdle.

¹⁴ His head and *his* hairs *were* white like wool, as white as snow; and his eyes *were* as a flame of fire;

¹⁵ And his feet like unto fine brass, as if they burned in a furnace; and his voice as the sound of many waters.

¹⁶ And he had in his right hand seven stars: and out of his mouth went a sharp twoedged sword: and his countenance *was* as the sun shineth in his strength.

¹⁷ And when I saw him, I fell at his feet as dead. And he laid his right hand upon me, saying unto me, Fear not; I am the first and the last:

¹⁸ I *am* he that liveth, and was dead; and, behold, I am alive for evermore, Amen; and have the keys of hell and of death.

¹⁹ Write the things which thou hast seen, and the things which are, and the things which shall be hereafter;

²⁰ The mystery of the seven stars which thou sawest in my right hand, and the seven golden candlesticks. The seven stars are the <u>angels</u> of the seven churches: and the seven candlesticks which thou sawest are the seven churches.

Revelation 2:1-29 - The Angel of the Chruch of Ephesus, Smyrna, Pergamo and Thyatira Writes

¹ Unto the <u>angel</u> of the church of Ephesus write; These things saith he that holdeth the seven stars in his right hand, who walketh in the midst of the seven golden candlesticks;

² I know thy works, and thy labour, and thy patience, and how thou canst not bear them which are evil: and thou hast tried them which say they are apostles, and are not, and hast found them liars:

³ And hast borne, and hast patience, and for my name's sake hast laboured, and hast not fainted.

⁴ Nevertheless I have *somewhat* against thee, because thou hast left thy first love.

⁵ Remember therefore from whence thou art fallen, and repent, and do the first works; or else I will come unto thee quickly, and will remove thy candlestick out of his place, except thou repent.

⁶ But this thou hast, that thou hatest the deeds of the Nicolaitans, which I also hate.

⁷ He that hath an ear, let him hear what the Spirit saith unto the churches; To him that overcometh will I give to eat of the tree of life, which is in the midst of the paradise of God.

⁸ And unto the <u>angel</u> of the church in Smyrna write; These things saith the first and the last, which was dead, and is alive;

⁹ I know thy works, and tribulation, and poverty, (but thou art rich) and *I know* the blasphemy of them which say they are Jews, and are not, but *are* the synagogue of Satan.

¹⁰ Fear none of those things which thou shalt suffer: behold, the devil shall cast *some* of you into prison, that ye may be tried; and ye shall have tribulation ten days: be thou faithful unto death, and I will give thee a crown of life.

¹¹ He that hath an ear, let him hear what the Spirit saith unto the churches; He that overcometh shall not be hurt of the second death.

¹² And to the <u>angel</u> of the church in Pergamos write; These things saith he which hath the sharp sword with two edges;

¹³ I know thy works, and where thou dwellest, *even* where Satan's seat *is*: and thou holdest fast my name, and hast not denied my faith, even in those days wherein Antipas *was* my faithful martyr, who was slain among you, where Satan dwelleth.

¹⁴ But I have a few things against thee, because thou hast there them that hold the doctrine of Balaam, who taught Balac to cast a stumblingblock before the children of Israel, to eat things sacrificed unto idols, and to commit fornication.

¹⁵ So hast thou also them that hold the doctrine of the Nicolaitans, which thing I hate.

¹⁶ Repent; or else I will come unto thee quickly, and will fight against them with the sword of my mouth.

¹⁷ He that hath an ear, let him hear what the Spirit saith unto the churches; To him that overcometh will I give to eat of the hidden manna, and will give him a white stone, and in the stone a new name written, which no man knoweth saving he that receiveth *it*.

¹⁸ And unto the <u>angel</u> of the church in Thyatira write; These things saith the Son of God, who hath his eyes like unto a flame of fire, and his feet *are* like fine brass;

¹⁹ I know thy works, and charity, and service, and faith, and thy patience, and thy works; and the last *to be* more than the first.

²⁰ Notwithstanding I have a few things against thee, because thou sufferest that woman Jezebel, which calleth herself a prophetess, to teach and to seduce my servants to commit fornication, and to eat things sacrificed unto idols.

²¹ And I gave her space to repent of her fornication; and she repented not.

²² Behold, I will cast her into a bed, and them that commit adultery with her into great tribulation, except they repent of their deeds.

²³ And I will kill her children with death; and all the churches shall know that I am he which searcheth the reins and hearts: and I will give unto every one of you according to your works.

²⁴ But unto you I say, and unto the rest in Thyatira, as many as have not this doctrine, and which have not known the depths of Satan, as they speak; I will put upon you none other burden.

²⁵ But that which ye have *already* hold fast till I come.

²⁶ And he that overcometh, and keepeth my works unto the end, to him will I give power over the nations:

²⁷ And he shall rule them with a rod of iron; as the vessels of a potter shall they be broken to shivers: even as I received of my Father.

²⁸ And I will give him the morning star.

²⁹ He that hath an ear, let him hear what the Spirit saith unto the churches.

Revelation 3:1-22 - The Angel of the Church of Sardis, Philadelphia and Laodicean Writes

¹ And unto the angel of the church in Sardis write; These things saith he that hath the seven Spirits of God, and the seven stars; I know thy works, that thou hast a name that thou livest, and art dead.

² Be watchful, and strengthen the things which remain, that are ready to die: for I have not found thy works perfect before God.

³ Remember therefore how thou hast received and heard, and hold fast, and repent. If therefore thou shalt not watch, I will come on thee as a thief, and thou shalt not know what hour I will come upon thee.

⁴ Thou hast a few names even in Sardis which have not defiled their garments; and they shall walk with me in white: for they are worthy.

⁵ He that overcometh, the same shall be clothed in white raiment; and I will not blot out his name out of the book of life, but I will confess his name before my Father, and before his angels.

⁶ He that hath an ear, let him hear what the Spirit saith unto the churches.

⁷ And to the <u>angel</u> of the church in Philadelphia write; These things saith he that is holy, he that is true, he that hath the key of David, he that openeth, and no man shutteth; and shutteth, and no man openeth;

⁸ I know thy works: behold, I have set before thee an open door, and no man can shut it: for thou hast a little strength, and hast kept my word, and hast not denied my name.

⁹ Behold, I will make them of the synagogue of Satan, which say they are Jews, and are not, but do lie; behold, I will make them to come and worship before thy feet, and to know that I have loved thee.

¹⁰ Because thou hast kept the word of my patience, I also will keep thee from the hour of temptation, which shall come upon all the world, to try them that dwell upon the earth.

¹¹ Behold, I come quickly: hold that fast which thou hast, that no man take thy crown.

¹² Him that overcometh will I make a pillar in the temple of my God, and he shall go no more out: and I will write upon him the name of my God, and the name of the city of my God, *which is* new Jerusalem, which cometh down out of heaven from my God: and *I will write upon him* my new name.

¹³ He that hath an ear, let him hear what the Spirit saith unto the churches.

¹⁴ And unto the <u>angel</u> of the church of the Laodiceans write; These things saith the Amen, the faithful and true witness, the beginning of the creation of God;

¹⁵ I know thy works, that thou art neither cold nor hot: I would thou wert cold or hot.

¹⁶ So then because thou art lukewarm, and neither cold nor hot, I will spue thee out of my mouth.

¹⁷ Because thou sayest, I am rich, and increased with goods, and have need of nothing; and knowest not that thou art wretched, and miserable, and poor, and blind, and naked:

[18] I counsel thee to buy of me gold tried in the fire, that thou mayest be rich; and white raiment, that thou mayest be clothed, and *that* the shame of thy nakedness do not appear; and anoint thine eyes with eyesalve, that thou mayest see.

[19] As many as I love, I rebuke and chasten: be zealous therefore, and repent.

[20] Behold, I stand at the door, and knock: if any man hear my voice, and open the door, I will come in to him, and will sup with him, and he with me.

[21] To him that overcometh will I grant to sit with me in my throne, even as I also overcame, and am set down with my Father in his throne.

[22] He that hath an ear, let him hear what the Spirit saith unto the churches.

Revelation 5:1-14 - Strong Angel Proclaiming Who is Worthy to Open the Book - Many Angels Around the Throne Praising God and the Lamb

[1] And I saw in the right hand of him that sat on the throne a book written within and on the backside, sealed with seven seals.

[2] And I saw a strong <u>angel</u> proclaiming with a loud voice, Who is worthy to open the book, and to loose the seals thereof?

[3] And no man in heaven, nor in earth, neither under the earth, was able to open the book, neither to look thereon.

[4] And I wept much, because no man was found worthy to open and to read the book, neither to look thereon.

[5] And one of the elders saith unto me, Weep not: behold, the Lion of the tribe of Juda, the Root of David, hath prevailed to open the book, and to loose the seven seals thereof.

⁶ And I beheld, and, lo, in the midst of the throne and of the four beasts, and in the midst of the elders, stood a Lamb as it had been slain, having seven horns and seven eyes, which are the seven Spirits of God sent forth into all the earth.

⁷ And he came and took the book out of the right hand of him that sat upon the throne.

⁸ And when he had taken the book, the four beasts and four *and* twenty elders fell down before the Lamb, having every one of them harps, and golden vials full of odours, which are the prayers of saints.

⁹ And they sung a new song, saying, Thou art worthy to take the book, and to open the seals thereof: for thou wast slain, and hast redeemed us to God by thy blood out of every kindred, and tongue, and people, and nation;

¹⁰ And hast made us unto our God kings and priests: and we shall reign on the earth.

¹¹ And I beheld, and I heard the voice of many <u>angels</u> round about the throne and the beasts and the elders: and the number of them was ten thousand times ten thousand, and thousands of thousands;

¹² Saying with a loud voice, Worthy is the Lamb that was slain to receive power, and riches, and wisdom, and strength, and honour, and glory, and blessing.

¹³ And every creature which is in heaven, and on the earth, and under the earth, and such as are in the sea, and all that are in them, heard I saying, Blessing, and honour, and glory, and power, *be* unto him that sitteth upon the throne, and unto the Lamb for ever and ever.

¹⁴ And the four beasts said, Amen. And the four *and* twenty elders fell down and worshipped him that liveth for ever and ever.

Revelation 7:1-17 - Four Angels Standing on the Four Corners of the Earth, Another Angel Ascending from the East, Crying not to Hurt the 144,000 - All Angels Around the Throne Worshipping God

¹ And after these things I saw four <u>angels</u> standing on the four corners of the earth, holding the four winds of the earth, that the wind should not blow on the earth, nor on the sea, nor on any tree.

² And I saw another <u>angel</u> ascending from the east, having the seal of the living God: and he cried with a loud voice to the four <u>angels</u>, to whom it was given to hurt the earth and the sea,

³ Saying, Hurt not the earth, neither the sea, nor the trees, till we have sealed the servants of our God in their foreheads.

⁴ And I heard the number of them which were sealed: *and there were* sealed an hundred *and* forty *and* four thousand of all the tribes of the children of Israel.

⁵ Of the tribe of Juda *were* sealed twelve thousand. Of the tribe of Reuben *were* sealed twelve thousand. Of the tribe of Gad *were* sealed twelve thousand.

⁶ Of the tribe of Aser *were* sealed twelve thousand. Of the tribe of Nepthalim *were* sealed twelve thousand. Of the tribe of Manasses *were* sealed twelve thousand.

⁷ Of the tribe of Simeon *were* sealed twelve thousand. Of the tribe of Levi *were* sealed twelve thousand. Of the tribe of Issachar *were* sealed twelve thousand.

⁸ Of the tribe of Zabulon *were* sealed twelve thousand. Of the tribe of Joseph *were* sealed twelve thousand. Of the tribe of Benjamin *were* sealed twelve thousand.

⁹ After this I beheld, and, lo, a great multitude, which no man could number, of all nations, and kindreds, and people, and tongues, stood before the throne, and before the Lamb, clothed with white robes, and palms in their hands;

¹⁰ And cried with a loud voice, saying, Salvation to our God which sitteth upon the throne, and unto the Lamb.

¹¹ And all the <u>angels</u> stood round about the throne, and *about* the elders and the four beasts, and fell before the throne on their faces, and worshipped God,

¹² Saying, Amen: Blessing, and glory, and wisdom, and thanksgiving, and honour, and power, and might, *be* unto our God for ever and ever. Amen.

¹³ And one of the elders answered, saying unto me, What are these which are arrayed in white robes? and whence came they?

¹⁴ And I said unto him, Sir, thou knowest. And he said to me, These are they which came out of great tribulation, and have washed their robes, and made them white in the blood of the Lamb.

¹⁵ Therefore are they before the throne of God, and serve him day and night in his temple: and he that sitteth on the throne shall dwell among them.

¹⁶ They shall hunger no more, neither thirst any more; neither shall the sun light on them, nor any heat.

¹⁷ For the Lamb which is in the midst of the throne shall feed them, and shall lead them unto living fountains of waters: and God shall wipe away all tears from their eyes.

Revelation 8:1-13 - Seven Angels Which Stood Before God and Sound Four of Seven Trumpets

¹ And when he had opened the seventh seal, there was silence in heaven about the space of half an hour.

² And I saw the seven <u>angels</u> which stood before God; and to them were given seven trumpets.

³ And another <u>angel</u> came and stood at the altar, having a golden censer; and there was given unto him much incense, that he should offer *it* with the prayers of all saints upon the golden altar which was before the throne.

⁴ And the smoke of the incense, *which came* with the prayers of the saints, ascended up before God out of the <u>angel's</u> hand.

⁵ And the <u>angel</u> took the censer, and filled it with fire of the altar, and cast *it* into the earth: and there were voices, and thunderings, and lightnings, and an earthquake.

⁶ And the seven <u>angels</u> which had the seven trumpets prepared themselves to sound.

⁷ The first <u>angel</u> sounded, and there followed hail and fire mingled with blood, and they were cast upon the earth: and the third part of trees was burnt up, and all green grass was burnt up.

⁸ And the second <u>angel</u> sounded, and as it were a great mountain burning with fire was cast into the sea: and the third part of the sea became blood;

⁹ And the third part of the creatures which were in the sea, and had life, died; and the third part of the ships were destroyed.

¹⁰ And the third <u>angel</u> sounded, and there fell a great star from heaven, burning as it were a lamp, and it fell upon the third part of the rivers, and upon the fountains of waters;

¹¹ And the name of the star is called Wormwood: and the third part of the waters became wormwood; and many men died of the waters, because they were made bitter.

¹² And the fourth <u>angel</u> sounded, and the third part of the sun was smitten, and the third part of the moon, and the third part of the stars; so as the third part of them was darkened, and the day shone not for a third part of it, and the night likewise.

¹³ And I beheld, and heard an <u>angel</u> flying through the midst of heaven, saying with a loud voice, Woe, woe, woe, to the inhabiters of the earth by reason of the other voices of the trumpet of the three <u>angels</u>, which are yet to sound!

Revelation 9:1-21 - Three More Angels Which Stood Before God and Sound Trumpets

¹ And the fifth <u>angel</u> sounded, and I saw a star fall from heaven unto the earth: and to him was given the key of the bottomless pit.

² And he opened the bottomless pit; and there arose a smoke out of the pit, as the smoke of a great furnace; and the sun and the air were darkened by reason of the smoke of the pit.

³ And there came out of the smoke locusts upon the earth: and unto them was given power, as the scorpions of the earth have power.

⁴ And it was commanded them that they should not hurt the grass of the earth, neither any green thing, neither any tree; but only those men which have not the seal of God in their foreheads.

⁵ And to them it was given that they should not kill them, but that they should be tormented five months: and their torment *was* as the torment of a scorpion, when he striketh a man.

⁶ And in those days shall men seek death, and shall not find it; and shall desire to die, and death shall flee from them.

⁷ And the shapes of the locusts *were* like unto horses prepared unto battle; and on their heads *were* as it were crowns like gold, and their faces *were* as the faces of men.

⁸ And they had hair as the hair of women, and their teeth were as *the teeth* of lions.

⁹ And they had breastplates, as it were breastplates of iron; and the sound of their wings *was* as the sound of chariots of many horses running to battle.

¹⁰ And they had tails like unto scorpions, and there were stings in their tails: and their power *was* to hurt men five months.

¹¹ And they had a king over them, *which is* the <u>angel</u> of the bottomless pit, whose name in the Hebrew tongue *is* Abaddon, but in the Greek tongue hath *his* name Apollyon.

¹² One woe is past; *and*, behold, there come two woes more hereafter.

¹³ And the sixth <u>angel</u> sounded, and I heard a voice from the four horns of the golden altar which is before God,

¹⁴ Saying to the sixth <u>angel</u> which had the trumpet, Loose the four <u>angels</u> which are bound in the great river Euphrates.

¹⁵ And the four <u>angels</u> were loosed, which were prepared for an hour, and a day, and a month, and a year, for to slay the third part of men.

¹⁶ And the number of the army of the horsemen *were* two hundred thousand thousand: and I heard the number of them.

¹⁷ And thus I saw the horses in the vision, and them that sat on them, having breastplates of fire, and of jacinth, and brimstone: and the heads of the horses *were* as the heads of lions; and out of their mouths issued fire and smoke and brimstone.

¹⁸ By these three was the third part of men killed, by the fire, and by the smoke, and by the brimstone, which issued out of their mouths.

¹⁹ For their power is in their mouth, and in their tails: for their tails *were* like unto serpents, and had heads, and with them they do hurt.

²⁰ And the rest of the men which were not killed by these plagues yet repented not of the works of their hands, that they should not worship devils, and idols of gold, and silver, and brass, and stone, and of wood: which neither can see, nor hear, nor walk:

²¹ Neither repented they of their murders, nor of their sorceries, nor of their fornication, nor of their thefts.

Revelation 10:1-11 - A Mighty Angel Came Down From Heaven

¹ And I saw another mighty <u>angel</u> come down from heaven, clothed with a cloud: and a rainbow *was* upon his head, and his face *was* as it were the sun, and his feet as pillars of fire:

² And he had in his hand a little book open: and he set his right foot upon the sea, and *his* left *foot* on the earth,

³ And cried with a loud voice, as *when* a lion roareth: and when he had cried, seven thunders uttered their voices.

⁴ And when the seven thunders had uttered their voices, I was about to write: and I heard a voice from heaven saying unto me, Seal up those things which the seven thunders uttered, and write them not.

⁵ And the <u>angel</u> which I saw stand upon the sea and upon the earth lifted up his hand to heaven,

⁶ And sware by him that liveth for ever and ever, who created heaven, and the things that therein are, and the earth, and the things that therein are, and the sea, and the things which are therein, that there should be time no longer:

⁷ But in the days of the voice of the seventh <u>angel</u>, when he shall begin to sound, the mystery of God should be finished, as he hath declared to his servants the prophets.

⁸ And the voice which I heard from heaven spake unto me again, and said, Go *and* take the little book which is open in the hand of the <u>angel</u> which standeth upon the sea and upon the earth.

⁹ And I went unto the <u>angel</u>, and said unto him, Give me the little book. And he said unto me, Take *it*, and eat it up; and it shall make thy belly bitter, but it shall be in thy mouth sweet as honey.

¹⁰ And I took the little book out of the <u>angel</u>'s hand, and ate it up; and it was in my mouth sweet as honey: and as soon as I had eaten it, my belly was bitter.

¹¹ And he said unto me, Thou must prophesy again before many peoples, and nations, and tongues, and kings.

Revelation 11:1-19 - Seventh Angel Sounded

¹ And there was given me a reed like unto a rod: and the <u>angel</u> stood, saying, Rise, and measure the temple of God, and the altar, and them that worship therein.

² But the court which is without the temple leave out, and measure it not; for it is given unto the Gentiles: and the holy city shall they tread under foot forty *and* two months.

³ And I will give *power* unto my two witnesses, and they shall prophesy a thousand two hundred *and* threescore days, clothed in sackcloth.

⁴ These are the two olive trees, and the two candlesticks standing before the God of the earth.

⁵ And if any man will hurt them, fire proceedeth out of their mouth, and devoureth their enemies: and if any man will hurt them, he must in this manner be killed.

⁶ These have power to shut heaven, that it rain not in the days of their prophecy: and have power over waters to turn them to blood, and to smite the earth with all plagues, as often as they will.

⁷ And when they shall have finished their testimony, the beast that ascendeth out of the bottomless pit shall make war against them, and shall overcome them, and kill them.

⁸ And their dead bodies *shall lie* in the street of the great city, which spiritually is called Sodom and Egypt, where also our Lord was crucified.

⁹ And they of the people and kindreds and tongues and nations shall see their dead bodies three days and an half, and shall not suffer their dead bodies to be put in graves.

¹⁰ And they that dwell upon the earth shall rejoice over them, and make merry, and shall send gifts one to another; because these two prophets tormented them that dwelt on the earth.

¹¹ And after three days and an half the Spirit of life from God entered into them, and they stood upon their feet; and great fear fell upon them which saw them.

¹² And they heard a great voice from heaven saying unto them, Come up hither. And they ascended up to heaven in a cloud; and their enemies beheld them.

¹³ And the same hour was there a great earthquake, and the tenth part of the city fell, and in the earthquake were slain of men seven thousand: and the remnant were affrighted, and gave glory to the God of heaven.

¹⁴ The second woe is past; *and*, behold, the third woe cometh quickly.

¹⁵ And the seventh <u>angel</u> sounded; and there were great voices in heaven, saying, The kingdoms of this world are become *the kingdoms* of our Lord, and of his Christ; and he shall reign for ever and ever.

16 And the four and twenty elders, which sat before God on their seats, fell upon their faces, and worshipped God,

17 Saying, We give thee thanks, O Lord God Almighty, which art, and wast, and art to come; because thou hast taken to thee thy great power, and hast reigned.

18 And the nations were angry, and thy wrath is come, and the time of the dead, that they should be judged, and that thou shouldest give reward unto thy servants the prophets, and to the saints, and them that fear thy name, small and great; and shouldest destroy them which destroy the earth.

19 And the temple of God was opened in heaven, and there was seen in his temple the ark of his testament: and there were lightnings, and voices, and thunderings, and an earthquake, and great hail.

Revelation 12:1-17 - Heavenly War between Michael and His Angels Fought Against the Dragon

1 And there appeared a great wonder in heaven; a woman clothed with the sun, and the moon under her feet, and upon her head a crown of twelve stars:

2 And she being with child cried, travailing in birth, and pained to be delivered.

3 And there appeared another wonder in heaven; and behold a great red dragon, having seven heads and ten horns, and seven crowns upon his heads.

4 And his tail drew the third part of the stars of heaven, and did cast them to the earth: and the dragon stood before the woman which was ready to be delivered, for to devour her child as soon as it was born.

5 And she brought forth a man child, who was to rule all nations with a rod of iron: and her child was caught up unto God, and *to* his throne.

6 And the woman fled into the wilderness, where she hath a place prepared of God, that they should feed her there a thousand two hundred *and* threescore days.

⁷ And there was war in heaven: Michael and his <u>angels</u> fought against the dragon; and the dragon fought and his <u>angels</u>,

⁸ And prevailed not; neither was their place found any more in heaven.

⁹ And the great dragon was cast out, that old serpent, called the Devil, and Satan, which deceiveth the whole world: he was cast out into the earth, and his <u>angels</u> were cast out with him.

¹⁰ And I heard a loud voice saying in heaven, Now is come salvation, and strength, and the kingdom of our God, and the power of his Christ: for the accuser of our brethren is cast down, which accused them before our God day and night.

¹¹ And they overcame him by the blood of the Lamb, and by the word of their testimony; and they loved not their lives unto the death.

¹² Therefore rejoice, *ye* heavens, and ye that dwell in them. Woe to the inhabiters of the earth and of the sea! for the devil is come down unto you, having great wrath, because he knoweth that he hath but a short time.

¹³ And when the dragon saw that he was cast unto the earth, he persecuted the woman which brought forth the man *child*.

¹⁴ And to the woman were given two wings of a great eagle, that she might fly into the wilderness, into her place, where she is nourished for a time, and times, and half a time, from the face of the serpent.

¹⁵ And the serpent cast out of his mouth water as a flood after the woman, that he might cause her to be carried away of the flood.

¹⁶ And the earth helped the woman, and the earth opened her mouth, and swallowed up the flood which the dragon cast out of his mouth.

¹⁷ And the dragon was wroth with the woman, and went to make war with the remnant of her seed, which keep the commandments of God, and have the testimony of Jesus Christ.

Revelation 14:1-20 - Angels in the Midst of Heaven

¹ And I looked, and, lo, a Lamb stood on the mount Zion, and with him an hundred forty *and* four thousand, having his Father's name written in their foreheads.

² And I heard a voice from heaven, as the voice of many waters, and as the voice of a great thunder: and I heard the voice of harpers harping with their harps:

³ And they sung as it were a new song before the throne, and before the four beasts, and the elders: and no man could learn that song but the hundred *and* forty *and* four thousand, which were redeemed from the earth.

⁴ These are they which were not defiled with women; for they are virgins. These are they which follow the Lamb whithersoever he goeth. These were redeemed from among men, *being* the firstfruits unto God and to the Lamb.

⁵ And in their mouth was found no guile: for they are without fault before the throne of God.

⁶ And I saw another <u>angel</u> fly in the midst of heaven, having the everlasting gospel to preach unto them that dwell on the earth, and to every nation, and kindred, and tongue, and people,

⁷ Saying with a loud voice, Fear God, and give glory to him; for the hour of his judgment is come: and worship him that made heaven, and earth, and the sea, and the fountains of waters.

⁸ And there followed another <u>angel</u>, saying, Babylon is fallen, is fallen, that great city, because she made all nations drink of the wine of the wrath of her fornication.

⁹ And the third <u>angel</u> followed them, saying with a loud voice, If any man worship the beast and his image, and receive *his* mark in his forehead, or in his hand,

¹⁰ The same shall drink of the wine of the wrath of God, which is poured out without mixture into the cup of his indignation; and he shall be tormented with fire and brimstone in the presence of the holy <u>angels</u>, and in the presence of the Lamb:

¹¹ And the smoke of their torment ascendeth up for ever and ever: and they have no rest day nor night, who worship the beast and his image, and whosoever receiveth the mark of his name.

¹² Here is the patience of the saints: here *are* they that keep the commandments of God, and the faith of Jesus.

¹³ And I heard a voice from heaven saying unto me, Write, Blessed *are* the dead which die in the Lord from henceforth: Yea, saith the Spirit, that they may rest from their labours; and their works do follow them.

¹⁴ And I looked, and behold a white cloud, and upon the cloud *one* sat like unto the Son of man, having on his head a golden crown, and in his hand a sharp sickle.

¹⁵ And another <u>angel</u> came out of the temple, crying with a loud voice to him that sat on the cloud, Thrust in thy sickle, and reap: for the time is come for thee to reap; for the harvest of the earth is ripe.

¹⁶ And he that sat on the cloud thrust in his sickle on the earth; and the earth was reaped.

¹⁷ And another <u>angel</u> came out of the temple which is in heaven, he also having a sharp sickle.

¹⁸ And another <u>angel</u> came out from the altar, which had power over fire; and cried with a loud cry to him that had the sharp sickle, saying, Thrust in thy sharp sickle, and gather the clusters of the vine of the earth; for her grapes are fully ripe.

¹⁹ And the <u>angel</u> thrust in his sickle into the earth, and gathered the vine of the earth, and cast *it* into the great winepress of the wrath of God.

²⁰ And the winepress was trodden without the city, and blood came out of the winepress, even unto the horse bridles, by the space of a thousand *and* six hundred furlongs.

Revelation 15:1-8 - Seven Angels and the Seven Plagues

¹ And I saw another sign in heaven, great and marvellous, seven <u>angels</u> having the seven last plagues; for in them is filled up the wrath of God.

² And I saw as it were a sea of glass mingled with fire: and them that had gotten the victory over the beast, and over his image, and over his mark, *and* over the number of his name, stand on the sea of glass, having the harps of God.

³ And they sing the song of Moses the servant of God, and the song of the Lamb, saying, Great and marvellous *are* thy works, Lord God Almighty; just and true *are* thy ways, thou King of saints.

⁴ Who shall not fear thee, O Lord, and glorify thy name? for *thou* only *art* holy: for all nations shall come and worship before thee; for thy judgments are made manifest.

⁵ And after that I looked, and, behold, the temple of the tabernacle of the testimony in heaven was opened:

⁶ And the seven <u>angels</u> came out of the temple, having the seven plagues, clothed in pure and white linen, and having their breasts girded with golden girdles.

⁷ And one of the four beasts gave unto the seven <u>angels</u> seven golden vials full of the wrath of God, who liveth for ever and ever.

⁸ And the temple was filled with smoke from the glory of God, and from his power; and no man was able to enter into the temple, till the seven plagues of the seven <u>angels</u> were fulfilled.

Revelation 16:1-21 - Seven Angels and the Seven Plagues

¹ And I heard a great voice out of the temple saying to the seven <u>angels,</u> Go your ways, and pour out the vials of the wrath of God upon the earth.

² And the first went, and poured out his vial upon the earth; and there fell a noisome and grievous sore upon the men which had the mark of the beast, and *upon* them which worshipped his image.

³ And the second angel poured out his vial upon the sea; and it became as the blood of a dead *man*: and every living soul died in the sea.

⁴ And the third angel poured out his vial upon the rivers and fountains of waters; and they became blood.

⁵ And I heard the angel of the waters say, Thou art righteous, O Lord, which art, and wast, and shalt be, because thou hast judged thus.

⁶ For they have shed the blood of saints and prophets, and thou hast given them blood to drink; for they are worthy.

⁷ And I heard another out of the altar say, Even so, Lord God Almighty, true and righteous *are* thy judgments.

⁸ And the fourth angel poured out his vial upon the sun; and power was given unto him to scorch men with fire.

⁹ And men were scorched with great heat, and blasphemed the name of God, which hath power over these plagues: and they repented not to give him glory.

¹⁰ And the fifth angel poured out his vial upon the seat of the beast; and his kingdom was full of darkness; and they gnawed their tongues for pain,

¹¹ And blasphemed the God of heaven because of their pains and their sores, and repented not of their deeds.

¹² And the sixth angel poured out his vial upon the great river Euphrates; and the water thereof was dried up, that the way of the kings of the east might be prepared.

¹³ And I saw three unclean spirits like frogs *come* out of the mouth of the dragon, and out of the mouth of the beast, and out of the mouth of the false prophet.

¹⁴ For they are the spirits of devils, working miracles, *which* go forth unto the kings of the earth and of the whole world, to gather them to the battle of that great day of God Almighty.

¹⁵ Behold, I come as a thief. Blessed *is* he that watcheth, and keepeth his garments, lest he walk naked, and they see his shame.

¹⁶ And he gathered them together into a place called in the Hebrew tongue Armageddon.

¹⁷ And the seventh <u>angel</u> poured out his vial into the air; and there came a great voice out of the temple of heaven, from the throne, saying, It is done.

¹⁸ And there were voices, and thunders, and lightnings; and there was a great earthquake, such as was not since men were upon the earth, so mighty an earthquake, *and* so great.

¹⁹ And the great city was divided into three parts, and the cities of the nations fell: and great Babylon came in remembrance before God, to give unto her the cup of the wine of the fierceness of his wrath.

²⁰ And every island fled away, and the mountains were not found.

²¹ And there fell upon men a great hail out of heaven, *every stone* about the weight of a talent: and men blasphemed God because of the plague of the hail; for the plague thereof was exceeding great.

Revelation 17:1-18 - Seven Angels and the Seven Vials

¹ And there came one of the seven <u>angels</u> which had the seven vials, and talked with me, saying unto me, Come hither; I will shew unto thee the judgment of the great whore that sitteth upon many waters:

² With whom the kings of the earth have committed fornication, and the inhabitants of the earth have been made drunk with the wine of her fornication.

³ So he carried me away in the spirit into the wilderness: and I saw a woman sit upon a scarlet coloured beast, full of names of blasphemy, having seven heads and ten horns.

⁴ And the woman was arrayed in purple and scarlet colour, and decked with gold and precious stones and pearls, having a golden cup in her hand full of abominations and filthiness of her fornication:

⁵ And upon her forehead *was* a name written, MYSTERY, BABYLON THE GREAT, THE MOTHER OF HARLOTS AND ABOMINATIONS OF THE EARTH.

⁶ And I saw the woman drunken with the blood of the saints, and with the blood of the martyrs of Jesus: and when I saw her, I wondered with great admiration.

⁷ And the <u>angel</u> said unto me, Wherefore didst thou marvel? I will tell thee the mystery of the woman, and of the beast that carrieth her, which hath the seven heads and ten horns.

⁸ The beast that thou sawest was, and is not; and shall ascend out of the bottomless pit, and go into perdition: and they that dwell on the earth shall wonder, whose names were not written in the book of life from the foundation of the world, when they behold the beast that was, and is not, and yet is.

⁹ And here *is* the mind which hath wisdom. The seven heads are seven mountains, on which the woman sitteth.

¹⁰ And there are seven kings: five are fallen, and one is, *and* the other is not yet come; and when he cometh, he must continue a short space.

¹¹ And the beast that was, and is not, even he is the eighth, and is of the seven, and goeth into perdition.

¹² And the ten horns which thou sawest are ten kings, which have received no kingdom as yet; but receive power as kings one hour with the beast.

¹³ These have one mind, and shall give their power and strength unto the beast.

¹⁴ These shall make war with the Lamb, and the Lamb shall overcome them: for he is Lord of lords, and King of kings: and they that are with him *are* called, and chosen, and faithful.

¹⁵ And he saith unto me, The waters which thou sawest, where the whore sitteth, are peoples, and multitudes, and nations, and tongues.

¹⁶ And the ten horns which thou sawest upon the beast, these shall hate the whore, and shall make her desolate and naked, and shall eat her flesh, and burn her with fire.

¹⁷ For God hath put in their hearts to fulfil his will, and to agree, and give their kingdom unto the beast, until the words of God shall be fulfilled.

¹⁸ And the woman which thou sawest is that great city, which reigneth over the kings of the earth.

Revelation 18:1-24 - Angel Come Down From Heaven

¹ And after these things I saw another <u>angel</u> come down from heaven, having great power; and the earth was lightened with his glory.

² And he cried mightily with a strong voice, saying, Babylon the great is fallen, is fallen, and is become the habitation of devils, and the hold of every foul spirit, and a cage of every unclean and hateful bird.

³ For all nations have drunk of the wine of the wrath of her fornication, and the kings of the earth have committed fornication with her, and the merchants of the earth are waxed rich through the abundance of her delicacies.

⁴ And I heard another voice from heaven, saying, Come out of her, my people, that ye be not partakers of her sins, and that ye receive not of her plagues.

⁵ For her sins have reached unto heaven, and God hath remembered her iniquities.

⁶ Reward her even as she rewarded you, and double unto her double according to her works: in the cup which she hath filled fill to her double.

⁷ How much she hath glorified herself, and lived deliciously, so much torment and sorrow give her: for she saith in her heart, I sit a queen, and am no widow, and shall see no sorrow.

⁸ Therefore shall her plagues come in one day, death, and mourning, and famine; and she shall be utterly burned with fire: for strong *is* the Lord God who judgeth her.

⁹ And the kings of the earth, who have committed fornication and lived deliciously with her, shall bewail her, and lament for her, when they shall see the smoke of her burning,

¹⁰ Standing afar off for the fear of her torment, saying, Alas, alas, that great city Babylon, that mighty city! for in one hour is thy judgment come.

¹¹ And the merchants of the earth shall weep and mourn over her; for no man buyeth their merchandise any more:

¹² The merchandise of gold, and silver, and precious stones, and of pearls, and fine linen, and purple, and silk, and scarlet, and all thyine wood, and all manner vessels of ivory, and all manner vessels of most precious wood, and of brass, and iron, and marble,

¹³ And cinnamon, and odours, and ointments, and frankincense, and wine, and oil, and fine flour, and wheat, and beasts, and sheep, and horses, and chariots, and slaves, and souls of men.

¹⁴ And the fruits that thy soul lusted after are departed from thee, and all things which were dainty and goodly are departed from thee, and thou shalt find them no more at all.

¹⁵ The merchants of these things, which were made rich by her, shall stand afar off for the fear of her torment, weeping and wailing,

¹⁶ And saying, Alas, alas, that great city, that was clothed in fine linen, and purple, and scarlet, and decked with gold, and precious stones, and pearls!

¹⁷ For in one hour so great riches is come to nought. And every shipmaster, and all the company in ships, and sailors, and as many as trade by sea, stood afar off,

¹⁸ And cried when they saw the smoke of her burning, saying, What *city is* like unto this great city!

¹⁹ And they cast dust on their heads, and cried, weeping and wailing, saying, Alas, alas, that great city, wherein were made rich all that had ships in the sea by reason of her costliness! for in one hour is she made desolate.

[20] Rejoice over her, *thou* heaven, and *ye* holy apostles and prophets; for God hath avenged you on her.

[21] And a mighty <u>angel</u> took up a stone like a great millstone, and cast *it* into the sea, saying, Thus with violence shall that great city Babylon be thrown down, and shall be found no more at all.

[22] And the voice of harpers, and musicians, and of pipers, and trumpeters, shall be heard no more at all in thee; and no craftsman, of whatsoever craft *he be*, shall be found any more in thee; and the sound of a millstone shall be heard no more at all in thee;

[23] And the light of a candle shall shine no more at all in thee; and the voice of the bridegroom and of the bride shall be heard no more at all in thee: for thy merchants were the great men of the earth; for by thy sorceries were all nations deceived.

[24] And in her was found the blood of prophets, and of saints, and of all that were slain upon the earth.

Revelation 19:1-21 - Angel Calling Standing in the Sun

[1] And after these things I heard a great voice of much people in heaven, saying, Alleluia; Salvation, and glory, and honour, and power, unto the Lord our God:

[2] For true and righteous *are* his judgments: for he hath judged the great whore, which did corrupt the earth with her fornication, and hath avenged the blood of his servants at her hand.

[3] And again they said, Alleluia. And her smoke rose up for ever and ever.

[4] And the four and twenty elders and the four beasts fell down and worshipped God that sat on the throne, saying, Amen; Alleluia.

[5] And a voice came out of the throne, saying, Praise our God, all ye his servants, and ye that fear him, both small and great.

[6] And I heard as it were the voice of a great multitude, and as the voice of many waters, and as the voice of mighty thunderings, saying, Alleluia: for the Lord God omnipotent reigneth.

⁷ Let us be glad and rejoice, and give honour to him: for the marriage of the Lamb is come, and his wife hath made herself ready.

⁸ And to her was granted that she should be arrayed in fine linen, clean and white: for the fine linen is the righteousness of saints.

⁹ And he saith unto me, Write, Blessed *are* they which are called unto the marriage supper of the Lamb. And he saith unto me, These are the true sayings of God.

¹⁰ And I fell at his feet to worship him. And he said unto me, See *thou do it* not: I am thy fellowservant, and of thy brethren that have the testimony of Jesus: worship God: for the testimony of Jesus is the spirit of prophecy.

¹¹ And I saw heaven opened, and behold a white horse; and he that sat upon him *was* called Faithful and True, and in righteousness he doth judge and make war.

¹² His eyes *were* as a flame of fire, and on his head *were* many crowns; and he had a name written, that no man knew, but he himself.

¹³ And he *was* clothed with a vesture dipped in blood: and his name is called The Word of God.

¹⁴ And the armies *which were* in heaven followed him upon white horses, clothed in fine linen, white and clean.

¹⁵ And out of his mouth goeth a sharp sword, that with it he should smite the nations: and he shall rule them with a rod of iron: and he treadeth the winepress of the fierceness and wrath of Almighty God.

¹⁶ And he hath on *his* vesture and on his thigh a name written, KING OF KINGS, AND LORD OF LORDS.

¹⁷ And I saw an angel standing in the sun; and he cried with a loud voice, saying to all the fowls that fly in the midst of heaven, Come and gather yourselves together unto the supper of the great God;

¹⁸ That ye may eat the flesh of kings, and the flesh of captains, and the flesh of mighty men, and the flesh of horses, and of them that sit on them, and the flesh of all *men, both* free and bond, both small and great.

¹⁹ And I saw the beast, and the kings of the earth, and their armies, gathered together to make war against him that sat on the horse, and against his army.

²⁰ And the beast was taken, and with him the false prophet that wrought miracles before him, with which he deceived them that had received the mark of the beast, and them that worshipped his image. These both were cast alive into a lake of fire burning with brimstone.

²¹ And the remnant were slain with the sword of him that sat upon the horse, which *sword* proceeded out of his mouth: and all the fowls were filled with their flesh.

Revelation 20:1-15 - Angel Casting Down Satan for 1,000 Years

¹ And I saw an <u>angel</u> come down from heaven, having the key of the bottomless pit and a great chain in his hand.

² And he laid hold on the dragon, that old serpent, which is the Devil, and Satan, and bound him a thousand years,

³ And cast him into the bottomless pit, and shut him up, and set a seal upon him, that he should deceive the nations no more, till the thousand years should be fulfilled: and after that he must be loosed a little season.

⁴ And I saw thrones, and they sat upon them, and judgment was given unto them: and *I saw* the souls of them that were beheaded for the witness of Jesus, and for the word of God, and which had not worshipped the beast, neither his image, neither had received *his* mark upon their foreheads, or in their hands; and they lived and reigned with Christ a thousand years.

⁵ But the rest of the dead lived not again until the thousand years were finished. This *is* the first resurrection.

⁶ Blessed and holy *is* he that hath part in the first resurrection: on such the second death hath no power, but they shall be priests of God and of Christ, and shall reign with him a thousand years.

⁷ And when the thousand years are expired, Satan shall be loosed out of his prison,

⁸ And shall go out to deceive the nations which are in the four quarters of the earth, Gog and Magog, to gather them together to battle: the number of whom *is* as the sand of the sea.

⁹ And they went up on the breadth of the earth, and compassed the camp of the saints about, and the beloved city: and fire came down from God out of heaven, and devoured them.

¹⁰ And the devil that deceived them was cast into the lake of fire and brimstone, where the beast and the false prophet *are*, and shall be tormented day and night for ever and ever.

¹¹ And I saw a great white throne, and him that sat on it, from whose face the earth and the heaven fled away; and there was found no place for them.

¹² And I saw the dead, small and great, stand before God; and the books were opened: and another book was opened, which is *the book* of life: and the dead were judged out of those things which were written in the books, according to their works.

¹³ And the sea gave up the dead which were in it; and death and hell delivered up the dead which were in them: and they were judged every man according to their works.

¹⁴ And death and hell were cast into the lake of fire. This is the second death.

¹⁵ And whosoever was not found written in the book of life was cast into the lake of fire.

Revelation 21:1-27 - Seven Angels and the Seven Vials

¹ And I saw a new heaven and a new earth: for the first heaven and the first earth were passed away; and there was no more sea.

² And I John saw the holy city, new Jerusalem, coming down from God out of heaven, prepared as a bride adorned for her husband.

³ And I heard a great voice out of heaven saying, Behold, the tabernacle of God *is* with men, and he will dwell with them, and they shall be his people, and God himself shall be with them, *and be* their God.

⁴ And God shall wipe away all tears from their eyes; and there shall be no more death, neither sorrow, nor crying, neither shall there be any more pain: for the former things are passed away.

⁵ And he that sat upon the throne said, Behold, I make all things new. And he said unto me, Write: for these words are true and faithful.

⁶ And he said unto me, It is done. I am Alpha and Omega, the beginning and the end. I will give unto him that is athirst of the fountain of the water of life freely.

⁷ He that overcometh shall inherit all things; and I will be his God, and he shall be my son.

⁸ But the fearful, and unbelieving, and the abominable, and murderers, and whoremongers, and sorcerers, and idolaters, and all liars, shall have their part in the lake which burneth with fire and brimstone: which is the second death.

⁹ And there came unto me one of the seven <u>angels</u> which had the seven vials full of the seven last plagues, and talked with me, saying, Come hither, I will shew thee the bride, the Lamb's wife.

¹⁰ And he carried me away in the spirit to a great and high mountain, and shewed me that great city, the holy Jerusalem, descending out of heaven from God,

¹¹ Having the glory of God: and her light *was* like unto a stone most precious, even like a jasper stone, clear as crystal;

¹² And had a wall great and high, *and* had twelve gates, and at the gates twelve <u>angels</u>, and names written thereon, which are *the names* of the twelve tribes of the children of Israel:

¹³ On the east three gates; on the north three gates; on the south three gates; and on the west three gates.

¹⁴ And the wall of the city had twelve foundations, and in them the names of the twelve apostles of the Lamb.

¹⁵ And he that talked with me had a golden reed to measure the city, and the gates thereof, and the wall thereof.

¹⁶ And the city lieth foursquare, and the length is as large as the breadth: and he measured the city with the reed, twelve thousand furlongs. The length and the breadth and the height of it are equal.

¹⁷ And he measured the wall thereof, an hundred *and* forty *and* four cubits, *according to* the measure of a man, that is, of the angel.

¹⁸ And the building of the wall of it was *of* jasper: and the city *was* pure gold, like unto clear glass.

¹⁹ And the foundations of the wall of the city *were* garnished with all manner of precious stones. The first foundation *was* jasper; the second, sapphire; the third, a chalcedony; the fourth, an emerald;

²⁰ The fifth, sardonyx; the sixth, sardius; the seventh, chrysolite; the eighth, beryl; the ninth, a topaz; the tenth, a chrysoprasus; the eleventh, a jacinth; the twelfth, an amethyst.

²¹ And the twelve gates *were* twelve pearls; every several gate was of one pearl: and the street of the city *was* pure gold, as it were transparent glass.

²² And I saw no temple therein: for the Lord God Almighty and the Lamb are the temple of it.

²³ And the city had no need of the sun, neither of the moon, to shine in it: for the glory of God did lighten it, and the Lamb *is* the light thereof.

²⁴ And the nations of them which are saved shall walk in the light of it: and the kings of the earth do bring their glory and honour into it.

²⁵ And the gates of it shall not be shut at all by day: for there shall be no night there.

²⁶ And they shall bring the glory and honour of the nations into it.

²⁷ And there shall in no wise enter into it any thing that defileth, neither *whatsoever* worketh abomination, or *maketh* a lie: but they which are written in the Lamb's book of life.

Revelation 22:1-21 - John Worshipping at the Feet of the Angel

¹ And he shewed me a pure river of water of life, clear as crystal, proceeding out of the throne of God and of the Lamb.

² In the midst of the street of it, and on either side of the river, *was there* the tree of life, which bare twelve *manner of* fruits, *and* yielded her fruit every month: and the leaves of the tree *were* for the healing of the nations.

³ And there shall be no more curse: but the throne of God and of the Lamb shall be in it; and his servants shall serve him:

⁴ And they shall see his face; and his name *shall be* in their foreheads.

⁵ And there shall be no night there; and they need no candle, neither light of the sun; for the Lord God giveth them light: and they shall reign for ever and ever.

⁶ And he said unto me, These sayings *are* faithful and true: and the Lord God of the holy prophets sent his <u>angel</u> to shew unto his servants the things which must shortly be done.

⁷ Behold, I come quickly: blessed *is* he that keepeth the sayings of the prophecy of this book.

⁸ And I John saw these things, and heard *them*. And when I had heard and seen, I fell down to worship before the feet of the <u>angel</u> which shewed me these things.

⁹ Then saith he unto me, See *thou do it* not: for I am thy fellowservant, and of thy brethren the prophets, and of them which keep the sayings of this book: worship God.

¹⁰ And he saith unto me, Seal not the sayings of the prophecy of this book: for the time is at hand.

¹¹ He that is unjust, let him be unjust still: and he which is filthy, let him be filthy still: and he that is righteous, let him be righteous still: and he that is holy, let him be holy still.

¹² And, behold, I come quickly; and my reward *is* with me, to give every man according as his work shall be.

¹³ I am Alpha and Omega, the beginning and the end, the first and the last.

¹⁴ Blessed *are* they that do his commandments, that they may have right to the tree of life, and may enter in through the gates into the city.

¹⁵ For without *are* dogs, and sorcerers, and whoremongers, and murderers, and idolaters, and whosoever loveth and maketh a lie.

¹⁶ I Jesus have sent mine <u>angel</u> to testify unto you these things in the churches. I am the root and the offspring of David, *and* the bright and morning star.

¹⁷ And the Spirit and the bride say, Come. And let him that heareth say, Come. And let him that is athirst come. And whosoever will, let him take the water of life freely.

¹⁸ For I testify unto every man that heareth the words of the prophecy of this book, If any man shall add unto these things, God shall add unto him the plagues that are written in this book:

¹⁹ And if any man shall take away from the words of the book of this prophecy, God shall take away his part out of the book of life, and out of the holy city, and *from* the things which are written in this book.

²⁰ He which testifieth these things saith, Surely I come quickly. Amen. Even so, come, Lord Jesus.

²¹ The grace of our Lord Jesus Christ *be* with you all. Amen.

Acknowledgements

Thank you -

Kay Stitzel for your tireless proofreading efforts and friendship.

Deanna Leah, of HBG Productions, for your efforts to give these books angel flight around the world.

Jo Ann Decker, editor and agent, for your valuable editing suggestions that make the best books possible.

Mike White, Publishing Consultant of Ghost River Images, thank you for continuing to share your knowledge and talent in taking an ordinary manuscript and turning it into a beautiful book.

Sara Jess, for assisting me with the organization of this book and my life.

Rev. Glenna Shepherd, Rev. Dr. Charlie Arehart, my MCC family and my loving friends for your support and blessings.

Ambika Wauters, for sharing your mutual experience and love of the angelic realm.

And to the Angels . . . how do I thank you for your constant presence and guidance. I love you so very much.

About the Author

Kermie Wohlenhaus, Ph.D. is an author, TV producer and angelologist. She teaches workshops, classes and gives angel presentations nationally and hosts a TV show in Tucson, Arizona on public access called *Kermie & the Angels* which is available on YouTube. As an angelologist, Dr. Wohlenhaus is regularly being interviewed on TV, radio, podcasts, and for newspapers and magazines throughout the United States. She is popular in live performance and with radio and TV audiences for her accurate angel messages and knowledge. Dr. Wohlenhaus is the Founder and Director of the School of Angel Studies.

Dr. Wohlenhaus's first book *How to Talk and Actually Listen to Your Guardian Angel* is based on her popular workshop of the same name. This book is now available in Spanish, French, and German. *The Complete Reference to Angels in the Bible* is the expanded, companion book to *A Quick Reference Guide to Angels in the Bible*. The forthcoming *Angels in Sacred Texts* includes not only Angels in the Bible, but many other angelic sacred texts.

Dr. Wohlenhaus received a Bachelor of Science (BS) from Colorado State University, a Master of Divinity (MDIV) from the Iliff School of Theology and a Doctor of Philosophy (Ph.D.) in Religion/Metaphysics at the College of Metaphysical Studies. She is currently living in Tucson, Arizona.

For further information: www.KermieandtheAngels.com